הרב דוד ב"ר קק"י

Donald D. Glass

THE LIVING BIBLE

A TOPICAL APPROACH
TO THE JEWISH SCRIPTURES

THE LIVING

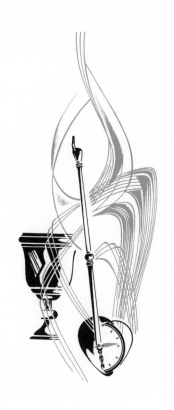

BIBLE

A TOPICAL APPROACH
TO THE JEWISH SCRIPTURES

by
RABBI SYLVAN D. SCHWARTZMAN, PH.D.
Professor, Jewish Religious Education
Hebrew Union College–Jewish Institute of Religion

and
RABBI JACK D. SPIRO, D.H.L.
Anshe Emeth Memorial Temple

Illustrated by BRUNO FROST

Union of American
Hebrew Congregations, New York

EDITOR'S INTRODUCTION

EVERY GENERATION OF JEWS HAS AFFIRMED THE CONTINUING RELE-
vance of the Bible, yet every generation has faced the problem of
learning to read it anew. The earliest centuries of Jewish Bible
reading produced translations into Aramaic and Greek and then
opened the world of Midrash. We, today, must see ourselves as
part of that continuing chain of Jewish Bible study, though the
problems which confront us are far more difficult and serious than
those of another day. We cannot accept any form of literal revelation which might give the words of our text authority, but neither
can we rest satisfied with simple historical or literary descriptions
which would sacrifice God's meaning for man's accuracy.

What does God say to us in the Bible? With all our philological
and historic knowledge, this remains the ultimate question for the
believing Jew. The authors of this volume have sought to respond
to that question by dealing with the biblical message neither
chronologically nor by literary style. They have rather identified
the great biblical themes and presented them both in their occasional and their major statement. They have set before the reader
the Bible's shifting moods as well as its steady affirmation. They
have not sacrificed its ambiguities and problems in their effort to
make its message clear, and in the process they have sought
neither to simplify the realities of existence nor turned from them.
Such an approach should open the Bible to many an inquiring
mind and ready heart. The Commission on Jewish Education is
privileged therefore to sponsor this as another one of its many
pioneering ventures in translating the relevance of Judaism to yet
another generation.

RABBI EUGENE B. BOROWITZ
Director of Education

PREFACE

THIS VOLUME IS BASED UPON THE RABBINICAL THESIS OF RABBI Jack D. Spiro, prepared in 1958 for the Department of Jewish Religious Education of the Hebrew Union College–Jewish Institute of Religion. Thoroughly rewritten, it was utilized experimentally under agreement with the Commission on Jewish Education as a religious school text for three years. The present edition, therefore, incorporates the many worthwhile comments of teachers, administrators, and rabbis whose schools used the experimental version, as well as the valuable observations and criticisms of the following members of the Reading Committee of the Commission: Rabbis Leon Fram, Eric Friedland, Samuel Glasner, and Drs. Toby K. Kurzband and Harry M. Orlinsky.

The incentive to create such a text came from research conducted by our Department which indicated the need for a new method of teaching Bible in our Reform program of education. Beyond the customary treatment of biblical personalities in the primary grades, practically all schools carried on either a chapter-by-chapter approach to the Bible as a whole, or concentrated upon the study of particular books, such as some of the Prophets and Writings. Neither proved very satisfactory, as the results of a detailed study conducted in 1957 by Rabbi Morris M. Hershman revealed. In the course of his investigation, he also discovered that the great majority of those charged with responsibility for Reform Jewish education preferred a topical approach to the Bible.

To fill these needs, *The Living Bible* was created. Here, dealing with a series of basic questions that many students had indicated were of genuine interest, the text seeks to provide an introduction to the Bible as a whole, rather than concern itself with the specifics of particular chapters, books, or sections. Thereby, it is believed, more satisfying results can be achieved.

For one thing, it is observed that a topical approach serves to stimulate greater interest in the Bible itself as well as transmit more extensive knowledge of its contents. For another, this approach contributes to a better understanding of the nature of biblical literature and the process of its creation and transmission as Reform Judaism views it. But no less important is the conviction that this kind of approach promotes a deeper appreciation of the Bible's relevance for life today, thereby helping to make the Scriptures once again THE LIVING BIBLE for our people.

A word of explanation is in order regarding the translation of biblical passages. The objective throughout has been to provide a clear and meaningful rendition of the text. Basically the Jewish Publication Society translation, with modifications suggested by the Revised Standard Version, has been followed. Frequently, however, to bring out the full sense of the passage, the authors provide their own translation.

We wish to thank all those whose many contributions are reflected in this volume—the members of the Reading Committee and, particularly, Rabbi Eugene B. Borowitz, Director of the Commission on Jewish Education; the teachers, directors, and rabbis of the schools which used the experimental edition; and Dr. Sheldon Blank, Professor of Bible at the Hebrew Union College–Jewish Institute of Religion, who gave us the benefit of his wise suggestions in preparing the original text.

To Esther P. Kaplan we offer a special word of appreciation for her careful preparation of the typescript and the supervision and distribution of the experimental edition. The splendid format of this volume is testimony to the skill and devotion of Mr. Ralph Davis, whose staff is also responsible for the excellent copy editing and proofreading. The art work was done by Bruno Frost. The illustrations were deliberately designed to capture the spirit of the various chapters. They are not meant to be taken literally, but rather they are thought-provoking. We hope the reader will find them challenging. We are grateful, too, for the deft literary style which Edith Brodsky Samuel contributed in the final stages of the manuscript. To all of them go our warmest thanks.

Finally, in the preparation of this book, a great many works were consulted. To all their authors and publishers, far too numerous to mention individually, we express our indebtedness. Specifically, however, we wish to acknowledge our appreciation to the following (where page numbers are given they refer to the pages of *The Living Bible* where material has been utilized):

Bible Translations

The Holy Scriptures, Jewish Publication Society.
Old Testament, Revised Standard Version, Thomas Nelson and Sons.
The Old Testament, An American Translation, University of Chicago Press.

References

ALBRIGHT, WILLIAM FOXWELL, *From Stone Age to Christianity*, Doubleday, pp. 21, 23, 165, 191.

Apocrypha, The, translated by Edgar J. Goodspeed, University of Chicago Press, p. 78.

BARTON, GEORGE A., *Archaeology and the Bible*, American Sunday School Union, pp. 192–194, 248, 253–255.

BLANK, SHELDON H., *Prophetic Faith in Isaiah*, Harper and Brothers, p. 115.

BUBER, MARTIN, *Tales of the Hasidim—The Early Masters*, Schocken Press, pp. 42–43.

BURROWS, MILLAR, *The Dead Sea Scrolls*, Viking Press, pp. 223–224, 226.

EWER, WILLIAM N., *The Week-End Book*, cited by Joseph L. Baron, *A Treasury of Jewish Quotations*, Crown Publishers, p. 43.

FELDMAN, ABRAHAM J., "Contributions of Judaism to Modern Society," No. 29, *Popular Studies in Judaism*, Union of American Hebrew Congregations, pp. 5–7.

FREEHOF, SOLOMON B., *Preface to Scripture*, Union of American Hebrew Congregations, pp. 4–7.

GLUECK, NELSON, *Rivers in the Desert*, Farrar, Straus and Cudahy, pp. 191, 253.

GOLDMAN, SOLOMON, *The Book of Books: An Introduction*, Harper and Brothers, pp. 4–5.

Josephus, Complete Works of, World Library Edition, World Publishing Co., pp. 216, 227.

KAPLAN, MORDECAI M., *The Future of the American Jew*, Macmillan Co., p. 44.

KELLER, WERNER, *The Bible as History*, William Morrow and Co., pp. 253–255.

KOHLER, KAUFMANN, *Jewish Theology*, Macmillan Co., p. 17.

Koran, The, translated by George Sale, Frederick Warne and Co., p. 8.

MACARTNEY, CLARENCE E., *Macartney's Illustrations*, Abingdon-Cokesbury Press, pp. 259–260.

MAZAR, BENJAMIN, editor, *Views of the Biblical World*, Vol. 2, International Publishing Co., pp. 253–254.

MILLER, MILTON G., and SCHWARTZMAN, SYLVAN D., *Our Religion and Our Neighbors*, Union of American Hebrew Congregations, pp. 165–166.

MOORE, WALTER L., *Courage and Confidence from the Bible*, New American Library, p. 3.

MURROW, EDWARD R., *This I Believe*, Simon and Schuster, pp. 7, 260–261.

New Testament, Revised Standard Version, Thomas Nelson and Sons, p. 7.

PFEIFFER, ROBERT H., *Introduction to the Old Testament*, Harper and Brothers, pp. 195–196, 208–210, 220.

PRITCHARD, JAMES B., *Ancient Near Eastern Texts Relating to the Old Testament*, Princeton University Press, pp. 191–194.

SCHWARTZMAN, SYLVAN D., *Reform Judaism in the Making*, Union of American Hebrew Congregations, pp. 40, 60, 101, 244.

TOYNBEE, ARNOLD J., *A Study of History*, Oxford University Press, p. 44.

Union Prayerbook, Vol. I, Central Conference of American Rabbis, pp. 141, 266.

WITT, LOUIS, "Judaism and Democracy," No. 11, *Popular Studies in Judaism*, Union of American Hebrew Congregations, pp. 6–7.

World's Most Famous Court Trial, The—Tennessee Evolution Case, National Book Co., pp. 241–242.

WRIGHT, GEORGE ERNEST, and FILSON, FLOYD VIVIAN, *The Westminster Historical Atlas to the Bible*, Westminster Press, pp. 27, 29, 33, 195–197, 253–255.

SYLVAN D. SCHWARTZMAN
JACK D. SPIRO

Cincinnati, 1962

CONTENTS

xii   Contents

CHARTS AND MAPS

THE LIVING BIBLE

A TOPICAL APPROACH
TO THE JEWISH SCRIPTURES

.

$\mathcal{O}_{ne}$

WHY STUDY THE BIBLE?

A Book Worth Studying

AS YOU START THIS BOOK YOU MAY PERHAPS BE WONDERING, "WHY study the Bible?"

There are a lot of good reasons. The fact is that because the Bible is no ordinary book, people attach all sorts of value to the study of it. Here is one example:

A young man was about to go on a long and difficult journey A friend came by to wish him good luck.

"I'm almost finished packing," the young man told him. "Now all I have to put in my suitcase are a guide book, a lamp, a mirror, a microscope, a telescope, a volume of great poetry, a few biographies, a song book and prayer book, some law books, a few works on ethics. . . ."

"Stop!" his friend cried. "You'll never be able to get all of that into one suitcase!"

"Sure I can," was the reply, and with that the young man put a Bible in his bag and closed it.

Obviously the young man of this story valued the Bible not only as an effective instrument through which one seeks to comprehend God, the universe, and life itself, but also as a "book of books," offering rare understanding in many different areas of human experience.

All of this is reminiscent of something one of the sages of the Mishnah once said. Speaking of the Torah he urged:

> Turn it and keep turning it, for everything is in it. Grow
> gray and old over it and do not turn away from it for there
> is no better rule for living than this. —Ovos 5:25

The sage was simply reminding us that the Torah, and for that matter the Bible as a whole, is well worth studying because it is an ever-living book.

The Bible and Our Culture

The truth is that the Bible does "live" in a great many ways.

For one thing there is its enormous impact upon the culture of the Western world. We must remember that the Bible is the oldest and most widely read book in our civilization. In continuous circulation for almost two thousand years, the Bible appears today in more than eleven hundred different languages and dialects, and it heads the best-seller list each year with an estimated six million copies sold annually. This means that over the centuries our language, literature, art, and various other phases of our culture have been greatly affected by the writings of Scripture.

Take the English language, for instance. It is richly colored with biblical expressions which have become part of our every day speech. Undoubtedly you yourself use such terms as "a Jonah" for someone who brings bad luck [see Jonah 1:11–12], "by the skin of our teeth" [Job 19:20], "sour grapes" [Ezekiel 18:2], "nothing new under the sun" [Ecclesiastes 1:9], "lick the dust" [Psalm 72:9], and "by the sweat of your brow" [Genesis 3:19]. You're probably also familiar with "eat, drink, for tomorrow we die" [Isaiah 22:13], "spare the rod and spoil the child" [Proverbs 13:24], "an eye for an eye" [Exodus 21:24], "my brother's keeper" [Genesis 4:9], or the reference to death as "the grim reaper" [based upon the statement in Jeremiah 9:21].

Throughout the English-speaking world practically every famous dramatist, novelist, poet, and orator has studied the Bible for basic ideas, style, and language. William Shakespeare referred to it in most of his works and he used at least one biblical quotation in every play. So greatly did it influence him that a noted scholar has said,

"If the Bible were lost, much of its language and incident, together with much of its spirit would be preserved to us in Shakespeare."

Another writer who drew heavily upon it was John Milton, the blind English poet of the seventeenth century. His most famous works, such as *Paradise Lost* and *Samson Agonistes,* are based entirely upon biblical themes. And among the long list of others whose works show a strong biblical influence are John Bunyan, Robert Burns, Samuel Taylor Coleridge, Ralph Waldo Emerson, Charles Lamb, Abraham Lincoln, Daniel Webster, John Greenleaf Whittier, and William Wordsworth.

Nor is this true only with writers of the past. We are constantly finding the Bible reflected in modern literature and drama. The title of Ernest Hemingway's great novel, *The Sun Also Rises,* was taken from the first chapter of Ecclesiastes [1:5]. That of John Steinbeck's *The Grapes of Wrath,* comes from Deuteronomy 32:32, and Leon Uris' *Exodus* gets its name, of course, from the second book of the Bible. Literally thousands of novels have been written around the lives of biblical characters. Among the finest are the works of Thomas Mann, distinguished Nobel Prize winner in literature, which deal with the life of Joseph as portrayed in Genesis 37–50.

The theater, movies, and television often use biblical titles, plots, and themes. The titles of *The Little Foxes* [Song of Songs 2:15], *The Voice of the Turtle* [Song of Songs 2:12], and *Inherit the Wind* [Proverbs 11:29]—all with long runs on Broadway—come directly from the Bible. Marc Connelly's *The Green Pastures* [Psalm 23:2], a Negro folk version of the Bible, and Thornton Wilder's drama, *The Skin of Our Teeth,* based upon the story of Noah [Genesis 6:9–9:29] are two well-known Pulitzer Prize winners. Another, *J.B.,* by Archibald MacLeish retells the story of Job in modern form. And Hollywood has used the Bible for some of its most successful productions, such as *The Ten Commandments, David and Bathsheba, Samson and Delilah,* and many others.

To be really educated in Western culture one requires a sound knowledge of the Bible.

Our Nation and the Bible

Without the Bible, one would have difficulty understanding the foundations and development of our American democracy. For it is an established fact that the political ideas and institutions of American life have been shaped by the teachings of the Bible.

The Pilgrims who sailed on the "Mayflower" and landed at Plymouth in December, 1620, looked upon the Bible as the proper basis for their laws and system of government. Speaking about its teachings, they asserted:

> They are for the mayne [main] so exemplary [outstanding], being grounded on principles of moral equitie [equity] as that all Christians especially ought alwaies [always] to have an eye thereunto in the framing of their politique [political] constitutions.

A well-known expert on Puritan life has said, "It [the Bible] moulded their speech, their thoughts, and their lives, and on it they built all their hopes of a better future. . . ."

All during the period of the American Revolution and the founding of the United States the colonists drew example and inspiration from this book that they so deeply cherished. Thomas Paine whose *Common Sense* did so much to stir up the colonists against Britain declared, "Monarchy is ranked in Scriptures as one of the sins of the Jews. . . . Gideon not only declines the honor [of the kingship offered him by the elders] but denies the right [of the Jews] to give it [see Judges 8:22–23]. . . . Here the Almighty has entered His protest against monarchical government. . . ."

From the Bible came other convincing arguments in favor of independence. To justify the principles of equality for all men and of freedom of speech, the colonists pointed to various incidents in the lives of the prophets of ancient Israel. Two of their favorite examples were Nathan rebuking King David [II Samuel 12:1–15] and Elijah condemning King Ahab [I Kings 21].

The patriots drew heavily upon the Bible for courage and guidance. Upon the Liberty Bell in Philadelphia they inscribed these words from Leviticus: "Proclaim liberty throughout all the land unto all the inhabitants thereof" [25:10]. And it is well-known that many of Washington's soldiers derived the spiritual strength to continue the seemingly hopeless fight from the Bibles they carried with them.

Popular among the people, too, were comparisons of King George of England to Pharaoh, and General Washington to Moses. A committee made up of Benjamin Franklin, John Adams, and Thomas Jefferson appointed to prepare a seal for the new nation, proposed that it show Pharaoh sitting in an open chariot passing through the divided Red Sea, with Moses on the opposite shore causing the waters to overwhelm him [Exodus 14].

In establishing laws for the new nation, the people naturally turned to the Bible. For instance, they adopted the legal principle that a man accused of a crime cannot be tried without a judge and competent witnesses—a principle which comes directly from Exodus 18 and Deuteronomy 19:15–19.

Little wonder then that George Washington once said, "It is impossible to rightly govern the world without God and the Bible." A later President, Andrew Jackson, declared to a friend, "That book, sir [referring to the Bible], is the rock on which our republic rests."

Today the Bible continues to serve as a powerful force for democracy. Quentin Reynolds, the well-known foreign correspondent and author, summarized the Bible's import when he said:

> If I were a dictator, the first book I would burn would be the Bible. I'd burn it because I'd realize that the whole concept of democracy came out of that book. "Democracy" is a Greek word which means rule by the people, but even at the height of its ancient glory Athens was not a democracy. The Greeks gave us the word for it but the Bible gave us the philosophy and the way we call democracy.

The Bible and Religion

Yet as influential as the Bible is in American legal, cultural, and moral spheres, it is really in the realm of religion, particularly in the religions of the entire Western world, that its importance will always be paramount.

To the Christians, of course, the Bible is the most sacred of all books, representing the word of God Himself. The largest portion of their Scriptures is the Jewish Bible which the followers of Christianity call the "Old Testament." They have long claimed to find passages in the Old Testament which they believe foretold the coming of Jesus.

The influence of the Jewish Scriptures, however, is felt even in the New Testament, which makes up the rest of the Christian Bible. This is especially true of the Gospels, the four books dealing with the life of Jesus, and the writings of Paul, who it is believed was originally a Jew. For instance, here is a passage from the Gospel of Matthew, the first book of the New Testament. When asked by his opponents what he considered the greatest commandment of all, Jesus replied:

> "You shall love the Lord your God with all your heart, and with all your soul, and with all your mind." This is the great and first commandment. And a second is like it, "You shall love your neighbor as yourself." On these two commandments depend all the law and the prophets.
> —Matthew 22:37–40

You needn't be surprised that this sounds familiar. These command-ments, taken directly from Deuteronomy 6:5 and Leviticus 19:18, are part of our own temple worship.

Christianity has also drawn heavily upon the Hebrew Scriptures for many of its beliefs and practices. Its conception of a God of love stems directly out of the teachings of Hosea [see especially Hosea 14:2–5]. The worship service of practically all Christian churches includes many passages from the Prophets and Psalms. Almost the whole of Christian ethics, including the Ten Commandments [Exo-dus 20:2–14 and Deuteronomy 5:6–18], comes from the Hebrew Scriptures. The practice of Baptism originates there [see Ezekiel 36:25], and Christian Communion symbolizes the Last Supper of Jesus [described by the New Testament in Luke 22:7–19] in which he seems to have been fulfilling the Passover observance com-manded by Exodus 12:14–20.

The Moslems, too, consider the Bible one of their sacred books, and it has considerable effect upon their faith. The followers of Islam proudly trace back their origins to Ishmael, the son of Abra-ham and Hagar [Genesis 16; 17:23–27; 21:8–21]; and on almost every page of the Koran, the Moslem Scriptures, we observe the influence of the style, personalities, legends, themes, beliefs, laws, and practices of our Bible. Here, for example, is a passage taken directly from the Koran:

> We believe in Allah [the Moslem name for "God"] and that which is revealed unto us and that which was revealed unto Abraham, and Ishmael, and Isaac, and Jacob, and the tribes, and that which Moses and Jesus received, and that which the Prophets received from their Lord. We make no distinction between any of them, and unto Him we have surrendered. —Surah II:136

But, while the Bible is cherished by both Moslems and Christians, it stands at the very heart of Judaism. This even Mohammed, the founder of Islam, recognized when he called the Jews "the People of the Book," referring, of course, to the Bible.

The Bible and the Practice of Judaism

The famous teacher Hillel, who lived around the time of Jesus, de-clared that a person ignorant of his tradition could not be a good Jew. Herein lies the chief answer to our question, "Why study the Bible?"

We do it so that we may be knowledgeable Jews, aware of our heritage, and alert to our responsibilities as Jews. Study of our Book helps us to achieve this goal in four essential ways:

1. Study of the Bible enables us to understand precisely what our religion demands of us. Contained within the Bible are most of our basic beliefs, such as Judaism's insistence upon our worship of only one God [see Exodus 20:3–6 and Deuteronomy 6:4] and the requirements of ethical living as an essential part of His worship [see, for example, Isaiah 58:1–8]. Our code of personal conduct is likewise largely prescribed by the Bible, as for instance in the Ten Commandments and many of the requirements of the so-called "Holiness Code" [see Leviticus 19:11–18]. And our whole value system is rooted in the Bible's demand for righteousness, justice, mercy, peace, concern for our fellow man, and the like.

Much of our present-day religious practice likewise stems from Bible times. The Sabbath, for example, is called for in Exodus 20:8–11; Sukos, in Deuteronomy 16:13–15; Purim, toward the end of the Book of Esther [9:26–28]; and so on. Our prayer book, too, is largely made up of biblical statements, as we find in the case of the *Sh'ma* and *v'Ohavto*, both of which are taken from Deuteronomy 6:4–9. And as part of every major synagogue worship service a section of the first five books of the Bible, the Torah, is always read.

But we must also remember that whatever was introduced into Judaism after the completion of the Bible was done mainly through the process of reinterpreting its meaning. So during the period beginning around the turn of the Common Era and continuing on through the fifth century, rabbis living in Palestine and Babylonia ardently engaged in studying and interpreting the Scriptures. From their discussions came, first, the Mishnah about 200 c.e., which reinterpreted biblical law for the changed conditions of the times. About 500 c.e., in Babylonia, the G'moro, explanations of these modified laws, was completed. Together, the Mishnah and G'moro comprise the Talmud which is still the most important collection of post-biblical Jewish law.

An example of this process is seen in connection with the following biblical passage:

> And when you reap the harvest of your land, you shall not completely reap the corner of your field, neither shall you gather the gleanings of your harvest. You shall not glean your vineyard, neither shall you gather the fallen fruit of your vineyard. You shall leave them for the poor and the stranger. —Leviticus 19:9–10

Originally this was to apply chiefly to the Jews, but the rabbis extended its provisions to include all the poor among the non-Jews as well. Thus, the Mishnah states, "We do not prevent the poor of the Gentiles from benefitting from these regulations about gleanings, fallen produce, and the corners of the field" [Gittin 5:8]; and the Talmud expands this even further by declaring, "We must support the poor of the Gentiles with the poor of Israel . . ." [Gittin 61a].

Interpretation of the Bible never ceased. From this process came large collections of midrashim offering the interpretation of biblical verses as they were preached in the synagogue. Important commentaries on the Bible were also produced, such as the ones by Rashi, who lived in Southern France during the eleventh century, and by Abraham ibn Ezra and Nachmanides, both of whom lived in Spain during the twelfth century. Even those who led the Reform movement in the nineteenth century turned to the Bible to justify many of the changes they were proposing. Thus, in advocating the elimination of the so-called "extra days" of the Jewish holidays introduced in post-biblical times, they pointed out that the Bible itself called for the observance of only seven days of Passover, not eight [Exodus 23:14], and one day of Shovuos, not two [Leviticus 23:21].

Today, as in the past, the Bible still stands at the very center of the Jewish faith. Without sound knowledge of it, therefore, the proper understanding and practice of our religion are inconceivable.

A Means of Jewish Self-Identification

2. At the same time, study of the Bible is fundamental in coming to identify oneself as a Jew.

Judaism, as we know, represents both a religion, a way of life that reflects God's will, and a people, pledged to carry out that will. Both are indispensable. Without a Jewish people Judaism could not long endure; without the Jewish religion there would be no purpose to Jewish survival.

Study of the Bible helps us to understand both the Jewish religion and the Jewish people. We have already seen what Bible study can do for our understanding of Jewish belief and practice. But it also contributes to the preservation of the Jewish group by strengthening our sense of identification as Jews. Here we come to associate ourselves with our great ancestors. We journey to Canaan with our forefather Abraham and experience God's ancient promise to all generations of Israel [Genesis 12:1–9]. With our people we undergo the suffering of Egyptian slavery and glory in our deliverance into freedom [Exodus 1:8–14:31]. We struggle with the Judges against our ancient enemies in Palestine and triumph with Deborah and Barak over the Canaanites [Judges 4:1–24], and with Gideon over the Midianites [Judges 6:1–7:25]. We battle with David against the Amalekites [I Samuel 30:1–20] and rejoice with Solomon in the dedication of God's Temple [I Kings 8:19–66]. We share the plea of Hosea for the return of our people to righteousness [Hosea 14:2–3], and in their darkest hour we go into exile with them to Babylonia [II Kings 24:8–25:22].

Inevitably in the course of our study of the Bible we link ourselves to our ancestors of thousands of years ago and endure their hardships, breathe their hopes, and share their ideals. In the process they cease being quaint personalities from an ancient book but become our very own kin with whom we are forever joined in the common peoplehood and destiny of Israel.

The more we come to identify ourselves with that biblical past, the greater inner pride we take in our people's achievements and the more deeply committed we are to our continuing role as Jews in the world today. For out of the pages of the Bible, as we shall see, comes our sense of mission as a people bound to God in an eternal covenant.

Awareness of God and His Role

3. Study of the Bible helps us to develop a greater sense of awareness of God and His role in the universe. For above everything else, the Bible reports the repeated encounters of our forefathers with Him.

God, as we shall see in greater detail later on, revealed Himself to our forefathers in a variety of ways, in keeping with their capacities and the realities of their times. He was envisioned by all of them, however, as the great Creator of the cosmos, the Fashioner of all existence [Genesis 1–3]. Natural phenomena—the sun, moon, stars [see Psalm 136:8–9], the winds, rain, and lightning [see Psalm 135:7], even the rainbow [Genesis 9:12–15]—reminded them of His universal presence and power. They encountered Him everywhere they turned—on the flaming peak of Sinai [Deuteronomy 4:12], in the visions of the prophets [see, for example, Isaiah 6], the voice of conscience [see, for example, Psalm 77:2–7], even in Israel's victories and defeats [see, for example, Judges 4:23–5:3 and 6:1–6]. The hand of the Almighty operated throughout all of human existence, in both life and death [see Job 1:21], in the abundance of the harvest [see Psalm 65:10–14], and the blessings of marriage [Proverbs 18:22].

Inevitably, study of the Bible focuses one's attention upon this. Increasingly conscious of God's existence everywhere, we begin to catch something of His presence in our own lives as well. He becomes as much a part of *our* universe as He was to our forefathers. With the opening verses of Genesis we see Him as the Creator of the heavens and the earth. With the saga of the Exodus we feel His guidance over the destiny of our people from ancient Egypt down to the very present. With the statutes of Leviticus and Deuteronomy we come to know Him as the Giver of those moral laws by which alone the human race can hope to find a life of blessing and peace. And with the psalmist we are comforted by Him in our trials and sorrows. Yes, everywhere we turn in the Bible—from the still, small voice heard by Elijah [I Kings 19:9–12] to the roar of the whirlwind in the ears of Job [Job 38]—God speaks. In the process, our own hearts and minds become attuned to hear Him in our own experiences of life.

In this sense, the encounters of our forefathers with God affect our own lives, and we become more and more sensitive to His presence until at last we, too, can say with the psalmist:

> O Lord, our Lord,
> How glorious is Your name in all the earth! —Psalm 8:2

Basic Questions and Answers

4. The Bible seeks to answer some of man's most important questions about himself, the nature of life, and God. This is our fourth reason for studying it.

Like ourselves, our forefathers also faced many profound questions to which they sought answers. No doubt at some time or other you have wondered about things like these:

—Who is God?
—Are the Jews really God's chosen people?
—Is man free to do as he wishes?
—Does prayer help?
—Why is there evil in the world?
—What purpose is there to life?
—Who is a religious person?
—Is death the end?

Those who wrote the Bible grappled with these very questions.

Of course these are questions of real concern to religious people, but finding answers to many of them is also essential to a wholesome and inwardly satisfying life in general. Thus, in connection with one of these questions, a number of leading psychiatrists have called attention to this fundamental truth: without a sense of worthwhile purpose in life, a person cannot expect to enjoy emotional well-being. Therefore, each individual must find a satisfactory answer to the question, "What purpose is there to life?"

The fact is that in the answers which the Bible offers we do find those beliefs by which we are better able to lead our lives. For it is still true, as the Bible itself pointed out thousands of years ago, "As a man thinks within himself, so he is" [Proverbs 23:7]. What we believe *is* important! What we think about man, life in general, religion, prayer, God, and many other things can determine what we are and what we do. If, for example, we think only of ourselves and ignore the needs and welfare of others, we can easily develop into self-centered, unsympathetic, and greedy people.

Study of the Bible and especially of those insights gained from more than two thousand years of wrestling with such questions has proved a blessing to countless generations. From it has come a hopeful outlook upon life and a way of living that has brought rich inner satisfaction and untold spiritual benefits to the individual and mankind generally.

Surely this must have been what Abraham Lincoln had in mind when, during the terrible trials of the Civil War, he wrote to a friend:

> I am profitably engaged in reading the Bible. Take all of this book upon reason that you can and the balance upon faith, and you will live and die a better man.

The Bible as a Living Book

Far from being old fashioned and out of date, the Bible, as we have now seen, turns out to be a very "live" book indeed.

Not only is it a vital force in Western culture, democracy, and religion in general, but for us as Jews, in particular, the Bible remains our great source of faith. Through it we are strengthened both in our practices and beliefs, and in our sense of self-identification with our people. Moreover through the spiritual experiences of our forefathers our own lives are infused with a consciousness of God. And from their quest for answers to the deeper questions of life we draw purpose and meaning for our own existence. In a very real sense, then, the Bible lives through our thoughts and actions as Jews.

Finally, let us not forget that as a document with a history going back some four thousand years, the Bible has a long independent existence of its own. In this sense it possesses a "life" of its own that likewise warrants consideration.

Imagine that some archaeologist were to discover a manuscript of more than a thousand pages going back nearly two thousand years before the Common Era. Everyone would surely want to know who wrote it, when and where it was written, how it managed to be preserved, and what it had to tell us about the past.

What a stir, for example, has been created by the recent discovery of a number of comparatively brief scrolls describing the life and practices of a small settlement of Jews living around 100 B.C.E. near the shores of the Dead Sea! During the past decade thousands of articles have already been written about their discovery, age, authorship, style, and contents, and we can be sure that there will be many, many more.

Yet, when we realize that the Bible is by far the longest and oldest written record we have of ancient times, we should be no less curious about such questions as:

—Who wrote the Bible?
—How and when did it become "holy"?
—How did it come down to us?
—Is the Bible a *true* record of fact and history?

Study of a "living" Bible involves these questions as well.

Where to Start?

By now you can understand why it is important to study the Bible. But what is the best way to go about it?

In the course of this book we can scarcely hope to cover every page of the Bible from beginning to end. And concentrating on just one particular section or only certain books might not give us a broad enough view of its contents.

Instead, suppose we approach the Bible *topically;* that is, in terms of key questions that are of immediate interest to us. And what better ones are there than those that have already been mentioned? The first set, you will recall, had to do with those basic issues concerning God, life, the Jews, man, prayer, and the like, with which the writers of the Bible themselves struggled. The second set involves the Bible itself, its authors, its manner of transmission, and its essential accuracy.

Using this topical approach, then, we shall be dealing with a more limited number of passages. But culled from all sections of the Bible, these passages will give us a better perspective on the Bible as a whole. At the same time we will also be getting the benefit of the Bible's answers to some very important questions.

Which question shall we explore first? Why not the one that is probably of greatest concern to most people, "Who is God?" Certainly over the centuries no subject has been of more vital interest to the human race. And it is no less so today.

Here we can be sure that those who wrote the Bible have a great deal to tell us. Especially since God was so central in their thinking. . . .

THINGS TO TALK OVER

1. In what respects has the Bible had a direct influence upon the life of each member of the class?

2. If the Bible had not been written, in what ways might Reform Jewish worship, religious observance, and belief differ today?

3. How is the culture, thinking, and behavior of the average American affected by the Bible?

4. In what ways can knowledge of the Bible enable the members of the class to become better Jews?

SOME OTHER BIBLE PASSAGES TO CONSIDER

1. What familiar expressions do you encounter in these selections: Leviticus 19:18; Deuteronomy 6:4; Isaiah 2:4; Isaiah 6:3; Jeremiah 13:23; Joel 3:1; Psalm 19:15; Proverbs 16:18?

2. With what current Jewish religious practices are the following passages connected: Genesis 2:3; Genesis 17:9–14; Exodus 25:31–37; Exodus 27:20–21; Leviticus 16:29–34; Leviticus 23:39–42; Deuteronomy 14:3–20?

3. In what ways do these selections contribute to our own consciousness of God: Isaiah 40:27–31; Jeremiah 23:23–24; Psalm 8; Psalm 23; Psalm 62:6–9?

4. What connection do you see between the American system of justice today and the biblical teachings found in the following passages: Exodus 18:13–26; Exodus 21:33–34, 37; Exodus 23:1–3; Leviticus 19:15; Deuteronomy 19:15–20?

1. THE NATURE OF SCRIPTURE: See A. Cohen, *Everyman's Talmud*, pp. 132–142, 154–157; and C. G. Montefiore and H. Loewe, *A Rabbinic Anthology*, [305–333] pp. 116–126.

2. THE "ORAL LAW": See A. Cohen, *Everyman's Talmud*, pp. xxii–xxiii, 154–157; and C. G. Montefiore and H. Loewe, *A Rabbinic Anthology*, [350] p. 131, [430–435] pp. 159–162.

3. STUDY OF SCRIPTURE: See A. Cohen, *Everyman's Talmud*, pp. 142–148; and C. G. Montefiore and H. Loewe, *A Rabbinic Anthology*, [336–341] pp. 127–128, [364–370] pp. 135–137, [379] p. 140, [382] pp. 140–141, [386–395] pp. 142–144.

————————— OTHER THINGS TO READ —————————

FELDMAN, ABRAHAM J., "Contributions of Judaism to Modern Society," No. 29, *Popular Studies in Judaism*, Union of American Hebrew Congregations.

FEUERLICHT, MORRIS M., "Judaism's Influence in the Founding of the Republic," No. 8, *Popular Studies in Judaism*, Union of American Hebrew Congregations.

FREEHOF, SOLOMON B., *Preface to Scripture*, Union of American Hebrew Congregations, Chap. 1: "The Book of Books," pp. 3–12; Chap. 7: "The Bible and the Modern Reader," pp. 65–78; Chap. 8: "The Bible as Literature," pp. 79–90; Chap. 9: "Treasures in the Bible," pp. 91–108.

GOLDMAN, SOLOMON, *The Book of Books: An Introduction*, Harper, Chap. 1: "The Achievement and the Instrument— The Hebrew Bible," pp. 1–12; Chap. 6: "An Eternally Effective Book," pp. 104–126.

WITT, LOUIS, "Judaism and Democracy," No. 11, *Popular Studies in Judaism*, Union of American Hebrew Congregations.

$\mathcal{T}wo$

WHO IS GOD?

An Impossible Task, But . . .

A FABLE OUT OF THE EAST TELLS OF A WISE MAN WHO TRIED TO answer the question, "Who is God?" For many months he thought about it, and finally he began to despair.

Then one day as he was walking along the seashore, he came upon some children playing in the sand. He saw that they were digging deep holes and pouring water from the sea into them. He asked them what they were doing.

"We're emptying the ocean of its water," one of the children replied.

The sage said nothing, but smiled. "How foolish," he thought to himself, "trying to empty the ocean of its water. . . ." But then his smile vanished, for he realized, "Am I not just as foolish as they? For how can I, with my limited knowledge, hope to understand who God really is?"

To know everything about God, as this wise man saw, is an impossible task. The authors of the Bible also came to the same conclusion. The Book of Exodus pictures Moses at the foot of Mount Sinai pleading with God to reveal Himself, but God replies, "You cannot see My Presence, for man shall not see Me and live" [Exodus 33:12–23].

Other biblical authors were no less aware of the impossibility of knowing God completely. For example, a friend asks Job:

> Can you discover the deep things of God? Can you find out the limit of the Almighty? It is as high as heaven; what can you do? Deeper than the netherworld; what can you know? —Job 11:7–8

And later Job himself admits:

> He [God] suspends the earth upon nothing.
> He binds up the waters in His thick clouds. . . .
> He covers the face of the moon. . . .
> By His power He stilled the sea. . . .
> By His wind the heavens were made fair. . . .
> And yet, these are but bare indications of His ways;
> And how small a whisper do we hear of Him!
> And who can understand His thunderous power?
> —Job 26:7–14

The point is clear. The Almighty is far beyond the comprehension of humans.

Yet this does not mean that those who wrote the Bible felt that people could learn *nothing* about God. Far from it!

Three Underlying Convictions

Actually, the Bible has a great deal to tell us about Him, mostly because those who wrote it began with three underlying convictions.

First, God really existed—of this they had not the least doubt. Consequently, nowhere in the Bible do we come across the slightest reference to "atheism," the belief that there is no God. To the biblical authors, no sensible person could hold such an opinion. Why, exclaimed one psalmist, "Only a fool would say to himself, 'There is no God' " [Psalm 14:1].

Nor did they ever attempt to "prove" that God existed. This was self-evident. The very heavens themselves revealed His glory [Psalm 19:2], and the whole of nature, including man himself, showed His handiwork [Psalm 8]. God's reality was confirmed by many things—by man's existence [Job 33:4], the history of the Jewish people [Exodus 15:13], the testimony of Israel's great leaders and prophets [Exodus 4:1–16 and Amos 7:12–15], one's own inner feelings [Psalm 42:2 and 73:25–26] and sense of faith [Psalm 23].

Second, while those who wrote the Bible recognized that man

could never fully know God, they were equally sure that He did reveal aspects of Himself through both His deeds and demands. Hence it was possible for people to learn various things about Him.

Many came to know something of God's nature by His response in the deeply moving experiences of their own life and those of their people. Abraham, at the sacrifice of Isaac, found that God rejected the cruelty of child-sacrifice [Genesis 22:1–14]. Thus He showed Himself to be compassionate. In the midst of disappointment and despair over his people's worship of the Golden Calf, Moses found Him wrathful at idolatry, yet ultimately forgiving of human weakness [Exodus 32:1–14]. Each revelation of His will added to man's knowledge of Him.

To a great extent, the authors of the Bible approached the subject of God much like a modern scientist who deals with things he cannot observe directly. A physicist, for instance, is unable to say precisely what "light" is. But, by studying its performance under many conditions, he can measure its speed and describe some of its more important characteristics.

Similarly, the biblical writers believed they could learn about God by observing the workings of His universe, the history of mankind, and the lives of people. Here, in relation to His actions, they were sure they could discover various aspects of Him. So, to one of the psalmists, the sun's warmth and light symbolized God's essential goodness to man:

> O give thanks unto the Lord for He is good. . . .
> To Him that made great lights,
> For His mercy endures forever;
> The sun to rule by day,
> For His mercy endures forever. . . . —Psalm 136:1–8

Or, in the historical experience of nations, and especially that of Israel, they saw the hand of God directing the course of human events, as the following passage discloses:

> And because He loved your fathers and chose their descendants He brought you out with His presence, with His great power, out of Egypt. He drove out nations from before you who were greater and mightier than you . . . to give you their land for an inheritance.
> —Deuteronomy 4:37–38

Third, the authors of the Bible recognized that man's conception of God could not be static. Rather, knowledge of Him is dynamic, growing with man's greater awareness of himself and his world. In this respect their concept of God is much like our view of the universe; thanks to every new scientific discovery, the universe appears to be greater and more complex than we had imagined. So in every age, the thought, observation, and experience of gifted individuals like the prophets inevitably lead to the expanding and refining of man's understanding of God. Indeed, we observe such a continuing trend toward an ever higher concept of Him within the Bible itself.

Basic to the biblical approach to God, then, are these three beliefs—God exists, man can indeed discover some of His characteristics as He reveals them through His deeds and demands, and with ever-increasing understanding, man can expect his knowledge of God to grow.

Hence the God-concept we find within the pages of the Bible is something that grows with the experience of centuries, beginning during the time of the Patriarchs.

God Establishes a Covenant with Israel

The Hebrews' worship of God commenced, we are told, with Abraham. It was at His command that Abraham and his family left their native land, and it was to Him that Abraham offered up his first sacrifice [Genesis 12:1-8].

Abraham and the other Patriarchs seem to have enjoyed a close personal relationship with God, whom they regarded as the Protector of their families. Apparently they knew God by various names, for in different places He is called *Elohim, El, El Elyon,* and *El Shaddai.* However, we must remember that in early times each nation or group of peoples identified itself with particular deities who, like individuals, bore personal names. In fact, it is interesting that when Moses first encountered God he immediately asked Him His name [Exodus 3:13].

It was with Moses that the Hebrews began calling their God by a new name. The Bible supplies us simply with the letters Y-H-V-H, and we can only guess at the original pronunciation because it has not been sounded since Temple days, when the High Priest used it to bless the people on Yom Kippur. The vowels now appearing with it in the Hebrew text belong to a different word: *Adonoi,* "my Lord," which Jews traditionally substituted for the sacred name. Not realizing this, however, Christians who tried reading the word with these vowels came up with the Hebraically impossible name *Y'hovah,* more commonly written "Jehovah."

The consensus of scholarly opinion today is that Y-H-V-H was probably pronounced *Yahveh*, derived from a form of the verb "to be," used in a causative sense. Hence, though we cannot be certain, the likely meaning is "the One who causes [everything] to be."

At any event, it is only with Moses that the name *Yahveh* begins to appear. The Bible, in fact, has God actually inform him:

> "I am the Lord [*Yahveh*]; and I appeared unto Abraham, Isaac, and Jacob as *El Shaddai*, but by My name *Yahveh* I did not make Myself known to them." —Exodus 6:2–3

Though this particular name was unknown to him, Moses promptly identified Him as the ancient God of the Patriarchs.

Scholars differ about how Moses came to learn of Yahveh. Many believe that He was originally the God of the Kenites, a desert tribe related to the Hebrews. The Bible tells us that after fleeing Egypt for killing a taskmaster, Moses dwelt in the land of Midian among the Kenites and even married one of them [Exodus 2:11–21]. His father-in-law was a Kenite priest [Exodus 2:16; 3:1], and it was probably from him that Moses learned of Yahveh.

At any event, the Bible reports that one day, while Moses was tending the flocks near Mount Sinai, he experienced a revelation from Yahveh. A small bush nearby suddenly burst into flames, but strangely, it was not consumed! As Moses drew closer to it, he heard a voice say:

> "Do not come near . . . for the place where you are standing is holy ground. . . . I am the God of your father, the God of Abraham, the God of Isaac, and the God of Jacob." —Exodus 3:5–6

It was in the name of this God that Moses eventually led the Hebrew people out of Egypt. Then at Mt. Sinai they entered into an agreement with Him. They promised to be His people if He would be their God.

From this time on, their religion remained rooted in that covenant.

A Living, Personal God

Though God was henceforth to be known as "the Lord," in essentials He was the same Deity the Patriarchs had worshiped. Moreover, His basic qualities were destined to remain characteristic of the Jew's God-concept.

He was felt to be a "living," personal Being, never some abstract "spirit" or natural force. His name itself, Yahveh, was associated in the Bible with the Hebrew verb "to be" and emphasized the fact that He was an existing, feeling, acting God who related to people. This "living" quality is stressed, for instance, at the scene of the burning bush. Here, when Moses was commanded to go to Pharaoh to secure the freedom of the Hebrew slaves, he questioned, "What shall I tell the people when they ask me the name of the God who has sent me?" The answer was:

> And God said unto Moses: "I AM THAT I AM." And He said, "You shall say to the children of Israel: I AM has sent me to you." —Exodus 3:14

The God of the Hebrews, then, was conceived of as a living Being directly concerned with the world. This, in turn, gave Him the kind of "personality" that made Him an intimate part of the lives of the Hebrews.

True, those with more limited conceptual powers thought of Him chiefly in human terms. This is seen in the story of Adam and Eve in the Garden of Eden. Here, after telling how they ate of the forbidden fruit, the Bible goes on to say:

> And they heard the voice of the Lord God walking in the garden toward the cool of the day; and the man and his wife hid themselves from the presence of the Lord God among the trees of the garden. —Genesis 3:8

In another passage we are told that Moses desired to see God's physical appearance. Though God refused, the Bible does have Him tell Moses:

> "Behold, there is a place by Me where you shall stand upon the rock; and while My glory passes by I will put you in a cleft of the rock, and I will cover you with My hand until I have passed by. Then I will take away My hand and you shall see My back; but My face shall not be seen."
> —Exodus 33:21–23

In both these passages, God appears quite human. Likewise in many other passages we come across references to His hands, arms, feet, face, eyes, ears, and nose. Such conceptions of God are called "anthropomorphic," a term coming from two Greek words, *anthropos*, "man," and *morphe*, "form." Hence, "anthropomorphic" means "having human characteristics."

Yet even as God came to be conceived in more spiritual and less physical terms, this sense of Him as a distinct "personality" remained. The writers of the Bible never ceased to look upon Him as a living Being with feelings and concerns. Long centuries after, in speaking of the faithlessness of Israel, the prophet Jeremiah portrays Him as an anguished "Father" in these words:

> "I [God] contemplated how I would set you among
> My sons,
> And give you a pleasant land;
> A heritage most beauteous of all nations
> And I thought you would call Me 'my Father,'
> And would not turn from following Me.
> Surely as a faithless wife leaves her husband
> So have you been faithless to Me, O house of Israel,"
> Says the Lord. —Jeremiah 3:19–20

The psalmist conceives of Him in a similar fashion when he declares:

> As a father pities his children,
> So the Lord pities those who revere Him. —Psalm 103:13

Characteristic, then, of the biblical conception of God is the continuing feeling that He is a living Being who is personally involved in the lives of His children and constantly concerned for their ultimate well-being.

God and the Forces of Nature

Moreover, God operated through the very forces of nature that He created.

From the very first, natural phenomena were seen as expressions of God's great power and glory. In fact, various Patriarchs conceived of Him as a deity whose presence inhabited the mountaintops. The word *Shaddai* in "El Shaddai," one of the names they called Him, came from a Mesopotamian word that meant "mountain." In the time of Moses and long after, God was said to dwell atop Mount Sinai (also called Horeb) where He revealed His presence with thunder, lightning, and earthquakes [Judges 5:5 and I Kings 19:8–12]. Thus, in picturing the covenant scene at Mount Sinai, the Book of Exodus states:

> On the morning of the third day there was thunder and lightning, and a thick cloud upon the mountain, and a very loud trumpet blast, so that all the people who were in the camp trembled. Then Moses brought the people out of the camp to meet God; and they took their stand at the foot of

the mountain. And Mount Sinai was wrapped in smoke because the Lord descended upon it in fire; and the smoke of it went up like the smoke of a kiln, and the whole mountain quaked greatly. And as the sound of the trumpet grew louder and louder, Moses spoke and God answered him in thunder. —Exodus 19:16–19

This conception of a God who reveals Himself through the power of nature and the marvels of His universe remained characteristic. So, long centuries after Sinai, the psalmist says:

For I know that the Lord is great,
And that one Lord is above all gods.
Whatever the Lord pleases He does
In heaven and on earth, in the seas and all deeps.
It is He who makes the clouds rise at the end of the earth,
Who makes lightnings for the rain
And brings forth the wind from His storehouses.
    —Psalm 135:5–7

And one of the friends of Job describes God's power in nature as follows:

Listen to the voice of His thunder,
And the rumbling that comes from His mouth.
Under the whole heaven He lets it go,
And His lightning to the corner of the earth. . . .
God thunders wondrously with His voice;
He does great things which we cannot comprehend.
To the snow He says, "Fall on the earth,"
And to the shower and the rain, "Be strong". . . .
From His chamber comes the whirlwind,
And cold from the scattering winds.
By the breath of God ice is given,
And the broad waters are frozen fast.
He loads the thick cloud with moisture;
And clouds scatter His lightning. —Job 37:2–11

Indeed, God's presence stands revealed through all the majesty and might of nature.

The God of History

But God also operates in the experiences of nations.

Almost from the very beginning, God is said to have created separate nations by dispersing the peoples of the earth and making them speak different languages [see Genesis 11:1–9 and Deuteronomy 32:8]. With the appearance of Abraham, He promises to make him the founder of a great nation [Genesis 12:2], and it is He who helps him defeat the kings who have kidnaped his nephew, Lot [Genesis 14:1–20].

As the Protector of Israel, God never ceases to watch over them. When they are deserving, He brings them victory over their enemies [see, for example, I Samuel 17:1–51]. "The Lord is a man of war," proclaims an ancient poem describing His mighty triumph over the armies of the Egyptians [Exodus 15:3]. And as the Hebrews journey through the wilderness, He helps them defeat other enemies. In one case, the people found themselves outnumbered by a fierce desert tribe known as the Amalekites, but Moses still had the "rod of God" which had helped free his people from Egypt [see Exodus 4:1–5]. With two assistants, Aaron and Hur, he went to the top of a hill overlooking the battle, and as long as he was able to hold the rod of God above his head, the Hebrews were successful. To commemorate the victory, Moses built an altar and called it *Adonoi-nisi,* "The Lord is my banner" [Exodus 17:8–16].

To all those who wrote the Bible, there was no denying that God operated through history.Thus the prophet Amos, who lived some five hundred years after the Exodus, saw the downfall of vanquished nations as His doing. "Shall evil befall a city and the Lord not be responsible?" he asks [Amos 3:6]. And still another prophet, five hundred years later, Ezekiel, promises that God will lay waste the land of Egypt, only to restore it after a time so that "they will know that I am the Lord" [Ezekiel 29:8–16].

Characteristic of God, then, is the fact that He carries out His will through the processes of history.

Where the God of the Hebrews Differed

Thus far, the Hebrews' conception of God was not too different from that of other peoples in the ancient Middle East. They, too, spoke of their deities in terms of "personality," nature, and history. In certain respects, however, the God of the Hebrews was unique.

To begin with, He was only one. Certain old biblical passages, to be sure, refer to the existence of angels and possibly other divine beings. One even mentions marriages between the so-called "sons of God" and the daughters of men [Genesis 6:1–2]. And from the repeated references of the Bible to the Jewish people's worship of other gods [for example, Deuteronomy 17:3 and Jeremiah 5:19], doubtlessly there were many Jews who gave credence to their existence.

But to the Patriarchs and Moses, there could only be one God, their own God. Nor once the people entered Palestine could they abandon the Lord for the gods of different localities or female deities. Such prohibitions as that found in Exodus 34:12–16 established the fact that they were to avoid polytheism in all its forms, including the immoral practices associated with the gods of their neighbors.

Another feature even of early biblical religion was the association of morality with the true worship of God. Although He was pictured as sometimes given to anger [I Samuel 6:19], jealousy [Genesis 11:6–9], and even favoritism [Genesis 15:1–5), He nevertheless was a moral Being who made moral demands upon His worshipers. So we observe in one of the oldest sets of laws in the Bible, called "the Book of the Covenant" [Exodus 20:22–23:33]. Here, in addition to all the ritual requirements, God also insists upon kindness to the stranger, the widow, the orphan, and the needy [Exodus 22:20–26], as well as the honest administration of justice [Exodus 23:1–3, 6–8]. These laws indicate that even during the time of Moses, God was believed to possess a strong sense of righteousness and justice.

Finally, again unlike other deities of the Middle East, the God of the Hebrews permitted no physical representations of Himself. While some people may have thought of Him in anthropomorphic terms, they were strictly forbidden to use images or other pictorial forms of God. So, among the Ten Commandments we read:

> You shall not make for yourself a graven image, nor any kind of likeness that is in the heavens above, or that is in the earth beneath, or that is in the water under the earth; you shall not bow down to them, nor serve them. . . .
> —Exodus 20:4–5

Though in some ways the Lord resembled the deities of other peoples, He was quite different in certain important respects. For, being strictly one, moral, and incapable of being represented by images, the God of the early Hebrews was already unique. And this uniqueness was consistently stressed by all the writers of the Bible.

The God of the Nation

It was inevitable that the Hebrew people's conception of God should be affected by their entry into Palestine. For one thing, an agricultural way of life replaced their former nomadic existence. But

DATES OF IMPORTANT BIBLICAL
EVENTS AND PERSONALITIES
(*indicates approximate date)

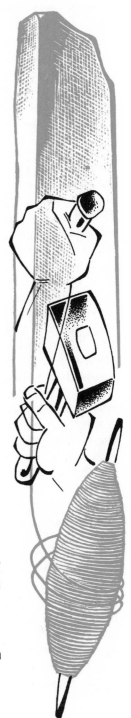

	B.C.E.	
Abraham	2000	(*2000-1700) Period of the Patriarchs
Isaac		(*1700-1300) Period of the Hebrew
Jacob		tribes in Egypt
Joseph	1500	
Moses		(*1300) Exodus from Egypt
Joshua		(*1250) Entry into Palestine
		(*1225-1020) Period of the Judges
Deborah		
Gideon		
Samson		
Samuel		(*1020-1004) Saul's reign
Saul		
Nathan	1000	(*998-965) David's reign
David		
Solomon		(*965-926) Solomon's reign
		(*926) Hebrew Kingdom Divided; Jeroboam, king of Israel
Elijah		(*882-871) Omri, king of Israel
		(*871-852) Ahab, king of Israel
Elisha		
Amos		
Isaiah		
Hosea		
Micah		(721) Assyrian destruction of Israel
		(621) Finding of Book of Deuteronomy
Jeremiah		(598) First Babylonian invasion of Judah
		(589) Final Babylonian invasion and and start of Exile
Ezekiel		
Second Isaiah		(*538) Edict of Cyrus permitting return of exiles
Ezra	500	(*450) Return of Ezra and Nehemiah
Nehemiah		

now they were also exposed to the influence of their new neighbors' religious ideas and practices.

So, as farmers, they came to expect the Lord to be more intimately concerned with the cycle of agricultural life. Therefore we are not surprised to find the Bible presenting various commandments in His name calling for harvest offerings [Exodus 22:28] and regulating farming practices [see, for example, Exodus 22:4–5 and Deuteronomy 22:9–10].

Like their neighbors, many of the Hebrews began to identify the Lord chiefly with their own land and own nation. For in the ancient Middle East, each nation had its own deities whom it considered sovereign over their people and territory. The Canaanites had Baal; the Babylonians, Bel; the Moabites, Chemosh; and so on. With the Hebrews, of course, it was the Lord. Not only was He the God who guided and protected the people of Israel, but in the popular mind He also possessed supreme power over the territory of the nation.

In II Kings 5:1–19 we find a good illustration of this kind of belief. Naaman, a captain in the Syrian army, was suffering from a serious disease. Thinking that a certain Hebrew prophet, Elisha, might be able to help him, Naaman left his own country for Palestine. There, with Elisha's aid, he was subsequently cured. Convinced that he owed his recovery to the prophet's God, Naaman resolved to continue worshiping the Lord. But how could he do this in Syria, outside the land of Palestine where the Hebrew God was supreme? He gathered together two muleloads of Palestinian soil to take back with him to Syria. There, upon the "territory" of the Hebrew God, he would now be able to worship Him.

Another example is seen in the conflict between the prophet Elijah and Jezebel, the foreign wife of King Ahab of Israel. Jezebel, we are told in I Kings 16:30–31, had been a princess of Phoenicia, a country to the north, before the Hebrew king married her. After she came to Palestine, she refused to give up her worship of Melkart (also known as Baal), the god of her own land. More than this, she even promoted his worship among the people of Israel.

Elijah was outraged. For one thing, there was the covenant between the Lord and His people. For another, there was the principle that it was the Lord alone who was sovereign over the nation and its land. But there was also the immorality associated with the worship of Melkart, something the Lord forbade. The Lord insisted upon righteous action by all the people of Israel, including the kings. As a matter of fact, the Bible relates how several early prophets sternly rebuked some of the kings for their misdeeds.

Palestine During the Divided Kingdom

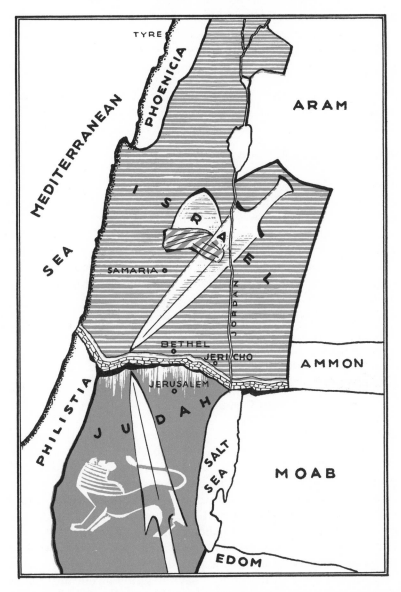

Nathan condemned King David for taking away the wife of another man [II Samuel 11–12:15]; Elijah himself berated King Ahab for murdering a man for his vineyard [I Kings 21:1–26].

Promptly Elijah challenged Queen Jezebel and her priests to a contest between Melkart and the Lord. The scene is described in I

Kings 18:1–40. There on Mt. Carmel, 450 priests of Melkart pleaded in vain with their god to show his power. Then, when Elijah's turn came, the Lord responded with a devastating display of His power:

> And when all the people saw it, they fell on their faces and
> said, "The Lord, He is God; the Lord, He is God!"
> —I Kings 18:39

To the thinking of the people of that day, the outcome proved the sovereignty of the Lord over the nation and its territory.

The Extent of God's Authority

There were others who arose from time to time to remind the people of the true character of their God. These were individuals like Amos, Hosea, and Isaiah, the first of the "literary" prophets. They are so named because, unlike Samuel, Elijah, Elisha, and other earlier prophets, they left written records of their own messages.

From the start, they protested against the introduction of the religious rites of neighboring peoples into the worship of the Lord. Hosea complains, "With their silver and their gold they have made idols" [Hosea 8:4], and Isaiah cries out:

> They [the people of Israel] are full of fortune-tellers from
> the east,
> And soothsayers like the Philistines. . . .
> Their land is filled with idols;
> They bow down to the work of their hands,
> To what their own fingers have made. —Isaiah 2:6–8

More than this, however, these prophets reasserted the sovereignty of the Lord not only over the territory of Israel but over all lands and peoples. And through the political events of the times, they forcefully brought home this fact to their people.

With the division of the country, after Solomon's reign, into two rival kingdoms, both Israel and Judah appealed to the Lord for support. The people of each believed that God would protect them from each other as well as from their more powerful enemies, like Assyria to the northeast and Egypt to the south.

Yet, in 721 B.C.E., the mighty Assyrian army swept into northern Palestine and killed or captured all of the people of the Kingdom of Israel. Those who survived were dragged off into exile from which they never returned. Did this mean, wondered the people of Judah to the south, that the Lord was no longer able to defend them against their enemies?

"Not at all," concluded Amos. Though he lived some years before the Assyrian disaster struck Israel, he was able to sense its coming. In fact, he even went up from his native land of Judah to warn the people of the Northern Kingdom of impending doom:

> An enemy shall surround the land,
> And bring down your defenses from you,
> And your strongholds shall be plundered! —Amos 3:11

> "On that day," says the Lord God, "I will make the sun go down at noon,
> And darken the earth in broad daylight.
> I will turn your feasts into mourning, and all your songs into wailing . . .
> I will make it like the mourning for an only son,
> And the end of it like a bitter day." —Amos 8:9–10

The "Day of the Lord" was fast approaching, he declared. Would it be a time of glorious victory over the Assyrian army, as the people confidently supposed? No, it would be a time of utter disaster to Israel. For the nation was guilty of many sins, among them oppression of the poor [Amos 2:6–7], immorality [Amos 2:7], the enjoyment of luxury by the leaders at the expense of their fellow man [Amos 6:1–6], and others.

And just as some day the Lord would repay other nations for their crimes, so would He use the Assyrians to punish the people of Israel:

> "For behold I will raise up against you a nation,
> O house of Israel," says the Lord, the God of Hosts; "and they shall afflict you. . . ." —Amos 6:14

The people needed to be assured that God's authority extended far beyond the borders of Israel and Judah. He was capable of demanding justice from the Syrians [Amos 1:3–5], the Philistines [Amos 1:6–8], the Tyrians [Amos 1:9–10], and all the other peoples [Amos 1:11–2:3]. Moreover, He was prepared to use these other nations to carry out His punishment of Israel.

A God of Justice . . . and Mercy

Eventually, Amos promised, God would see to it that all wicked nations would receive due punishment. But it would come even swifter in the case of the people of Israel because of their special relationship, their covenant, with the Lord. For, angrily, God points out:

"Only you [Israel] have I known of all the families of the
earth;
Therefore I will visit upon you all your iniquities."
—Amos 3:2

Is there then no hope whatever for the people? Indeed, yes, another
prophet asserts. Have the people forgotten the Lord is also merciful
and compassionate?

This prophet's name was Hosea. He was in complete agreement
with Amos that the Lord was indeed a God of justice. But he also
stressed that He was capable of love and mercy.

Perhaps it was the prophet's own personal experiences that reminded him of this fact. He tells us of his unhappy marriage to a
faithless wife whom he still deeply loved [Hosea 1:1–3]. He com-
pares his own situation with the relationship between God and His
people [Hosea 2:4–15]. Like the prophet's wife, Israel, too, has become faithless to its "husband," God. Yet the Lord loves His people
because of their "marriage," their long-standing covenant [Hosea
11:1–4]. Speaking in God's name, Hosea then says:

"How can I give you up, O Ephraim [another term for
'Israel']?
How can I hand you over, O Israel? . . .
My heart is turned within Me,
My compassion is warm and tender." —Hosea 11:8

It is too difficult for God to destroy the object of His love:

"I will not carry out my fierce anger,
Nor will I again destroy Ephraim;
For I am God, and not man,
The Holy One in the midst of you,
And I will not come to destroy." —Hosea 11:9

Yet His sense of justice compels Him to punish His faithless people;
that is, unless they mend their ways quickly:

Return, O Israel, unto the Lord your God;
For you have stumbled in your iniquity. —Hosea 14:2

If they will only reform by living righteously and abandoning the
worship of other gods, the Lord will spare them. For He loves His
people. Thinking of his own wife whom he would gladly take back,
the prophet reassures Israel that if they repent, God will surely receive them once more in love. "Yes," declares the Lord:

"I will betroth you to Me forever,
I will betroth you to Me in righteousness, and in justice, in

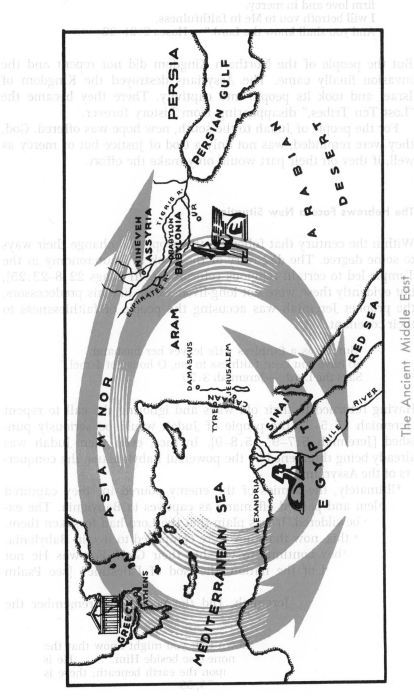

The Ancient Middle East

> firm love and in mercy.
> I will betroth you to Me in faithfulness,
> And you shall know the Lord." —Hosea 2:21–22

But the people of the Northern Kingdom did not repent and the invasion finally came. The Assyrians destroyed the Kingdom of Israel and took its people into captivity. There they became the "Lost Ten Tribes," disappearing from history forever.

For the people of Judah to the south, new hope was offered. God, they were reminded, was not only a God of justice but of mercy as well, if they on their part would only make the effort.

The Hebrews Face a New Situation

Within the century that followed, the people did change their ways to some degree. The discovery of the Book of Deuteronomy in the Temple led to certain religious reforms [see II Kings 22:8–23:25], but evidently these were not long-lived. Soon, like his predecessors, the prophet Jeremiah was accusing the people of faithlessness to their covenant:

> "Surely, as a faithless wife leaves her husband,
> So have you been faithless to me, O house of Israel,"
> Says the Lord. —Jeremiah 3:20

Having returned to their old ways and ignoring the call to repent [Jeremiah 15:5–7], the people of Judah would be seriously punished [Jeremiah 5:7–9; 15:8–9]. In fact, even then Judah was already being threatened by the powerful Babylonians, the conquerors of the Assyrians.

Ultimately, the armies of the enemy poured in; they captured Jerusalem and packed off many as captives to Babylonia. The exiles were bewildered. It was plain that the Lord had forsaken them. More than this, now that they were compelled to live in Babylonia, how could they continue to worship their God? For was He not chiefly the God of the nation, the God of Palestine? [see Psalm 137:1–4].

Not so, declared Jeremiah. Did the people not remember the words of Deuteronomy:

> To you [Israel] it was shown that you might know that the Lord, He is God; there is none else beside Him. . . . He is God in heaven above and upon the earth beneath; there is none else. —Deuteronomy 4:35, 39

Furthermore, the prophet pointed out:

> "Am I a God near at hand," says the Lord,
> "And not a God afar off?
> Can any hide himself in secret places
> That I shall not see him?" says the Lord;
> "Do I not fill heaven and earth?"
> Says the Lord. —Jeremiah 23:23–24

To make sure that the exiles understood, Jeremiah wrote them the following letter:

> Thus says the Lord of hosts, the God of Israel, to all the exiles whom I have sent into exile from Jerusalem to Babylon: "Build houses and live in them; plant gardens and eat their produce. Take wives and have sons and daughters; take wives for your sons, and give your daughters in marriage so that they may bear sons and daughters; multiply there, and do not decrease. But seek the welfare of the city where I have sent you into exile, and pray to the Lord on its behalf. . . ." —Jeremiah 29:4–7

Though the exiles dwelt on Babylonian soil, the prophet was reminding them, they could certainly worship the Lord there. For He was not the God merely of Palestine or even of the Hebrew people alone. He was also the God of Babylonia; in fact, He was the God of the whole universe! It was He alone who created the world and everything in it:

> It is He who made the earth by His power,
> Who established the world by His wisdom,
> And by His understanding stretched out the heavens. . . .
> —Jeremiah 10:12

The God Within Us

More than this, said Jeremiah, the Lord was also close to everyone. Actually, He was right within each person's heart.

Here the prophet drew upon the long-established belief in God as a "personal" Being, intimate and ever-present. Long before him, as I Kings 19:2–11 reports, Elijah had been deeply discouraged by Queen Jezebel's threat to kill him, and he complained to God. In reply, God commanded Elijah to stand before Him on a mountain. Suddenly a violent storm broke:

> . . . A great and strong wind shattered the mountains and broke the rocks in pieces, but the Lord was not in the wind. After the wind, an earthquake came, but the Lord

was not in the earthquake. And after the earthquake, a
fire, but the Lord was not in the fire. And after the fire
there was a still, small voice. —I Kings 19:11–12

God, Elijah found, was not only in and above nature; His presence
was also felt within each person. For evidently the "still, small
voice" he heard was that inward experience we call "conscience."
Especially when we do something wrong, we hear this voice speaking to us. Here is God within us, rebuking us and making known
His demands.

We catch something of this same understanding of the "God
within us" in these words of one of the psalmists:

Behold, You desire truth in the inward being;
Therefore teach me wisdom in my secret heart. . . .
Create in me a clean heart, O God,
And put a new and steadfast spirit within me.
Cast me not away from Your Presence,
And take not Your holy Spirit from me.
—Psalm 51:8, 12–13

Similarly with Jeremiah. He knew that God was the mighty Creator
and Ruler of the universe, but at the same time he also felt Him
to be part of his own being. Though he was beaten and imprisoned
in stocks for condemning the people for their sins and predicting
the nation's destruction [Jeremiah 19:14–20:6], this inner voice
demanded that he carry on:

If I say, "I will not mention Him [God],
Or speak any more in His name,"
There is in my heart as it were a burning fire
Shut up in my bones,
And I am weary with holding it in,
Nor can I. —Jeremiah 20:9

That "burning fire" was God. It was He who made him know the
difference between good and evil, who also demanded that he speak
the "word of the Lord" [see Jeremiah 1:4–10]. Indeed, as God dwelt
within him, so was He to be found within all human hearts!

The God of the Bible

Who, then, is God as the Bible conceives of Him?

The answer is summed up in the teachings of the unknown
prophet whom we call Second Isaiah because his message was
added on to that of the original Isaiah. Here in his own words are
ten of God's distinctive characteristics:

1. GOD IS ONE AND UNIQUE:

"Remember this and stand fast . . . :
That I am God, and there is none else;
I am God, and there is none like Me!"
—Isaiah 46:8–9

"Before Me no God was formed,
Nor shall there be any after Me.
I, I am the Lord,
And besides Me there is no savior."
—Isaiah 43:10–11

". . . I am the first and I am the last;
Besides Me there is no God.
Who is like Me? Let him proclaim it,
Let him declare and set it forth before Me."
—Isaiah 44:6–7

2. GOD IS THE CREATOR OF ALL:

". . . I am the Lord, who made all things,
Who stretched out the heavens alone,
And who spread out the earth. . . ."
—Isaiah 44:24

". . . I am He; I am the first,
And I am the last.
My hand laid the foundation of the earth,
And My right hand spread out the heavens. . . ."
—Isaiah 48:12–13

3. GOD IS ALL-KNOWING, ALL-POWERFUL, AND
   ETERNAL:

"Why do you say, O Jacob,
And speak, O Israel:
'My way is hidden from the Lord,
And my right is disregarded by my God?'
Have you not known? Have you not heard?
The Lord is the everlasting God . . .
He does not faint or grow weary,
His understanding is unsearchable.
He gives power to the faint,
And to him who has no might He increases
strength. . . ." —Isaiah 40:27–29

4. GOD IS THE RULER OF HISTORY:

"Remember this and consider . . . :
Remember the former things of old;
For I am God, and there is no other;
I am God, and there is none like Me,
Declaring the end from the beginning,
And from ancient times things not yet done,
Saying, 'My counsel shall stand,

And I will accomplish all My purpose,'
. . . I have spoken, and I will bring it to pass;
I have purposed, and I will do." —Isaiah 46:8–11

5. GOD IS HOLY:

"I am the Lord, your Holy One,
The Creator of Israel, your King." —Isaiah 43:15

6. GOD IS RIGHTEOUS AND JUST:

". . . There is no other God besides Me,
A righteous God and a Savior;
There is none besides Me,
A just God and a Savior. . . ." —Isaiah 45:21

"I the Lord speak the truth,
I declare what is right." —Isaiah 45:19

"Listen to Me, My people,
And give ear to Me, My nation;
For a law will go forth from Me,
And My justice for a light to the peoples."
    —Isaiah 51:4

7. GOD IS MERCIFUL:

Seek the Lord while He may be found,
And call upon Him while He is near;
Let the wicked forsake his way,
And the unrighteous man his thoughts;
Let him return to the Lord, that He may
have mercy upon him,
And to our God, for He will abundantly pardon.
    —Isaiah 55:6–7

8. GOD CARES FOR MAN:

Behold the Lord God comes with might,
And His arm rules for Him;
Behold, His reward is with Him,
And His recompense before Him.
He will feed His flock like a shepherd,
And He will gather the lambs in His arms,
He will carry them in His bosom,
And gently lead those that are with young.
    —Isaiah 40:10–11

"When the poor and needy seek water,
and there is none,
And their tongue is parched with thirst,
I the Lord will answer them,
I the God of Israel will not forsake them."
    —Isaiah 41:17

9. GOD IS THE SAVIOR OF ALL MANKIND:

"Turn to Me and be saved,
All the ends of the earth!
For I am God, and there is no other." —Isaiah 45:22

"My deliverance draws near speedily,
And My salvation has gone forth . . .
My salvation will be for ever,
And My deliverance will never be ended."
   —Isaiah 51:5–6

10. IN THE FINAL ANALYSIS, HOWEVER, GOD IS
    REALLY UNKNOWABLE:

"For My thoughts are not your thoughts,
Neither are your ways My ways," says the Lord.
"For as the heavens are higher than the earth,
So are My ways higher than your ways,
And My thoughts than your thoughts."
   —Isaiah 55:8–9

It remained only for Malachi, the little-known prophet who probably lived among the Jews who returned to Palestine after the exile, to note that, of course, God was really the Father of all mankind. For he pointed out:

> Have we not all one Father
> Has not one God created us? —Malachi 2:10

This was echoed by the Book of Job. Here, in speaking about the servant and his master, the writer asks, "Did not He who made me in the womb make him? And did not One fashion us [both] in the womb?" [Job 31:13, 15].

An Answer . . . But with Problems

The Bible's final answer on the subject of God is clear. Though man can never hope to know everything about Him, he can be sure that He is one, holy, righteous and just, merciful, all-knowing, all-powerful, and eternal. The Creator of all, He is the living God of the universe, the Ruler of history, and the Father and Savior of all mankind. Existing everywhere in the world, He also dwells within the heart of man.

Here the writers of the Bible laid down the principle of "ethical monotheism," the belief in the One universal God who is completely righteous and demands righteousness from those who worship Him. They also established the foundations for the concept that all people are the children of their common Heavenly Father. With this arose the hope that some day the world would see a lasting brotherhood of all mankind united in righteousness, justice, and peace.

Essentially these remain our beliefs even today. For here, in *The Guiding Principles of Reform Judaism*, adopted by the Reform rabbinate in 1937, is a brief statement of our present-day view of God:

> The heart of Judaism and its chief contribution to religion is the doctrine of the One, living God, who rules the world through law and love. In Him all existence has its creative source and mankind its ideal of conduct. Though transcending [existing outside of] time and space, He is the indwelling Presence of the world. We worship Him as the Lord of the universe and as our merciful Father.

Nevertheless, with the completion of the Bible, the Jews did not cease thinking about the nature of God. Actually the spread of Greek culture, particularly the teachings of philosophy and their views of life and the universe, stimulated the rabbis to think all the more deeply about their beliefs. For example, the atheism of certain Greek thinkers challenged the rabbis to develop logical "proofs" for God's existence. And the different systems of Greek philosophy stimulated them to describe in more rational terms just how God operated in nature and history.

Still to some, even in Bible times, there appeared to be certain inconsistencies in their concept of God. One in particular had to do with the relationship between Him and the people of Israel. For, on the one hand, the Lord was proclaimed as the God of all mankind. Yet, on the other, Israel was considered His own chosen people. "Hear, O Israel," the Bible affirmed in the words of the Sh'ma, "the Lord [is] *our* God" [Deuteronomy 6:4].

But, we may ask, how can the God who is the Father of all mankind have a people of His own? And why should He?

These are questions to which the writers of the Bible also directed their attention. . . .

─────────── THINGS TO TALK OVER ───────────

1. In what respect is the "God of Abraham, Isaac, and Jacob" the God of the modern Jew?

2. How do the Bible's ideas about God confirm our view of it as a developing book of religion?

3. In what ways does the Reform Jew today draw upon the Bible for his conception of God?

4. With our scientific view of the universe, what position can we take regarding the biblical view of God's activity in nature and history?

———————— SOME OTHER BIBLE PASSAGES TO CONSIDER ————————

1. Contrast the prophets' view of God with that of the people described in II Kings 17:24–28.

2. To what extent would we share the point of view of Joshua 23 in urging our fellow Jews to remain faithful to God?

3. In what ways is the Lord different from idols? See Isaiah 40:18–26 and Jeremiah 10:1–10.

4. How did those who wrote the Bible conceive of God's effect on history? See Judges 3:7–11.

———————— FROM THE RABBIS' VIEWPOINT ————————

1. THE EXISTENCE OF GOD: See *Everyman's Talmud,* pp. 1–4; and *A Rabbinic Anthology,* [1–17] pp. 2–11, [21–22] p. 12, [1114] p. 405, [1332] p. 470.

2. GOD'S PRESENCE: See *Everyman's Talmud,* pp. 8–11; and *A Rabbinic Anthology,* [23–25] pp. 12–13, [27–41] pp. 15–21.

3. GOD'S JUSTICE AND MERCY: See *Everyman's Talmud,* pp. 17–21; and *A Rabbinic Anthology,* [19] p. 11, [620–632] pp. 234–238.

———————— OTHER THINGS TO READ ————————

BAMBERGER, BERNARD J., *The Story of Judaism,* Union of American Hebrew Congregations, Part 1: "The Foundations," pp. 5–55.

COHON, SAMUEL S., "The Jewish Idea of God," No. 28, *Popular Studies in Judaism,* Union of American Hebrew Congregations.

MILLER, MILTON G., and SCHWARTZMAN, SYLVAN D., *Our Religion and Our Neighbors,* Union of American Hebrew Congregations, Chap 2: "How Religion Began," pp. 19–29; Chap. 3: "Religion Develops Many Gods," pp. 31–41; Chap. 4: "The Hebrew God Demands Righteousness," pp. 42–54; Chap. 5: "Judaism Becomes a Missionary Faith," pp. 55–69.

STEINBERG, MILTON, *Basic Judaism,* Harcourt, Brace, Section 4: "God," pp. 31–58.

Three

DOES GOD HAVE A FAVORITE PEOPLE?

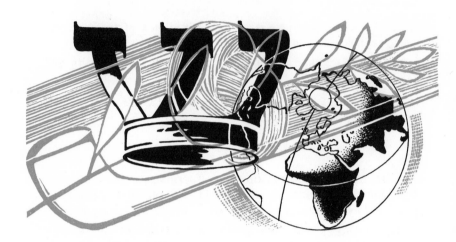

The Rabbi Questions God

THE TINY CHASIDIC SYNAGOGUE WAS CROWDED. IT WAS THE MORN-
ing of Rosh Ha-shono and all the worshipers were in the midst of
their prayers.

Suddenly the voice of the rabbi rang out—"I, Levi Yitzchok, son
of Sarah, speak to You, God. . . ."

A strange thing, indeed . . . interrupting the service. But the
congregation was not at all upset. Rabbi Levi Yitzchok of Berdit-
chev was often moved to speak out while praying. And this gifted
chasidic leader of the nineteenth century would frequently engage
God in conversation.

"What is he saying?" the people asked. They leaned forward to
catch his words. . . .

"Yes, I, Levi Yitzchok, am speaking to You, God. I have a question . . ."

A murmur ran through the congregation. "A question! He's asking God a question!"

"My question is: What do You, God of all the world, have
against the people of Israel? To whom do You always speak? To
the children of Israel! To whom do You give commandments? To

the children of Israel! Whom do You ask to worship You? The children of Israel! Are there not lots of other peoples that You could turn to? And so I ask You: What do You have against the children of Israel?"

"A good question!" ran through the congregation.

"Shh, the rabbi has an answer!" Quickly the synagogue became still.

"Ah," the rabbi was heard to say, "it is because the children of Israel are dear to You! Indeed, in Scripture do You not call them 'My children'? [Ezekiel 16:21]. Well, then, blessed are You, O Lord our God, Ruler of the world!"

Long afterwards the people recalled that particular Rosh Hashono day. "That was the time," they would say, "that our rabbi questioned God Himself!"

Are the Jews the "Chosen People"?

Although not quite so dramatically as Rabbi Levi Yitzchok, many have questioned God's relationship to the Jews. A certain poet put it this quaint way:

> How odd
> Of God
> To choose
> The Jews.

He calls attention here to two things. One is that God, the Father of all mankind, chose a particular people to be His very own. The other is, that of all peoples, He selected the Jews.

Both raise some real questions. How can the just and righteous God of the whole universe rightfully have a "favorite" people? Is this fair to the rest of mankind who are also His children?

Then, too, if the Almighty deems it necessary to have a people of His own, why should it be the Jews, a tiny, weak, and often persecuted group? And, in the long run, doesn't this give them an unfair advantage over others?

In the course of history, these questions have been raised many times. The early Christians, for example, vigorously disputed the Jews' claim of being the "chosen people," even to the point of calling their own sacred writings the "New Testament." Since the word "testament" really means "covenant," they maintained that God had entered into a new relationship with *them*, replacing His earlier covenant with the Jews. In fact, the Christians even called themselves the "New Israel," indicating that they now considered *themselves* God's chosen people.

The issue over God's selection of the Jews still arises from time to time. Not long ago, for instance, the famous English historian Arnold Toynbee termed this belief an "error" on the part of the Jews. "They [the Jews]," he wrote, "persuaded themselves that Israel's discovery of the One True God had revealed Israel to be God's Chosen People."

Even certain Jews have raised objections. One of them is Mordecai Kaplan, a retired professor of the Jewish Theological Seminary (Conservative) and leader of the Reconstructionist movement in Judaism. He holds that the Jewish religion has outgrown the notion of a chosen people, and in his book, *The Future of the American Jew,* he has written, "We . . . advocate the elimination from our own liturgy of all references to . . . Israel as the Chosen People."

Most Jews would not agree. This belief is too deeply rooted in our history and practice. In fact, because it is so meaningful, before we read the Torah in the synagogue we customarily recite:

> Praised are You, O Lord our God, Ruler of the universe, *who has chosen us from among all peoples* and has given us Your Torah. Praised are You, the Giver of the Torah.

For well over two thousand years, then, the Jews have looked upon themselves as chosen by God. Actually, as the Bible tells us, the idea goes all the way back to the beginnings of the Jewish people. And, like their beliefs about God, this, too, was a developing concept.

An Ancient Agreement with God

On the third month after the Hebrew slaves departed from Egypt, so the Book of Exodus relates, they were camped before Mount Sinai [Exodus 19:1–2]. And Moses made his way up the mountain. Then the voice of the Lord came to him, saying:

> ". . . Thus shall you say to the house of Jacob and tell the children of Israel: You have seen what I did to the Egyptians. . . . Now if you will indeed listen to My voice and keep My covenant, then you will be My own treasure from among all peoples. . . . These are the words which you shall tell the children of Israel."
>
> Then Moses came and called for the elders of the people, and set before them all these words which the Lord had commanded him. And all the people answered together and

said: "All that the Lord has spoken we will do." And Moses
reported the words of the people to the Lord.
—Exodus 19:3–8

In this manner did the people of Israel enter into an agreement
with their God. For their part, they were to worship only Him and
carry out His commandments. God, in turn, pledged Himself to
help His people in numerous ways—to defeat their enemies [Exodus 23:27–28], to keep them from sickness [Exodus 23:25–26], and
to secure the land of Palestine for them and their descendants [Exodus 23:30–31].

However, the establishment of a covenant with one's god by
other peoples of the Near East was not anything unusual. Many
scholars believe that the names of certain deities indicate a close
personal relationship between themselves and their peoples. Thus,
Moloch, the god of a people who lived in the neighborhood of
Jerusalem, is a name that really means "king," and Baal, the god
of the Canaanites, means "master" or "possessor of the land."

Actually, the Bible states that very early in the history of man,
God established a covenant with Noah that was to apply for all
times to the whole human race [Genesis 9:8–17]. For His part, God
promised never again to send a great flood upon earth. Though in
the preceding verses Noah is called upon only to refrain from murder and eating flesh cut from a living animal [Genesis 9:4–6], later
Jewish tradition claimed that God made it obligatory upon him as
well as all people to obey five other commandments. In addition to
the two already mentioned, the seven "Noachian Laws," as they are
called, required them to establish courts of justice and avoid idolatry, blasphemy, adultery, and robbery. Through this covenant.
God thereby established His relationship to all mankind.

But God also entered into a succession of covenants with the
Patriarchs. To Abraham He is said to have declared:

> "I am God Almighty [*El Shaddai*]; walk before Me and be
> blameless. And I will establish My covenant between you
> and Me, and will multiply you exceedingly."
> —Genesis 17:1–2

Moreover God had already promised him, ". . . Through you [and
your descendants] shall all the families of the earth bless themselves" [Genesis 12:3].

And Abraham, in turn, accepted the covenant:

> Then Abraham fell on his face, and God said to him, "Behold My covenant is with you. . . ." —Genesis 17:3–4

The Book of Genesis reports that God renewed this covenant with Isaac [Genesis 26:2–5]. Jacob, too, established a covenant with God, this time in the name of *Elohim* or *El* [Genesis 28:13–22]. Thus, the fact that the Hebrew people was chosen by God early in its history was plain to those who wrote the Bible.

The Conditions of Choice

But why did God select Israel?

Not because of any special merit on their part, but because of His love for them. Israel was to be His own special vehicle for His purposes, for they were told:

> . . . The Lord your God has chosen you to be His own treasure from among all of the peoples that are upon the face of the earth. The Lord did not set His love upon you, nor choose you, because you were more in number than any other people—for you were the fewest of all peoples—but because the Lord loved you. . . . —Deuteronomy 7:6–8

And what in return were the obligations that the people of Israel were expected to fulfil?

Many scholars believe that the original obligations are those found in the so-called "Book of the Covenant" of Exodus 20:22–23:19. As we see there, these call for carrying on certain forms of worship, the observance of three sacred festivals, and insuring the proper execution of justice. In this last regard, particularly, the covenant is unique. For basic to the worship of the Lord are fair treatment of strangers, widows, and orphans [Exodus 22:20–23], consideration for the poor [Exodus 22:24–26], and impartial administration of justice [Exodus 23:1–3, 6–9].

In God's sight, therefore, even from earliest times, the fulfilment of the covenant demanded a high degree of righteousness from His people. And over the years the Hebrew people were repeatedly reminded that the true worship of the Lord involved important moral and ethical obligations.

Later Jewish tradition came to look upon this as the very reason why God chose Israel to be His people. The rabbis of the early centuries of the Common Era said that when God decided to give His Torah to mankind, He approached all seventy nations of the world to see which would accept it. The Edomites, a fierce, warfaring people, refused to take the Torah when they learned that among its laws was "You must not kill." Because immorality was prohibited, the Moabites, who traced back their origin to an act of unchastity committed by the daughters of Lot, also declined. The Ishmaelites, noted for thievery, likewise rejected it because of the command not to steal. One by one all the rest of the nations refused the Torah, except the people of Israel. They promptly responded, "All that the Lord has spoken we will do and obey" [Exodus 24:7].

This, of course, is legend, but it does point to the key element in the choice of Israel. They were chosen to serve God through religious living, a fundamental obligation of which is the practice of righteousness.

The Emphasis of the Prophets

With the settlement of the Hebrews in the land of Palestine, God's demands upon them continued to increase until they eventually comprised the greater part of the Torah. In rabbinic times, these were said to number 613 commandments, of which 365 were prohibitions against certain acts, and the balance duties to be performed. Taken as a whole, these 613 commandments included almost every kind of law—ritual, moral, ethical, civil, and criminal.

Always central among the demands were those calling for righteous conduct. The Ten Commandments are a good example [see Exodus 20:1–14 or Deuteronomy 5:6–18]. In addition to banning idol-worship and insisting upon honoring one's parents and observing a day of rest, they sternly prohibit false oaths, murder, adultery, theft, bearing false witness, and "covetousness" or greed.

Nevertheless, as time passed and the separate Kingdoms of Israel and Judah came into existence, many people tended to place greater stress upon ritual observance. To them the worship of the Lord was thought of mainly in terms of the celebration of festivals and the offering of sacrifices. Less and less attention was paid to the moral demands of the covenant.

This was particularly disturbing to the prophets, and they did not hesitate to voice their objection. Samuel protested against the greed with which the people took spoil of the Amalekites, a direct violation of God's command [I Samuel 15]. Though King Saul tried to excuse the people on the grounds that they seized all the animals because they were eager to offer them up as sacrifices, Samuel rejected this, saying:

> . . . Has the Lord as great a delight in burnt-
> offerings and sacrifices,

As in listening to the voice of the Lord?
Behold, to obey is better than sacrifice,
And to listen, than the fat of rams. —I Samuel 15:22

Nathan, as we have seen, condemned King David for taking away another man's wife and thereby sinning against the Lord [II Samuel 11–12:15], and Elijah likewise predicted the doom of King Ahab for stealing the vineyard of Naboth [I Kings 21:1–24]. But it was Amos, one of the first of the literary prophets, who placed the issue squarely before the Hebrew people as a whole.

This Judean shepherd had made his way to the city of Beth-El in the Kingdom of Israel. There at the royal shrine he addressed the crowd and proceeded to describe their more serious transgressions:

> . . . They sell the righteous for silver,
> And the needy for a pair of shoes;
> They trample the head of the poor into the
> dust of the earth,
> And drive the afflicted out of the way;
> And a man and his father have relations
> with the same maiden. . . . —Amos 2:6–7

Instead of obeying the moral obligations of the covenant, the people have stressed ritual observance. Thus does the prophet taunt the Israelites:

> Come to Beth-El and transgress;
> To Gilgal [another shrine] and multiply
> transgression.
> Bring your sacrifices every morning,
> Your tithes every three days;
> Offer a sacrifice of thanksgiving of that
> which is leavened;
> Proclaim freewill-offerings and announce them.
> For so you love to do, O people of Israel. . . .
> —Amos 4:4–5

But, says the prophet, God Himself protests:

> "I hate, I despise your feasts,
> And I take no delight in your religious gatherings.
> Even though you offer Me your burnt-offerings
> and your meal-offerings,
> I will not accept them;
> And the peace-offerings of your fatted beasts
> I will not look upon.
> Take away from Me the noise of your hymns;

> I will not listen to the melody of your harps.
> But let justice roll down like waters,
> And righteousness like an ever-flowing stream!"
> —Amos 5:21–24

The issue is clear. If Israel's covenant with God calls for the performance of certain rituals, it also demands whole-hearted obedience to His laws of righteousness. Rites and sacrifices are not substitutes for justice and morality.

Consequently the people of Israel can no longer count upon the protection of the Lord. Certainly not, Amos thunders! For if the breaking of an agreement among men is a dishonorable act, how much the more so when it involves a covenant between God and His very own people. And speaking in the name of the Lord the prophet exclaims:

> "You only have I known of all the families
> of the earth;
> Therefore will I punish you for all your
> iniquities." —Amos 3:2

To enjoy the benefits of the covenant, the people must:

> Seek good and not evil, that you may live;
> And consequently the Lord, the God of hosts,
> will be with you, as you have said.
> Hate evil and love good,
> And establish justice in the gate;
> It may be [then] that the Lord, the God of hosts,
> Will be gracious to the remnant of Joseph. —Amos 5:14–15

To Amos, as to all the succeeding prophets, the covenant conferred responsibility, not privilege, upon the people. They were not chosen because they were superior. Rather, they were chosen to show how God's righteousness could be made the basis of everyday life. Therefore, similar protests against the people's misconduct were voiced by Hosea [4:1–2], Isaiah [1:4–6], Jeremiah [5:1–14], and others. They warned first the people of Israel, then Judah, of the consequences of breaking their covenant with the Lord. For God would surely revoke His part of the agreement if the people failed to live up to their obligations. So, one prophet puts it:

> If you are willing and obedient,
> You shall eat the good of the land;
> But if you refuse and rebel,
> You shall be devoured by the sword. . . .
> —Isaiah 1:19–20

The Necessity for Holiness

The downfall of Israel and the impending danger of a similar fate for the people of the Southern Kingdom led the prophets to call ever more vigorously for obedience to God's righteous demands.

Meanwhile over the years the requirements for righteous living had continued to expand. Among other things, they now included a stricter code of sexual morality [such as we find, for instance, in Leviticus 18] and even greater insistence upon fair and humane treatment of one's fellow man [such as, for instance, Leviticus 19:9–18 and 19:32–36].

The declining days of the Judean Kingdom, followed by its destruction and the exile of most of its people, saw a new emphasis upon the necessity for "holiness" as God's chosen people. "Sanctify yourselves and be holy, for I am the Lord your God," is the way it is expressed in Leviticus 20:7. God is said to have informed the people that the terms of their covenant meant:

> "If you will obey My voice and keep My covenant, then you shall be My own treasure from among all peoples, for all the earth is Mine; and you shall be unto Me a kingdom of priests and a holy nation. . . ." —Exodus 19:5–6

Or as another passage states:

> You are a holy people unto the Lord your God, and the Lord has chosen you to be His own treasure from among all the peoples that are upon the face of the earth.
> —Deuteronomy 14:2

To be holy, then, was really the commitment that the children of Israel had made at Mount Sinai.

What was meant by "holiness"? In general, two things. Carrying on the ritual worship of God was one. Thus, after prescribing a series of religious rites, Chapter 15 of the Book of Numbers sums them up with:

> . . . Remember and do all My commandments and be *holy* unto your God. —Numbers 15:40

But no less imperative was proper ethical and moral conduct. Chapter 19 of the Book of Leviticus begins with the call to the children of Israel:

> You shall be holy; for I the Lord your God am holy.
> —Leviticus 19:2

And what follows is a listing of various impediments to holiness. Significantly these include neglect of the poor, acting falsely and lying, dealing unjustly with one's employees, perverting justice, and the like [see Leviticus 19:9–18].

To maintain the covenant with God, then, meant being holy in matters of both ritual practice and personal conduct.

A Holy People . . . Forever

The obligation to be holy was of concern to more than just the individual Jew. Just as the covenant was made with the *entire* people of Israel, so one's *personal* holiness, or lack of it, affected the character of the *whole* people. "You," God says to all the household of Israel, "shall be unto Me a kingdom of priests and a holy nation" [Exodus 19:6]. And Amos reminds the people that because of the transgressions of individuals, the nations of Israel and Judah must pay [Amos 2:4–8].

Moreover the obligation to be a holy people is an eternal one. The covenant between Israel and the Lord, Moses reports, has not been made solely with his own generation:

> "Nor is it with you alone that I make this covenant and this oath, but with him who is not here with us this day as well as with him who stands here with us this day before the Lord our God." —Deuteronomy 29:13–14

To confirm this, the covenant is renewed repeatedly—by Moses in the plains of Moab [see Deuteronomy 28:69; 29:9–14], by Joshua before his death [see Joshua 24:21–28], by the high priest Jehoiada when Jehoash is made King of Judah [see II Kings 11:17], and by King Josiah after he reads the book of the law that has been found in the Temple [II Kings 23:2–3].

Hence this is an everlasting agreement between God and the children of Israel [see also Genesis 17:7–9]. The observance of the Sabbath testifies to this [Exodus 31:16–17]. And, though God might permit the Babylonians to conquer Jerusalem, destroy the Temple, exile His people, and let them suffer, God, says Jeremiah, has no intention of abandoning His covenant with Israel:

> Thus says the Lord: "If you can break My covenant with the day and My covenant with the night, so that day and night will not come at their appointed time, then also My covenant with David My servant may be broken. . . ."
> —Jeremiah 33:20–21

The prophet also promises that in the future, when the Jewish people will have overcome its wickedness, God will establish a "new covenant," that is, a more perfect relationship with them [Jeremiah 31:31–32]. It is no new Law, or new "Testament" as the older English expression has it, that he speaks of here, as the Christians suggest. Rather it means that the people will become so inwardly attuned to all their moral responsibilities that they will carry them out automatically. For thus the prophet hears God declare:

> "This is the covenant which I will make with the house of Israel after those days . . . I will put My law within them, and I will write it upon their hearts. I will be their God and they shall be My people. And no longer shall each man [have to] teach his neighbor and his brother, saying, 'Know the Lord,' for they will all know Me, from the least of them to the greatest . . . I will forgive their iniquity, and I will no longer remember their sins." —Jeremiah 31:33–34

In the meantime, every Jew must constantly bear in mind his people's covenant with God, for the Bible insists:

> . . . These words [God's commandments] which I command you this day shall be upon your heart. And you shall teach them diligently to your children and talk of them when you sit in your house, when you walk on the way, when you lie down, and when you rise up.
> —Deuteronomy 6:6–7

Israel, Servant of the Lord

The nature of the relationship between Israel and God underwent a further development during the Babylonian exile. It was then that Second Isaiah pointed out that the ancient covenant also imposed a special "mission" upon the Jewish people. In fact, in a number of passages which have become known as the "Servant Songs," he describes Israel as the Servant of the Lord. So he has God say to the people:

> ". . . You, Israel My servant.
> Jacob, whom I have chosen,
> The seed of Abraham, My friend;
> You whom I have taken hold of from the ends of the earth,
> And called from the uttermost parts thereof,
> And said unto you: 'You are My servant,
> I have chosen you and not rejected you.'
> Fear not for I am with you;

> Be not dismayed, for I am your God.
> I will strengthen you; yes, I will help you. . . ."
>   —Isaiah 41:8–10

God has a particular reason for strengthening them. As His Servant, Israel:

> " . . . Shall make righteousness go forth
> to the nations. . . .
> He will not fail or be discouraged
> Until he has established justice throughout the world,
> And the coastlands wait for his teachings."
>   —Isaiah 42:1, 4

Yes, God's servant-people must bring knowledge of justice and righteousness to every nation. More than this, the whole world must know that the Lord is the God of the universe:

> "Declare and present your case;
> Let them [the nations] take counsel together!
> Who told this long ago?
> Who declared it of old?
> Was it not I, the Lord?
> And there is no other God besides Me,
> A righteous God and a Savior;
> There is none besides Me.
> Turn to Me and be saved,
> All the ends of the earth!
> For I am God and there is no other.
> By Myself I have sworn,
> From My mouth has gone forth in righteousness
> A word that shall not return:
> 'To Me every knee shall bow,
> Every tongue shall swear!'" —Isaiah 45:21–23

The Jews will perform their mission not simply by telling the word of God and His righteous demands, but by *living* them. In this way Israel will be "a light unto the nations":

> "I am the Lord, I have called you in righteousness,
> I have taken you by the hand and kept you;
> I have given you as a covenant to the people,
> For a light unto the nations,
> To open the eyes that are blind,
> To bring out the prisoners from the dungeon,
> From the prison those who sit in darkness. . . ."
>   —Isaiah 42:6–7

Hence, as the chosen people, Israel has not been singled out by God for special privileges and rewards, but for special responsibilities to mankind. Certainly the experience of exile shows that the Jews have not been accorded favored treatment. Actually they have suffered great punishment because of their selection [Isaiah 53:3–9]. But the Jew can derive satisfaction from the fact that:

> "By his knowledge [of God and His ways],
> My servant makes many to become righteous."
> —Isaiah 53:11

And it is this concept of the role of the Jewish people which unquestionably helped sustain their hopes all during the Exile.

The Promise of a Return

But the people were also encouraged by their faith that some day they would be restored to the Land of Israel.

Hadn't God promised the land to Abraham for all time? For in entering into the covenant with him He said:

> "And I will give to you and your descendants after you the land of your sojournings, all the land of Canaan, for an everlasting possession. . . ." —Genesis 17:8

And hadn't He renewed that pledge to Jacob? [see Genesis 35:12].

Once again, when He called Moses to take the children of Israel out of Egypt, He promised to restore them to the land of Canaan, "a land flowing with milk and honey" [Exodus 3:17]. "A good land," He called it [see Deuteronomy 8:7–9], and always under His watchful scrutiny [Deuteronomy 11:12]. And truly the people were led back to the land under Joshua. In return they pledged to serve only the Lord wholeheartedly [see Joshua 24].

But, as the prophets reminded them, they had not kept their word. Because, said Hosea:

> You have gone astray from your God. . . .
> Therefore you shall not dwell in the Lord's land.
> —Hosea 9:1–3

First the Kingdom of Israel to the north, then Judah to the south were destroyed and their people taken into exile. The long-promised punishment had befallen them.

To the exiles in Babylonia eventually came the word of the Lord through Jeremiah His prophet:

> "In the time to come," says the Lord, "the people of Israel and the people of Judah shall come together, weeping as they come; and they shall seek the Lord their God. They

shall ask the way to Zion with faces turned toward it, saying, 'Come, let us join ourselves to the Lord in an everlasting covenant that will never be forgotten.'"
—Jeremiah 50:4–5

Yes, when the people, God's flock, have fully paid for their sins
and are no longer wicked:

"I [the Lord] will restore Israel to his pasture,
He shall feed on Carmel and Bashan,
And his desires will be satisfied on the hills
of Ephraim and in Gilead." —Jeremiah 50:19

This promise that Israel would someday be restored to the land that
the Lord had given them sustained the people in their exile, and continued to comfort them during their sufferings down through the
ages. To this very day, the settlers of the modern State of Israel
have drawn their inspiration from this ancient promise.

The Reluctant Servant

What seemed utterly impossible to the Babylonian exiles actually
happened!

In the year 538 B.C.E., almost fifty years after the destruction of
Jerusalem, King Cyrus of Persia, the new master of Babylonia, gave
permission for some of the Jews to return to Palestine.

Those who returned—and they were a relatively small group—
found life in Palestine precarious. On the one hand they were
forced to protect themselves against hostile neighbors [Nehemiah
3:33–4:12] and the inroads of assimilation [Nehemiah 10:29–40].
On the other hand, they had to recultivate a barren land [see, for
example, Haggai 1 and Ezra 6:14–16]. As a result, their own self-
preservation and the safeguarding of Judaism began to claim all
their energies. Even those in Babylonia began to think less about
their mission to others and more about their own survival as a
people.

It was during this period, many believe, that the Book of Jonah
was written as a reminder to the people of their wider mission to
all mankind. In this interesting tale built upon the experience of a
reluctant prophet, the Jewish people is taken to task for neglecting
its role as servant of the Lord.

At the start of the book, God commands the prophet Jonah to go
to the city of Nineveh, the capital of Assyria, and condemn the people for their sins. But Jonah is unwilling to go; he sees no point in

prophesying to non-Jews. He tries to escape his duty by going on a long sea voyage where he thinks he will be out of the reach of the Lord. But a terrible storm arises. To save the rest of the crew and passengers, Jonah voluntarily offers to be thrown overboard into the sea. Three days later he is cast up on land, not too far from Nineveh.

Realizing now that he cannot escape his mission, the prophet makes his way to the city and there preaches his message of destruction. Moved by his words the people promptly begin fasting and begging God for forgiveness. God hears their pleas and forgives them, much to the despair and anger of the prophet. In fact, Jonah tells God:

> ". . . Is this not what I said when I was still in my own country? That is why I made haste to flee to Tarshish, for I know that You are a gracious God and merciful, slow to anger, and abounding in love, who repents of any harsh intentions.
>
> Therefore, now, O Lord, take my life, I beseech You, for it is better for me to die than live." —Jonah 4:2–3

And Jonah stubbornly sits himself down in a booth to see whether God will change His mind about the fate of Nineveh.

All day long the hot sun burns down upon him, and Jonah suffers greatly. Taking pity on him, God causes a large plant to spring up to shade him from the sun. But it soon perishes and Jonah laments over its destruction. Then God says to him:

> ". . . You have had pity on this plant which required no labor on your part and which you did not cause to grow. It came up in a night and withered in a night. Then should I not have pity on the great city of Nineveh . . . ?"
> —Jonah 4:10–11

This story, of course, is a parable; that is, fiction which tries to teach a moral lesson. In the mind of the author, Jonah represents the people of Israel. Like the prophet, their viewpoint has become narrow; they think only of themselves. But must they also not bear in mind the welfare of the other peoples of the world? Their existence and conduct must be such as to remind the non-Jews of their own moral responsibilities. For under the Noachian laws given to all mankind, they, too, have duties to God.

Therefore, in their concern only for themselves, the people of Israel have been shirking their wider responsibilities. But, as the Servant of the Lord, they, like Jonah, cannot escape them.

The Purpose of Israel's Mission

With the passing of time the people of Israel once more firmly established their own nation in Palestine. Though the majority continued to live in Babylonia, even they were moved by the prophets' promises that eventually all the Jews would be restored to the Promised Land in triumph. "All the outcasts of Israel and . . . the dispersed of Judah He [God] will gather from the four corners of the earth" [Isaiah 11:12]. "On that day," proclaims Zephaniah:

> "I [the Lord] will bring you [Israel] home,
> At the time when I gather you together.
> Yes, I will make you renowned and praised
> Among all the peoples of the earth,
> When I put an end to all your dispersion
> before your eyes,"
> Says the Lord. —Zephaniah 3:20

"You will enjoy the wealth of all the nations," promises another prophet [Isaiah 60:11], and "no more will there be violence in the land" [Isaiah 60:18]. More than this, the various enemies that still threaten the existence of the tiny nation already reestablished in Palestine must either serve Israel or face destruction, as we read:

> For the nation and kingdom that will not
> serve you [Israel] will perish;
> Those nations shall be utterly laid waste. —Isaiah 60:12

This continuing hope for a glorious national future in no way denied the wider purpose for the Jews' existence; rather this hope would really deepen and expand it because the restored nation would aid in spreading the knowledge of God and His ways. Faithfully carrying out this "Mission," as it came to be called, the people would ultimately bring about the appearance of the "Messianic Age," that time when God would reign over the entire earth.

A passage in the Book of Psalms describes that future age. It will be a time when:

> All the ends of the earth shall remember
> and turn unto the Lord;
> And all the families of the nations shall worship Him.
> For dominion belongs to the Lord,
> And He is the ruler over the nations. —Psalm 22:28–29

Does this mean that the Jews are to convert all the other peoples to Judaism? No, the idea of making converts actively arises only in the post-biblical period.

The Bible, to be sure, often mentions the "stranger" who dwells among the people of Israel [for example, Leviticus 24:22 and Numbers 15:15], and in a number of places it is clear that the term refers to a convert to Judaism. The prophet Isaiah speaks of "the stranger who shall join himself to them [the people of Israel] and shall cleave to the house of Jacob" [Isaiah 14:1], and the writer of Exodus 12:48 refers to "the stranger" who is circumcised and observes the Passover. The heroine of the Book of Ruth is, of course, a Moabite woman who has converted to Judaism [see Ruth 1], and the Book of Esther even makes mention of "many who became Jews" [Esther 8:17].

But within the Bible itself there is no real indication that the Mission of the Jews ever called for active "proselytizing." To lead exemplary lives so that other peoples would be mindful of the Lord and become faithful to their own moral commitment as required by His covenant with Noah was the essence of Israel's Mission.

For in this way the Kingdom of God would come to be established upon earth.

The Nature of God's Kingdom

How did the Jews envision that Kingdom?

It was to center about the worship of God in the Temple in Jerusalem. God's Kingdom would be established when:

> . . . The mountain of the Lord's house shall be established
> as the highest of the mountains,
> And shall be raised above the hills.
> All nations shall flow to it,
> And many peoples shall then say:
> "Come, let us go up to the mountain of the Lord,
> To the house of the God of Jacob;
> That He may teach us His ways,
> And we may walk in His paths. . . ." —Isaiah 2:2–3

Once having learned of God's demands:

> . . . The earth shall be full of the knowledge of the Lord,
> As the waters cover the sea. —Isaiah 11:9

And the consequences for mankind will be wonderful indeed! The nations will flock to the banner of a ruler upon whom:

> The spirit of the Lord shall rest . . .
> The spirit of wisdom and understanding,
> The spirit of counsel and might,

The spirit of knowledge and reverence for the Lord,
And his delight shall be in reverence for the Lord . . .
With righteousness he shall judge the poor,
And decide with fairness for the lowly of the earth . . .
With the breath of his lips will he slay the wicked.
Righteousness shall be the girdle of his waist,
And faithfulness the girdle of his loins. —Isaiah 11:2–5

And for the whole world there will be everlasting peace and security:

> . . . He [the Lord] will judge between the nations,
> And decide for many peoples,
> And they shall beat their swords into plowshares,
> And their spears into pruning-hooks.
> Nation shall not lift up sword against nation,
> Neither shall they learn war any more.
>   —Isaiah 2:4; Micah 4:3

> But they shall sit every man under his
> vine and under his fig-tree,
> And none shall make them afraid. . . . —Micah 4:4

With this glorious picture the concept of the Chosen People and their Mission reaches its climax. Truly God's promise to Abraham will then have been fulfilled:

> ". . . And through your descendants shall all the nations of the earth bless themselves, because you have obeyed My voice." —Genesis 22:18

Answering the Question

Well, then, what about the question with which we began? Does God have a favorite people?

If we understand the term correctly, then the answer of the Bible is "yes."

But this, as we have seen, does not mean that the Jews have been singled out for special favors. Far from it! We have been chosen for carrying out the exacting duties of being God's Servant. Ours is the task of being a holy people and thereby reminding the world of God and of His demands for righteousness. The Father of mankind entrusted this task to the Jews so that His Kingdom might ultimately be established on earth for the benefit of all His children. In this sense alone are we "favored."

All of this imposes heavy responsibilities upon us. Our ancient covenant requires that we be holy and live according to God's requirements. Setting an example of righteousness, justice, and brotherliness, we will thereby influence all mankind to worship the Lord as the true God.

This belief that God has selected the Jews appears to be amply confirmed by the course of history. That we have survived all these centuries in spite of every kind of hardship seems too remarkable to be accidental. Other more powerful peoples, like the Canaanites, Babylonians, Romans, and the rest, have long since disappeared. Yet the Jews, one of the tiniest and weakest of the peoples, continue to exist. In fact, after nearly two thousand years our people have even reestablished themselves in their ancient land. Certainly all this suggests something far deeper and more significant than mere accident.

The truth is that we have been preserved to carry on our Mission. Despite the fact that others, such as the Moslems and Christians, have joined with us by accepting much of the Bible's teachings, we are still needed to set the example as a holy people and to remind all others of God's will. For, while we welcome the assistance of others, we do not believe this can relieve us of our particular responsibility as God's special servant. To continue to know Him and His will in as true a way as possible, to strive to live our lives according to that knowledge, and to proclaim it constantly to the nations—all this remains our unique obligation as a people whose covenant with God is eternal.

That Mission has been vital throughout history, but never has it been more urgently required than today. The wholesale production of rockets, missiles, and hydrogen bombs urgently reminds us how much the survival of mankind depends upon the fulfilment of God's moral demands. For we still insist with the prophets of long ago that lasting peace can come only as His reign of righteousness, justice, and brotherhood is established upon earth. Hence, the Jews' task of spreading that message is imperative in our day.

Thus, nearly two thousand years after the completion of the Bible, the belief that we have been selected by God for a special Mission remains a central teaching of our religion. Here is the way *The Guiding Principles of Reform Judaism*, adopted by the Reform rabbinate in 1937, expresses it:

> Throughout the ages it has been Israel's mission to witness to the Divine in the face of every form of paganism and materialism. We regard it as our historic task to cooperate with all men in the establishment of the Kingdom of God, of universal brotherhood, justice, truth, and peace on earth. This is our Messianic goal.

We have survived to fulfil this Mission. Yet this very belief in a Mission also helped to insure that survival. In interpreting the Bible for succeeding generations, the rabbis often referred to it. From the concept of Israel's Mission as well as the promise of a return to Palestine they derived much comfort for the Jew in times of persecution and still greater challenge. In the selection of the people of Israel, for example, they saw one of the prime purposes for which God created the world. The continued existence of the Jews, they also held, was the one indispensable factor in the preservation of mankind. Moreover, in an age when various faiths, including Christianity as well as many pagan cults, were competing for people's spiritual allegiance, the rabbis encouraged proselytism as a means of bringing the non-Jew more fully under the will of God.

In these and other ways, then, did they build upon the teachings of the Bible for the continuing development of Judaism.

Does God Control Us?

We have now explored one of the problems involved in the biblical conception of God—that of His selection of Israel.

But this is only one. Another problem concerns man's freedom. For if, as the Bible maintains, God is the Ruler of history and the universe, doesn't He determine everything that happens to us? If so, how is it possible for man to make any of his own decisions?

Our answer here can have far-reaching consequences. If we hold that people can do as they wish, then what role does God play in human affairs? And, more than this, if man is free can God really rule over history and the universe?

But if God decides everything that happens to us, can we hold any human being responsible for his acts? If, for example, a criminal says, "God made me do it," can we rightfully punish him for his crime?

At this point we must be wondering how those who wrote the Bible dealt with this problem. Let us see. . . .

THINGS TO TALK OVER

1. Recently some Jews have advocated that our people should again actively seek to gain converts to Judaism. How do you think those who wrote the Bible would react to this?

2. What answer would you give someone who argued that the concept of Israel as the Chosen People shows favoritism on the part of God?

3. In what ways does history seem to confirm the biblical teachings concerning the Mission of Israel?

4. In the light of the Bible what connection is there between ourselves and the Jews of the modern State of Israel?

───────────── SOME OTHER BIBLE PASSAGES TO CONSIDER─────────

1. How do you think the writer of the Book of Jonah would have reacted to the situation described in Ezra 9–10:19?

2. For what main purposes did the writers of the Bible see the necessity for a restoration of Israel to Palestine? See Isaiah 11 and 52; Ezekiel 11:14–21; Haggai 1; Zechariah 8.

3. In what respects have the policies of the modern State of Israel been influenced by the following: Deuteronomy 8:7–10; Isaiah 61:4; 65:18–22; and Jeremiah 29:14?

4. Whom does Psalm 15 picture as holy to God?

───────────────── FROM THE RABBIS' VIEWPOINT─────────────

1. GOD'S CHOICE OF ISRAEL: See *Everyman's Talmud,* pp. 62–65; and *A Rabbinic Anthology,* [209–218] pp. 77–81.

2. ISRAEL'S MISSION: See *Everyman's Talmud,* pp. 64–67; and *A Rabbinic Anthology,* [289–304] pp. 110–115.

3. THE LAND OF ISRAEL: See *Everyman's Talmud,* pp. 374, 383–384, 390; and *A Rabbinic Anthology,* [35] p. 17, [1560] p. 557, [1650–1651] p. 600.

─────────────────── OTHER THINGS TO READ───────────────

BAMBERGER, BERNARD J., *The Story of Judaism,* Union of American Hebrew Congregations, pp. 17, 35, 39–40, 172, 282, 320–321, 375, 443–444.

FACKENHEIM, EMIL L., *Paths to Jewish Belief,* Behrman, Chap. 10, "Why Do We Remain Jews?" pp. 117–129.

GITTELSOHN, ROLAND B., *Little Lower Than the Angels,* Union of American Hebrew Congregations, pp. 208–210, 215.

HELLER, BERNARD, "The Jewish Concept of the Chosen People," No. 31, *Popular Studies in Judaism,* Union of American Hebrew Congregations.

SILVER, ABBA HILLEL, *Where Judaism Differed*, Macmillan, Chap. 2, "A Pattern in History," pp. 11–21.

STEINBERG, MILTON, *Basic Judaism*, Harcourt, Brace, Section 6: "Israel and the Nations," pp. 91–115.

ARE WE REALLY FREE?

Was God Fair to Pharaoh?

AS HE STOOD BEFORE THE BURNING BUSH, MOSES HEARD GOD SAY:

> "Come now and I will send you to Pharaoh that you may
> bring forth My people, the children of Israel, out of Egypt."
> —Exodus 3:10

Moses was by no means eager to go. First, there was the matter of
personal risk. Was he not a hunted man for having killed an
Egyptian taskmaster [Exodus 2:11–15]? Then, too, he questioned
his own ability to carry out the assignment. The people did not
know this God, Yahveh, who was sending him [Exodus 3:13]; nor
would they believe that he had really been sent by Him [Exodus
4:1]. And because of a speech impediment how would he even be
able to make himself understood to Pharaoh [Exodus 4:10]?

To each objection, God had an answer. Finally, the still reluctant
Moses agreed.

On the way to Egypt Moses received some new and very dis-
quieting information. God told him that Pharaoh would not be
easily convinced to free the Hebrews. As a matter of fact, God
would deliberately see to it that Pharaoh refused. So we learn from
Exodus 4:21 where He tells Moses:

". . . When you go back to Egypt, see to it that you do before Pharaoh all the wonders that I have put into your hand. But I will harden his heart and he will not let the people go."

The rest of the story bears this out. Time and again Pharaoh refuses Moses' request, and this in turn prompts God to send still another plague to afflict him and his people [Exodus 7:14–10:28]. All the while God continues to "harden Pharaoh's heart" [Exodus 9:12; 10:1, 20, 27; 11:10].

Finally, as a result of the tenth plague, the death of all the first-born males of Egypt, Pharaoh relents and permits Moses and his people to leave [Exodus 12:29–32]. But once the Hebrews are gone, Pharaoh undergoes a change of heart. "What have we done, letting Israel go from being our slaves?" he suddenly realizes [Exodus 14:5]. Little did he know that it was the Lord who had once more hardened his heart so that he and his army might meet their doom in the waters of the Red Sea [Exodus 14:4, 26–28].

We may well question the Bible's portrayal of God's actions here as the rabbis themselves did at a later period. How could God rightfully punish Pharaoh for not granting Moses' request when it was He who made him stubborn? Was God really fair to Pharaoh?

And with this we come face to face with the basic question of whether man is free.

The Heart of the Problem

In telling of God and His relationship to man and history, the authors of the Bible faced a dilemma. On the one hand, they came to conceive of Him as all-powerful. Thus, Moses is made to declare:

> O Lord God, You have begun to show Your servant Your greatness and Your strong hand; for what god is there in heaven or on earth that can do according to Your works and according to Your mighty acts? —Deuteronomy 3:24

One of the psalmists, too, testifies to the tremendous might of the Lord:

> Come and behold the works of the Lord,
> How He has made desolations in the earth.
> He makes wars cease to the end of the earth;
> He breaks the bow and shatters the spear,
> He burns chariots with fire! —Psalm 46:9–10

Yes, says another psalmist, God indeed rules over the nations [Psalm 66:7]. He gives power to whomever He wishes, declares the writer of Daniel, and none can prevent Him [Daniel 4:14, 31–32]. More than this, God knows all. The Book of Job points this out:

> For He [God] looks to the ends of the earth,
> And sees everything under the heavens. —Job 28:24

Amos and Jeremiah agree [see, for example, Amos 9:3 and Jeremiah 23:23–24]. In fact, God is aware of everything that takes place throughout the universe, for does He not also "fill the heavens"? [Jeremiah 23:24; see also Psalm 139:7–8.] He even knows the inner secrets of the individual [Psalm 44:22; 139:1–6].

He also has knowledge of everything that is going to happen. Thus, for instance, God reveals to Abraham His intention to destroy the wicked cities of Sodom and Gomorrah [Genesis 18:17–21], and as Amos says, He informs the prophets in advance of His actions:

> The Lord God will do nothing
> Without revealing His secret to His servants
> the prophets. —Amos 3:7

From this point of view, then, it would seem that God knows and determines everything that takes place.

Yet, on the other hand, the Bible also indicates that man has freedom from God's control. In an early passage of Genesis, for example, we are told that Adam and Eve willfully disobeyed God's command not to eat of the tree of the knowledge of good and evil [Genesis 3:2–6]. Obviously here they were free to follow their own impulses.

Likewise, shortly after, in the story of Cain and Abel, we have a definite statement that God does not determine the individual's deeds. When Cain became angry because the Lord was not as pleased with his offering as He had been with his brother's, God rebukes him with these words:

> "Why are you angry, and why has your countenance fallen?
> If you do well, will you not be accepted?
> But if you do not do well, sin waits for you at the door.
> Its desire is for you, but you must master it." —Genesis 4:6

The last sentence makes it plain, doesn't it, that it is man himself who has control over his evil desires and can overcome them if he wishes.

Certainly one of the Bible's clearest expressions of man's freedom is this statement in which God says to the people of Israel in the Wilderness:

> "I call heaven and earth to witness against you this day that I have set before you life and death, the blessing and the curse; therefore choose life, that you may live, you and your descendants." —Deuteronomy 30:19

Here the Hebrews are being told that they are free to choose between good and evil. The choice determines the consequences, but the decision is plainly theirs.

The heart of our problem, then, is the apparent contradiction that seems to exist in the Bible between the principle known as "determinism," that is, that God decides everything that happens to us, and "free-will," the belief that man may do as he wishes. In certain instances, as in the story of Adam and Eve, man appears to enjoy freedom of will. In others, as with Pharaoh, his actions are determined by God.

A Minority View—God Controls Man's Actions

Actually, very few writers of the Bible supported the position of determinism. Other than the incident with Pharaoh and with the exception of only one particular book, such expressions are quite rare. (Two are seen in Deuteronomy 2:30 and Proverbs 21:1.)

The great exception is the Book of Ecclesiastes, which, in many places, sees man's actions as controlled by God.

Its author, we are told, was Koheleth, a son of King David [see Ecclesiastes 1:1]. Koheleth was primarily concerned with finding some purpose to life:

> . . . I applied my mind to seek and search out by wisdom all that is done under heaven; it is an unhappy business that God has given to the sons of men to be busy with. . . .
> —Ecclesiastes 1:13

Therefore, he experimented with various ways of living, including hard work, pleasure-seeking, study, and other things.

In the course of his experiences, he came to certain conclusions. For one thing he saw no difference between the fate of the fool and that of the wise man, as he declares:

> The wise man has his eyes in his head, but the fool walks in darkness. And yet I noticed that one fate comes to all of them. Then I said to myself, "What happens to the fool

> will also happen to me. Why then have I been so very
> wise? . . ." —Ecclesiastes 2:14–15

The harder Koheleth worked, the more he became convinced that one's efforts are really useless. God controls our lives anyway, and whatever He desires will eventually take place. Man "is not able to dispute with One stronger than he" [Ecclesiastes 6:10].

In the following statements, Koheleth's conviction that determinism governs existence becomes even clearer:

> Consider the work of God; who can make straight what He
> has made crooked? In the day of prosperity be joyful, and
> in the day of adversity consider; God has made one as well
> as the other. . . . —Ecclesiastes 7:13–14

> Every matter has its time and way. . . . For man does not
> know what is to be; because who can tell him how it will
> be? —Ecclesiastes 8:6–7

> But all this I laid to heart, examining it all, how the right-
> eous and the wise and their deeds are in the hand of God;
> whether it is love or hate man does not know. . . .
> —Ecclesiastes 9:1

Thus, in the opinion of Koheleth, whatever we do makes no real difference; man's ways are already predetermined. Man might just as well not worry about his deeds or what will happen to him. Let him simply enjoy life as best he can.

This outlook led him to one final conclusion about life, which he states in these words:

> Go eat your bread with enjoyment,
> And drink your wine with a merry heart;
> For God has already determined what you do.
> —Ecclesiastes 9:7

From the point of view of the remainder of the Bible, this is an extreme position. It seems to reflect a spirit of world-weariness and resignation. But, while this attitude found a place in the Bible, it never became the accepted Jewish belief. If it had, the individual could no longer have been held accountable for his acts. God would have been responsible. After all, wasn't it He who determined in advance whatever one did?

Another Answer—God Controls History

Still, many of the other writers of the Bible were not ready to say that man was entirely free. Certainly God, they felt, exerted some control over him. To be sure, He did this indirectly, but His decisions affected him nevertheless. For God determined the course of history, or, as one of the psalmists put it, He was the "Ruler of the nations":

> The Lord is most high, awesome,
> A great King over all the earth.
> He subdues peoples under us
> And nations under our feet. . . .
> God reigns over the nations;
> He sits upon His holy throne. —Psalm 47:3–4, 9

As Sovereign over all the nations, God decides their destiny. Naturally, in the process, the life of every individual is also affected.

An illustration of this point of view is found in Isaiah's message to the people of Judah. In 721 B.C.E., you will recall, the Assyrian forces destroyed the Northern Kingdom of Israel and took the people captive. This was really God's doing, Isaiah told the people of Judah. For thus the Lord had said:

> "Ah, Assyria, the rod of My anger,
> The staff of My fury!
> Against a godless nation I send it,
> And against the people of My wrath I command it,
> To take spoil and seize plunder,
> And to tread them down like the mud of
> the streets." —Isaiah 10:5–6

Yes, the destruction of Israel is the result of God's anger. He has used the Assyrian nation as a weapon against His sinful people.

Naturally the Assyrians do not realize this; their king thinks that it is he who has earned the glorious victory. Therefore he boasts:

> ". . . By the strength of my hand I have done it,
> And by my wisdom, for I have understanding;
> I have removed the boundaries of peoples,
> And have plundered their treasures;
> Like the mighty I have brought down those
> who sat on thrones. . . ." —Isaiah 10:13

The ruler of Assyria is also confident that the Kingdom of Judah will be his next victim, for he says:

> "Shall I not do to Jerusalem and her idols
> As I have done to Samaria [the capital city
> of Israel] and her images?" —Isaiah 10:11

But he does not reckon with God whose instrument he really is. Does the king of Assyria think that he is free to do as he pleases, that he is not the agent of the Lord? To Isaiah the answer is very plain. Such a thing is impossible, for:

> Shall the ax raise itself up against him who cuts with it,
> Or the saw glorify itself over him who wields it?
> As if a rod should wield him who lifts it,
> Or as if a staff should lift him who is not wood!
> —Isaiah 10:15

Indeed! God will do with Assyria exactly as He pleases. In this instance, because of the boastfulness of the Assyrian ruler, He will humble his army:

> Therefore the Lord, the Lord of Hosts,
> Will send wasting sickness among his stout warriors;
> And under his glory a burning will be kindled,
> Like the burning of fire. —Isaiah 10:16

God will destroy his empire as well:

> The glory of his forest and of his fruitful land
> The Lord will destroy, both soul and body,
> And it will be as when a sick man wastes away.
> The remnant of the trees of his forest will be so few
> That a child will be able to write them down.
> —Isaiah 10:18–19

Throughout the Bible one finds many such passages picturing God as the Ruler of history. Thus Jeremiah declares that it is He who will give Jerusalem into the hands of Nebuchadrezzar, the king of Babylonia:

> Then came the word of the Lord to Jeremiah, saying: "Behold, I am the Lord, the God of all flesh; is there anything too hard for Me? Therefore, thus says the Lord: Behold I will give this city [Jerusalem] into the hand of Nebuchadrezzar, king of Babylon, and he shall come and set this city on fire and burn it with the houses upon whose roofs they have offered [sacrifices] to Baal and poured out drink-offerings to other gods to provoke Me. For the children of Israel and the children of Judah have done nothing but evil in My sight from their youth. . . ." —Jeremiah 32:26–30

But the Lord in turn will destroy the Babylonians [Jeremiah 51:1–4]. And it is Second Isaiah who sees Cyrus, the ruler of Persia, as God's instrument for the overthrow of Babylonia [Isaiah 45:1–3].

And what about the individual's freedom? To a large extent his fate is dependent upon whatever happens to his nation. God's action against the Syrians means that every one of the Syrian people will be sent into captivity [Amos 1:4–5]; His judgment against the Philistines will cause all of them to perish [Amos 1:6–8].

Such is the position of these biblical writers. We realize, of course, that there is much truth in what they said. The individual's life is certainly affected by what happens to his country. A severe economic depression, for example, could radically change many of our plans. Likewise the outbreak of war, especially in this atomic age. In this respect our lives are indeed influenced by everything that happens to our nation, or for that matter today in the world at large.

Still, we are not entirely powerless to do something about it. We can help direct the affairs of our country to avert catastrophes. We now have reason to believe, for instance, that some of the worst phases of economic depressions can be avoided. The United Nations, too, offers us at least one possibility of preventing global war. Hence we can no longer agree that the fate of nations and their peoples is as surely determined as some of the biblical writers believed.

And as if anticipating this, those who wrote the Bible countered with still another point of view. . . .

A Third Answer—Man Is Free

Although they were convinced that God did influence the course of history, practically all the authors of the Bible insisted that man, nevertheless, was free to do as he wished. Out of their maturity and wholesome respect for man's capacities, they could accept nothing less. Furthermore, their concept of God as just and merciful demanded this. Otherwise He was guilty of holding man responsible for acts which were not of his own making, the very height of injustice and cruelty!

That man has freedom of will is made quite clear almost from the beginning. God confirms this fact in connection with Adam and Eve. Here we are told that once they had eaten of the tree of knowledge He declared, "Behold man has become like one of us [Godlike], knowing good and evil" [Genesis 3:22]. In fact, their freedom compelled Him to expel them from the Garden of Eden "lest they also take of the tree of life" [Genesis 3:22].

The authors of the Bible began with the faith that man's deeds were of his own making, and they consistently held to this belief throughout their work. Man had the option of obeying the will of God. Speaking to the Hebrew people in the Wilderness, God was pictured as saying:

> "Behold, I set before you this day a blessing and a curse: the blessing, if you shall listen to the commandments of the Lord your God which I command you this day; and the curse, if you shall not listen to the commandments of the Lord your God, but turn aside out of the way which I command you this day, to go after other gods whom you have not known." —Deuteronomy 11:26–28

Certainly man may do what he pleases. He may choose the blessing or the curse, life or death. This is also made quite clear by Jeremiah. Here he is relaying God's word to the people of Jerusalem whose city is under siege by the Babylonians:

> ". . . Behold I set before you the way of life and the way of death. He who stays in this city shall die by the sword, by famine, and by pestilence; but he who goes out and surrenders to the Chaldeans [Babylonians] who are besieging you shall live and have his life as a prize of war. For I have set My face against this city for evil and not for good, says the Lord. It shall be given into the hand of the king of Babylon, and he shall burn it with fire." —Jeremiah 21:8–10

Though the fate of Jerusalem has already been settled, what will happen to its inhabitants remains strictly up to the individual. Each has freedom of choice.

Does God Care What We Do?

While man may make whatever decisions he wants, God is very much concerned with his choice. For those who wrote the Bible were convinced that He deeply cared about people's actions.

This is obvious from the very conduct of God Himself. In the face of the wickedness of the generation of the Flood He is seen as grieving and feeling resentful [Genesis 6:6–7]. To those who disobey His covenant He is "a devouring fire" [Deuteronomy 4:23–24]. And, says the psalmist:

> . . . We are consumed by Your [God's] anger,
> And we are overwhelmed by Your wrath. —Psalm 90:7

In contrast, God encourages people to choose ways that He desires. From the start He has provided them with knowledge of His will through His commandments in order that they may find well-being [see Deuteronomy 4:40]. Indeed:

> The law of the Lord is perfect, reviving the soul;
> The testimony of the Lord is sure, making
> wise the simple;
> The precepts of the Lord are right, rejoicing
> the heart;
> The commandment of the Lord is pure,
> enlightening the eyes;
> The fear of the Lord is clean, enduring forever;
> The ordinances of the Lord are true, and
> righteous altogether.
> More to be desired are they than gold,
> yes, even fine gold;
> Sweeter also than honey
> and drippings of the honeycomb. —Psalm 19:8–11

Those who choose to obey God's will will find Him merciful and compassionate, as the psalmist says:

> . . . The mercy of the Lord is from everlasting to
> everlasting upon those who revere Him,
> And His righteousness to children's children
> To those who keep His covenant
> And remember to do His commandments.
> —Psalm 103:17–18

Of course God cares what we do! Why else did He send the prophets? That people might heed His word, says Jeremiah [see Jeremiah 29:19]. For in line with His purposes, God does not want man to be destroyed but to live, declares Ezekiel [Ezekiel 18:23].

Yes, God shows that He cares through His own reactions, His covenant with Israel, the commandments He has given, the prophets He has sent. But this can also be seen in yet another way, in the fact that He has established a world in which there are consequences to our acts. . . .

The Consequences of Being Free

Though we enjoy freedom, said the authors of the Bible, we must also expect to reap the consequences of our actions. For they are determined by God as part of the order which He has established within the universe. So, in speaking about the nature of God, one of the psalmists says:

> You are not a God who delights in wickedness;
> Evil may not dwell with You.
> The boastful may not stand in Your sight;
> You hate all evildoers.
> You destroy those who speak lies;
> The Lord abhors bloodthirsty and deceitful men . . .
> But You do bless the righteous, O Lord;
> You cover him with favor as with a shield.
>   —Psalm 5:5–7, 13

Speaking in God's name, the prophet Ezekiel, too, points out:

> "Behold, all souls are Mine [God's]! The soul of the father
> as well as the soul of the son is Mine; the soul that sins
> shall die.
> "If a man be just and do that which is lawful and right
> . . . he shall surely live," says the Lord God.
> ". . . [But the person that does wicked deeds] he shall not
> live." —Ezekiel 18:4–9, 13

The fact that God has so ordered the world to bring about consequences to our acts shows how very much He cares about what we
do. These, as the writer of Proverbs put it, are like the punishments and rewards of a devoted father deeply concerned with the
proper conduct of his child. For he says:

> . . . Do not despise the Lord's discipline
> Or be weary of His reproof,
> For the Lord reproves him whom He loves,
> As a father a son in whom he delights.
>   —Proverbs 3:11–12

All of us, then, are free to do whatever we wish. But, because God
is concerned that we do what is right, He has established consequences to our deeds. Of this we are all aware. Suppose, for example, during finals at school someone decides not to take a particular
examination. He has that choice of action. At the same time he also
knows what will happen. He will undoubtedly fail the course and
be required to repeat it, and this in turn may postpone his gradua-
tion. So, though theoretically we are free to do as we please, realisti-
cally, in a world in which God has established consequences to man's
deeds, He wants us to act rightfully and responsibly.

This is stated time and again in the Bible. To some extent we
find it in the story of Elijah and Jezebel. Here the prophet challenges the Queen to a kind of contest to see who is the true God—
the Lord or Melkart, also known as Baal, Jezebel's deity. The people
are given the choice, for there gathered on Mount Carmel they hear
Elijah call out to them:

How long will you refuse to take sides between two different opinions? If the Lord is God, follow Him. But if Baal, follow him. —I Kings 18:21

For those who followed after Baal, the consequences were destruction [I Kings 18:40]. Those who accepted the Lord as God were sent rain to end the drought [I Kings 18:41–45]. Nevertheless the people were given the freedom to make their choice.

The same view is presented in the Book of Deuteronomy. In the following passage Moses conveys to the Hebrew people in the Wilderness God's words:

> "See, I have set before you this day life and good, death and evil. If you obey the commandments of the Lord your God . . . the Lord your God will bless you. . . . But if your heart turns away and you do not listen . . . then I declare to you this day that you shall perish. . . . I call heaven and earth as witness this day that I have set before you life and death, blessing and curse; therefore choose life that you and your descendants may live. . . ."
> —Deuteronomy 30:15–20

Yes, while our freedom is unrestricted, if we act foolishly or irresponsibly by turning our backs on what is right, we pay the penalty. Hence, man's more rewarding freedom consists in obeying God's laws of righteousness. Therefore one of the psalmists declares:

> I will keep Your law continually,
> For ever and ever;
> And I will walk in freedom.
> For I have sought Your precepts. —Psalm 119:44–45

The real freedom for man, as the psalmist sees it, lies in his obedience to God's righteous ways.

Freedom Even For Nations

Just as individuals possess freedom of choice, observed the authors of the Bible, so, too, do nations. But they, too, are subject to the moral laws God has established.

We have already seen this in connection with the Hebrew people. Judah, declared Amos, is to be destroyed:

> . . . Because they [the people] have rejected
> the law of the Lord.
> And have not kept His statutes,

And their lies have caused them to err,
After which their fathers did walk. —Amos 2:4

Israel, too, shall be conquered because of its serious moral misdeeds [see, for example, Amos 2:6–8].

The other nations are likewise held accountable for their acts,
and the decision to violate God's laws is bound to have serious consequences. The Lord's judgment against Syria and Philistia, described by Amos, is the result of their evil deeds [Amos 1:6, 9].
God's decision to destroy the Assyrian army, disclosed by Isaiah,
is based on the king's boastfulness [Isaiah 10:12]; Jeremiah predicts the conquest of Babylonia because of its insufferable arrogance
[Jeremiah 50:31]. And in speaking of Egypt, Ezekiel prophesies in
God's name:

"I will give it into the hand of a mighty one of the nations;
he shall surely deal with it as its wickedness deserves. . . ."
—Ezekiel 31:11

The nation, then, like the individual, is free to choose its own
course, but that choice carries with it certain consequences. The
principle remains:

Righteousness exalts a nation,
But sin is a reproach to any people. —Proverbs 14:34

Is There No Hope for Wrong-Doers?

But strive as they may to do the right, individuals and nations
may make mistakes. Once this happens, is God's law so inflexible
that the dread consequences automatically occur? Is there no hope
at all for forgiveness?

Yes, asserted the authors of the Bible, for God is not only just
but also merciful. It all depends upon how we react to our own
wrong-doing. Even though the people of Israel are "mighty in sins,"
says Amos, if they will now:

Hate evil and love good,
And establish justice in the gate,
It may be that the Lord, the God of hosts,
Will be gracious to the remnant of Joseph
[those of the people of Israel who remain]. —Amos 5:14–15

The worst consequences of their acts—the total destruction of the
nation—may be averted through God's compassion if the people will
only change their ways. So the prophet Hosea hears God saying:

"I will return again to My place [paying no attention
to the destruction of Israel],
Until they acknowledge their guilt and seek My presence,
And in their distress they seek Me saying:
'Come, let us return to the Lord. . . .' " —Hosea 5:15–6:1

For God cares and wants to help His people. But they will not refrain
from their evil-doing [see Hosea 7].

Here we have a teaching which some have termed the doctrine
of "BUT IF." The consequences of man's acts are determined, "BUT
IF" he recognizes his wrong-doing and earnestly seeks to amend his
ways there is hope that God will extend mercy to him. If we truly
repent, said the people of Nineveh when they became aware of
their evil ways, "Who knows whether God may not reconsider and
turn from His fierce anger so that we do not perish?" [Jonah 3:9].
And, as we know, God did have mercy upon them [Jonah 3:10].

In presenting this teaching of "BUT IF" to his listeners, Jeremiah
made use of a colorful illustration. He tells of his visit to a pottery-
making establishment where he watched the potter work away at
his wheel. Jeremiah noticed that when the vessel he was molding
did not come out as planned, the potter would rework the clay into
another vessel more to his liking. What happened to the clay, then,
depended upon the way it turned out. This, said Jeremiah, is like
the relationship between God and the nations, including His own
people, Israel. For, the prophet observes:

". . . O house of Israel, cannot I do with you as this potter?" says the Lord. "Behold, as the clay in the potter's
hand, so are you in My hand, O house of Israel. At one
instant I may speak concerning a nation, and concerning a
kingdom, to pluck up and break down and to destroy it;
but if that nation turn from their evil, because of that
which I have spoken against it, I repent of the evil that I
thought to do unto it. And at one instant I may speak
concerning a nation to build and to plant it; *but if* it do evil
in My sight, then I repent of the good with which I said I
would benefit it." —Jeremiah 18:5–10

Hence, as Jeremiah saw it, a people's freedom was unlimited. In
fact, it could even amend its sinful ways and thereby through God's
mercy alter its fate. Indeed, God tells the prophet:

"Now, therefore, say to the men of Judah and the inhabitants of Jerusalem: "Thus says the Lord: Behold, I am shap-
ing evil against you and devising a plan against you. Return, every one from his evil way, and amend your ways
and doings.' " —Jeremiah 18:11

Not only is the freedom of nations and individuals upheld, but with the teaching of "BUT IF," thanks to God's love and mercy, it now even becomes possible for the thoroughly repentant to escape the consequences of their former wicked ways.

Where Judaism Stands

Essentially, this position taken by the Bible is the one that Judaism finally adopted. Yes, God does rule over the universe, and through His law He ultimately determines the fate of people. But such decisions are based on their conduct, since men and nations are completely free to choose their course of action, and even to repent if they so desire.

Freedom to act brings with it certain *consequences*. Because God cares that people do the right, He has established the moral law in His universe. If they choose to do evil, they must ultimately pay the penalty, but those who obey Him can expect happier consequences. Therefore, though man is completely free, the choices he makes must be the right ones, for his own well-being.

An excellent summary of these views is offered by Ecclesiasticus. This, you will remember, is the book written by Ben-Sirach during the second century B.C.E. Today it may be found in the Apocrypha, the collection of writings not included in the Jewish Bible. Here Ben-Sirach says:

> Do not say, "It was because of the Lord that I transgressed,"
> For He will not do the things that He hates.
> Do not say, "It was He that led me astray,"
> For He has no need of a sinner.
> The Lord hates everything abominable;
> And it is not lived by those who revere Him.
> It was He who made man in the beginning,
> And left him in the hands of his own decisions.
> If you will, you can keep the commandments,
> And acting faithfully rests upon your own good pleasure.
> He has set fire and water before you;
> Stretch out your hand for whichever you wish.
> Life and death are before a man,
> And whichever he chooses will be given him.
> —Ecclesiasticus 15:11–17

And that God has created man free remains Judaism's position.

Yet, because He is also able to foresee everything that will happen, there is a problem. For if He knows what people will do, doesn't He thereby exert some control over their actions?

An answer to this difficulty is not found in the Bible. The problem was not resolved until the rabbis of the Talmud applied their wisdom. Here, they said, is a paradox, two beliefs that cannot be logically reconciled. Nevertheless, we must affirm the truth of each.

Sometimes, you see, we have to recognize that man with his limited knowledge is incapable of understanding the workings of God and must accept things that may even appear contradictory to the human mind. But this is also true in science. For example, physicists now work with two seemingly contradictory theories about the nature of light. One theory holds that light consists of waves, the other, of particles. Because each theory helps to answer certain questions, physicists find truth in both, even though the two cannot be logically reconciled.

Similarly with the problem of God's foreknowledge and human freedom. Here are two truths which, on the surface, seem to contradict one another. Yet, despite the paradox, we see that we must accept both as true. So in the Mishnah we find this statement by Rabbi Akiba, who lived during the early part of the second century C.E.: "All is foreseen [by God], yet freedom of choice is granted man" [Ovos 3:16]. Or as another rabbi of the Talmud put it, "Everything is in the power of Heaven [God] except the fear of Heaven [God]" [Berachos 33b]. By the term "fear of Heaven" he meant "adherence to God and His demands." Therefore, though God has power over all, the choice of one's conduct still belongs to each individual.

Reform Judaism subscribes to this view. Therefore in dealing with the question of God's power and man's freedom, the 1937 *Guiding Principles of Reform Judaism* has this to say:

> . . . God . . . rules the world through law and love. . . .

> [Man] is endowed with moral freedom and is charged with the responsibility of overcoming evil and striving after ideal ends.

Like those who wrote the Bible, we believe that God governs or rules the universe and that He has established His moral law throughout it. At the same time, we hold that He has also given man complete freedom of action. Because He cares about what we do, He has made known His ways and the consequences of disobedience, but He does not predetermine what to do. Each of us remains responsible for his own deeds.

We may, in a manner of speaking, say that God has limited His own powers for man's benefit. Surely, had He so desired, He could have controlled everything that happens to us, as Koheleth and a few others apparently believed. Rather, as the great majority of the writers of the Bible came to realize, God preferred to give man freedom to act for himself. Else the individual could not be held accountable.

What About Prayer?

This, then, is the Bible's final answer to an extremely difficult question.

The experience of history confirms the truth of this answer. Individuals and nations have indeed been free to act as they wished. Yet, when they conducted themselves wickedly, they ultimately paid a heavy price. In our own times, evil nations, such as Fascist Italy and Nazi Germany, have gone down to destruction, and their people have experienced much suffering. Similar fates have overtaken individuals, like Hitler and Mussolini. In the long run, wickedness brings misery and suffering not only to the wrong-doer himself, but to all those contaminated by him. Thus the freedom that God has given mankind is ours to enjoy only if we use it wisely, in keeping with His moral and ethical laws.

With this, however, new problems arise. For instance, if there are fearful consequences for evil-doing, why sometimes does it take so long for the evil-doer to be punished? This is a question that bothered those who wrote the Bible and it is one that we shall certainly want to consider later on.

Another problem is this—if man is truly free, can God intervene at all in human affairs? Or, having established His laws in the universe, has God now removed Himself entirely from people's lives?

This is an important question because of its bearing on the subject of prayer. For if God has removed Himself, how is it possible for Him to answer a man's prayers? Or if He responds, doesn't He deny some of man's freedom? Suppose, for instance, we pray and God helps us pass an examination for which we haven't studied? What happens to our right of choosing between studying or not studying? And what about the teacher's freedom to test a student's knowledge? Yet can we say that God doesn't answer prayer at all?

Well, what's the opinion of those who wrote the Bible?

——————————— THINGS TO TALK OVER ———————————

1. In what ways would life be different if everyone adopted the attitude of Koheleth?

2. Would life be liveable if God were not also a God of mercy as well as of justice?

3. If God has a plan for the universe that mankind must ultimately help to achieve, how is it possible for us to enjoy freedom?

4. How does the biblical approach to the problem of man's freedom illustrate: [a] the manner in which the Bible came to be written, and [b] why the development of Judaism did not cease with the completion of the Bible?

———————— SOME OTHER BIBLE PASSAGES TO CONSIDER ————————

1. How does the leadership of a nation affect the fate of its people? See Isaiah 3:12–15; 9:12–16; Jeremiah 23:1–6; Ezekiel 34.

2. How do the following passages reveal that God is concerned with our actions: Genesis 4:1–14; Judges 3:7–8. Micah 3:1–4; Job 5:17–26?

3. In what ways do the following passages confirm man's freedom: Genesis 1:26–30; Isaiah 1:18–20; Ezekiel 18:20–23; Psalm 8:4–9?

4. What can be some of the consequences of our freedom to do right or wrong? See Isaiah 54:13–14; Psalm 1:4–6; 4:4–9; Proverbs 3:1–4; 4:14–19.

———————— FROM THE RABBIS' VIEWPOINT ————————

1. THE POWER OF GOD: See *Everyman's Talmud*, pp. 11–15; and *A Rabbinic Anthology*, [67] pp. 28–29, [69] p. 30, [73–77] pp. 31–33, [686] p. 270, [689] p. 271.

2. MAN'S FREEDOM: See *Everyman's Talmud*, pp. 99–101; and *A Rabbinic Anthology*, [88–89] p. 36, [534–535] p. 198.

3. REPENTANCE: See *Everyman's Talmud*, pp. 110–117; and *A Rabbinic Anthology*, [813–841] pp. 316–322.

———————— OTHER THINGS TO READ ————————

BAMBERGER, BERNARD J., *The Story of Judaism*, Union of American Hebrew Congregations, pp. 140, 166 f., 288, 292.

FACKENHEIM, EMIL L., *Paths to Jewish Belief*, Behrman, Chap. 6: "What Is Man?" pp. 75–83; Chap. 7: "How Right Is Right? How Wrong Is Wrong? Can We Choose Between Them?" pp. 85–95.

GITTELSOHN, ROLAND B., *Little Lower Than the Angels*, Union of American Hebrew Congregations, Chap. 8: "God and You," pp. 115–139, 151–153.

SILVER, ABBA HILLEL, *Where Judaism Differed*, Macmillan, Chap. 13: "That Men Are Not Free," pp. 243–253.

STEINBERG, MILTON, *Basic Judaism*, Harcourt, Brace, pp. 59–65, 79–90.

DOES PRAYER HELP?

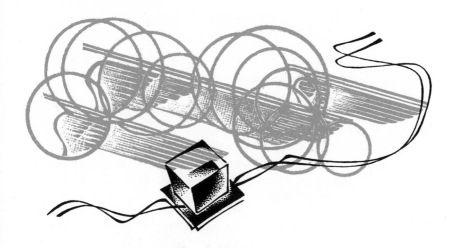

A Miracle-Producing Prayer!

THERE IS NO DOUBT THAT THE WRITERS OF THE BIBLE BELIEVED that God answered prayer. In fact, as we see from the account in I Kings 17, some of them felt that prayer could even produce miracles!

We are told in that passage that when Elijah's life was being threatened by Queen Jezebel he fled across the Jordan River. For a time he made his home near a flowing brook. Then a drought dried up the stream.

Forced to find food and water elsewhere, the prophet made his way to a small village where he persuaded a certain widow to shelter him. Even though she had only a limited supply of food for her son and herself, she agreed to share it with him. Somehow, all during the time they were together the food never ran out.

Then one day the widow's son fell ill and died. Bitter in her grief, she held Elijah responsible. Instead of defending himself, however, the prophet simply asked permission to take the child's body to his room.

Once upstairs, Elijah placed the child across the bed. Three times he stretched over him, praying, "O Lord, my God, let this child's soul come into him again." The passage then goes on:

> And the Lord listened to the voice of Elijah; and the soul of the child came into him again and he revived. And Elijah took the child and brought him down from the upper room into the house and delivered him to his mother; and Elijah said, "See, your son lives." And the woman said to Elijah, "Now I know that you are a man of God, and that the word of the Lord in your mouth is true."
> —I Kings 17:22–24

From this we know that at least one writer of the Bible was positive that prayer could indeed work miracles!

Belief in God's Power

To be sure, this sort of wonder-working prayer was exceptional, and undoubtedly that is why it is recorded in the Bible. It was intended to demonstrate the great power of the Lord.

The Bible contains other instances of such prayers. We are informed that as a result of his prayer to God the prophet Elisha, too, restored a dead child to life [II Kings 4:8–37]. Abraham's prayer in behalf of King Abimelech, who ruled over Gerar, in the southwestern part of Palestine, was responsible for healing both him and his family [Genesis 20:17–18]. Jacob prayed that his brother, Esau, whose birthright he had stolen, might not kill him [Genesis 32:4–12]; and the result was that he received a friendly reception at Esau's hands [Genesis 33:1–16]. The prayer of Moses healed the leprosy of his sister Miriam [Numbers 12:1–15].

In many instances the prayers of lesser people, sincerely offered, also achieved wonderful results. Destined for destruction, the people of Nineveh earnestly prayed to God and were spared [Jonah 3:4–10]. When King Hezekiah of Judah was on the verge of death, prayer secured for him an additional fifteen years of life [II Kings 20:1–7]. And one of the most touching stories in the Bible is that of the prayer of Hannah and her husband for a son.

According to I Samuel 1, both Hannah and her husband had longed for a son for many years, but without success. Once more the unhappy woman went to the shrine at Shiloh. This time she promised that if she should have a son she would surrender him to the lifelong service of God. Her prayer was answered and she gave birth to Samuel who eventually became one of God's most faithful prophets.

The fact that all of this appears in the Bible testifies to the profound belief of those who wrote it. Why, under certain circumstances, God could perform miracles! Thus, when Sarah scoffed at the idea of having a child in her old age, Abraham promptly reminded her, "Is anything too difficult for the Lord?" [Genesis 18:12–15]. And in telling of the parting of the Red Sea, the Bible includes the triumphant song the people sang which in part declares:

> Who is like unto You, O Lord, among the mighty?
> Who is like unto You, O Lord, glorious in holiness,
> Awesome in marvelous deeds, doing wonders?
> —Exodus 15:11

How the Ancients Saw It

Few of us today would resort to prayer to revive the dead, heal a leper, or satisfy a barren couple's desire for a child. That is because, in the first place, we have no need of equating God's power with performance of miracles. We find ample evidence of His greatness in the marvels of life itself, the universe, the human body, and the like. Surely there is no greater demonstration of God's wonderful work than the birth of a baby or the grandeur of a glorious sunset!

But, in the second place, we do not expect God to answer prayers that would require Him to set aside the very physical and moral laws that He has established. Such acts would not only turn the world topsy-turvy, but also deprive man of the very freedom of choice he has been given. For then, simply by praying to God, people could interfere in the lives of others or avoid the consequences of their own deeds.

By and large this was no problem to people of ancient times. They saw no contradiction between human freedom and the power of their deities. Practically all peoples of the Mediterranean world were convinced that their gods were moved by such things as sacrifice and prayer. If you have read Homer's *Iliad*, for example, you will recall that before every battle the Greek warriors would offer up sacrifices to their gods to insure a favorable outcome.

The early Hebrews shared such beliefs. The Bible tells us that prior to a battle with the Philistines, the prophet Samuel offered up a lamb as a sacrifice to God [I Samuel 7:7–11]. Abel, we are informed, found special favor with God because of the fine quality of his offering [Genesis 4:4]; and the father of Samson prayed and prepared a sacrifice to the Lord when he learned that he would eventually have a son [Judges 13:2–19]. Even the Book of Leviticus, dealing as it does with the various offerings, begins by declaring that to find favor with God it is necessary to offer an unblemished sacrifice [Leviticus 1:1–3]. One's offerings must also have a "pleasing odor to the Lord" [Leviticus 1:9].

In addition to sacrifices, prayer, too, was believed to influence the Deity. Thus, at the Red Sea, the children of Israel cried out to God and he saved them from the menacing Egyptians [Exodus 14:10–30]. Repeatedly we are told that the Hebrew tribes in Palestine prayed for deliverance from their enemies, and without their doing anything further a "judge," or military leader, appeared to rescue them [see, for example, Judges 3:9, 15; 4:3–4]. Displeased by the people's demand for a king, the prophet Samuel asked God to show His anger by sending thunder and rain. And so He did [I Samuel 12:1–19].

Prayers That Were Not Answered

Yet the ancients also observed that their prayers were not always answered as they desired. The writers of the Bible report several such cases.

We find, for instance, that King David prayed to God to spare the life of his sick child, but on the seventh day the boy died [II Samuel 12:16–18]. Isaiah pictured God as telling the people of the Northern Kingdom of Israel:

> "When you spread forth your hands [to Me],
> I will hide My eyes from you;
> Yes, when you offer up many prayers,
> I will not listen [to them]. . . ." —Isaiah 1:15

And one of the psalmists complains:

> . . . I, O Lord, cry to You;
> In the morning my prayer comes before You.
> O Lord, why do You cast me off?
> Why do You hide Your face from me? —Psalm 88:14–15

In his anguish, Job begs God to let him die. "Oh that I might have my request, and that God would grant my desire," he cries, "that it would please God to crush me, and that He would let loose His hand and cut me off!" [Job 6:8–9]. But his prayer goes unanswered.

The writers of the Bible, of course, wondered why God did not always grant people's wishes. Over the years they came to the conclusion that certain conditions had to be met before God would respond favorably.

The Demands of Proper Conduct

Even in earliest times it was recognized that the quality of one's worship was important. The proper rites had to be performed in the correct, approved manner. For instance, offering up blemished animals or grain of poor quality would not find favor with the Lord. This is implied in what the Bible tells us of God's displeasure with Cain's offering in contrast to that of Abel [Genesis 4:3–5]. But it is more explicitly brought out by the clear-cut prohibitions against inferior offerings mentioned in Leviticus 22:18–25.

The establishment of the covenant between the Lord and Israel served to reinforce this. Only if the people followed His commandments would their sacrifices and prayers be acceptable to Him. Thus, according to one biblical passage, God informs the people:

> "An altar of earth you shall make for Me, and you shall sacrifice thereon your burnt-offerings . . . [then] I will bless you." —Exodus 20:21

This and many other examples make it clear that obedience to God's commandments included the proper performance of religious rites [see, for example, Exodus 23:14–19 and Leviticus 7:37–38].

But over and beyond this was the matter of one's personal conduct, for here the covenant also made serious demands. And it was this that the prophets, in particular, stressed. So, in the words of Hosea, God states:

> ". . . I desire love [of Me] and not sacrifice.
> The knowledge of God, rather than burnt-offerings."
> —Hosea 6:6

Amos, too, holds that because of their conduct God is hostile to the people's sacrifices and prayers:

> "I hate, I despise your festivals,
> And I take no delight in your solemn assemblies.
> Even though you offer Me your burnt-offerings and cereal-offerings,
> I will not accept them.
> And the peace-offerings of your fatted beasts
> I will not look upon. . . .
> But let justice roll down like waters,
> And righteousness like an everflowing stream."
> —Amos 5:21–24

Similarly with Isaiah. Their offerings, the prophet tells the people of Israel, are a burden to God. What he really requires of them is righteousness [see Isaiah 1:11–17].

Hence, as the prophets saw it, the righteousness of the individual played a major part in determining the outcome of his prayers and sacrifices. Evil-doers, says the prophet Micah:

> . . . Will cry to the Lord,
> But He will not answer them;
> He will hide His face from them at that time,
> Because they have made their deeds evil. —Micah 3:4

And one of the psalmists declares:

> Come and hear, all you who fear God,
> And I will tell what He has done for me,
> I cried aloud to Him,
> And He was praised with my tongue.
> If I had cherished iniquity in my heart,
> The Lord would not have listened.
> But truly God has listened;
> He has given heed to the voice of my prayer.
> —Psalm 66:16–19

Some Other Requirements

While righteous living continued to be regarded as indispensable, other requirements for the acceptance of prayer were added over the years. Especially was this so when, with the destruction of the Temple by the Babylonians, sacrifices could no longer be offered.

First, proper prayer demanded the wholeheartedness of the individual. Isaiah complains that the prayers of the people of Israel are pointless because the worshipers:

> ". . . Draw near,
> And with their mouth and with their lips do honor Me
> [God],
> But have removed their heart far from Me,
> And their reverence of Me is [merely] a commandment of men
> learned by rote." —Isaiah 29:13

An essential condition for the acceptance of one's worship, as the later rabbis pointed out, is contained in the words of Deuteronomy 6:5, "And you shall love the Lord your God with all your heart, with all your soul, and with all your might." This, they said, meant "worship with one's full heart."

A second requirement laid down by various biblical writers was sincerity. "Now, therefore, revere the Lord and serve Him in sincerity and truth," demands one of them [Joshua 24:14]. The psalmist urges God to accept his prayer because it comes from his lips "without deceit" [Psalm 17:1].

Humility appears to be another condition. Eliphaz, one of Job's friends, assures him that God saves the humble person [Job 22:29], and one of the psalmists maintains:

> Lord, You have heard the desire of the humble;
> You will strengthen their heart, You will incline Your ear.
> —Psalm 10:17

As a sign of humility and repentance, fasting and wearing sackcloth seem to help. The Book of Judges tells us that prior to an important battle certain of the Hebrew tribes fasted and they were victorious [Judges 20:26–48]. The people of Nineveh also fasted and put on sackcloth, and God was moved to spare them [Jonah 3:5–10].

Certain passages require the person who prays to show proper respect for God and His law. As one biblical writer says:

> If one turns his ear from hearing the law,
> Even his prayer is worthless. —Proverbs 28:9

And others praise the glories of God's law and ask that their prayers be answered in order to uphold the law. [See, for example, Psalm 119:113–119 and 129–136.]

Finally, there is the matter of faith and trust in the Lord. "He that puts his trust in the Lord shall be abundantly satisfied," says the Book of Proverbs [Proverbs 28:25]. And one of the writers of the Book of Psalms puts it this way:

> For God alone my soul waits in silence,
> For my help is from Him.
> He only is my strength and my salvation,
> My fortress; I shall not be shaken.
> On God rests my deliverance and my honor;
> My mighty rock, my refuge is God.
> Trust in Him at all times, O people;
> Pour out your heart before Him;
> God is a refuge for us. —Psalm 62:6–9

Hence, it would appear that only as the individual fulfils these conditions may he count upon a favorable answer to his prayer. As if to summarize precisely what is demanded of the worshiper, one of Job's friends advises the stricken man to:

Receive, I pray you, instruction from His [God's] mouth,
And lay up His words in your heart,
If you return to the Almighty and humble yourself,
If you remove unrighteousness far from your tent. . . .
And if the Almighty is your treasure
And as precious silver to you,
Then you will delight yourself in the Almighty,
And lift up your face to God.
You will make your prayer to Him, and He will hear
you. . . . —Job 22:22–27

But Still No Real Assurance

Yet, as certain of the writers of the Bible recognized, even the fulfilment of these conditions gave no assurance that one's prayers
would meet with the sought-for response. They tried to explain why.

There were some who felt that the wicked deeds of one's ancestors
or of the nation as a whole affected God's answer. Thus, God states:

". . . I the Lord your God am a jealous God, visiting the
iniquity of the fathers upon the children to the third and
fourth generation of those who hate Me. . . ."
—Deuteronomy 5:9

The Book of Exodus [Exodus 20:5 and 34:7] as well as the prophet
Jeremiah [Jeremiah 32:18] repeat this; and one of the psalmists
urges God not to remember the "iniquities of our forefathers"
[Psalm 79:8].

As for the conduct of the people of Israel as a whole, their sinfulness, says the prophet Isaiah, means that when they pray, God will
not listen to them [Isaiah 1:15]. It will take seventy years of exile,
another prophet tells the people of Judah, before God will pay attention to their prayers [Jeremiah 29:10–14]. And the writer of Lamentations declares that God's anger against the people of Israel has
prevented his own prayer from being heard [Lamentations 3:8,
43–44].

On the other hand, certain of the writers of Psalms, in particular,
looked upon God's failure to grant one's wishes as only a temporary
delay. Typical of their belief that He would ultimately respond to
the petitions of the righteous are such statements as these:

Hear the right, O Lord, listen to my cry;
Give ear to my prayer from lips without deceit. . . .
. . . I call upon You, for You will answer me, O God. . . .
. . . I shall behold Your face in righteousness;
I shall be satisfied, when I awake, with Your likeness.
—Psalm 17:1, 6, 15

"Wait for the Lord," another Psalm advises [Psalm 27:14]: "Maintain your righteousness, for I have never seen the righteous forsaken," urges a second [Psalm 37:25]. "The Lord will accomplish that which concerns me," proclaims a third [Psalm 138:8]. Proper prayer, then, will eventually achieve its desires. It is merely a matter of time.

Another hindrance was one's unknown sins. For no matter how righteous the individual, as a frail human being made of flesh and blood, he could never be wholly pure in God's sight. This was the observation of Eliphaz to his suffering friend Job:

> Shall mortal man be just before God?
> Shall a man be pure before his Maker? —Job 4:17

Other biblical writers express the same thought. In his prayer dedicating the Temple, King Solomon begs God to forgive the sins of his people when they make atonement, "for there is no man that does not sin" [I Kings 8:46]. This is also the observation of those who wrote both Ecclesiastes [Ecclesiastes 7:20] and Chronicles [II Chronicles 6:36].

A final explanation for God's failure to grant our petitions is that He has His own reasons. This is the conclusion of the author of the Book of Job. Once God has spoken to Job from the whirlwind and pointed out man's inability even to comprehend the things in the world around him, Job realizes that it is impossible for human beings with their limited capacities to understand God's reasons for doing things. Job then replies:

> I know that You can do all things,
> And that no purpose of Yours can be thwarted. . . .
> Therefore, I have uttered what I did not understand,
> Things too wonderful to me, which I did not know.
> —Job 42:2–3

In this respect, God is like a parent who, out of his greater knowledge and experience, often finds it necessary to deny some of his child's wishes. Similarly, in His all-knowing wisdom God frequently sees fit to deny the desires of humans.

Thus many different reasons were offered to explain why one's petitions were not always granted. These include one's failure to meet the necessary conditions for proper prayer, the sinfulness of the nation or one's ancestors, one's unknown sins, a temporary delay on the part of God, or simply the denial of one's requests by Him whose purposes must remain unfathomable to man.

Our Prayers and God

Yet to those who wrote the Bible, four things were certain. First, God does hear man's prayers. Of this there is no doubt. The psalmist speaks of God as the One "who hears prayer" [Psalm 65:2], and the writer of Proverbs declares:

> The Lord is far from the wicked,
> But He hears the prayers of the righteous.
> —Proverbs 15:29

As further proof, the Bible records the evidence of all whose petitions had been granted. There was Moses who prayed for the people [Numbers 21:7] and Samuel who sought the Lord's guidance about their request for a king [I Samuel 8:6–9]. And there was the promise of God to Jeremiah:

> "And you shall call upon Me, and I will listen to you."
> —Jeremiah 29:12

Yes, God surely can hear man's prayer.

But, second, the authors of the Bible recognized that an all-knowing and all-powerful God could never be *compelled* by man to pay heed to his prayer. That was within the will of God Himself. So when Solomon dedicated the Temple he prayed:

> O Lord, my God, hearken to the cry and prayer which Your servant [Solomon] prays before You this day, that Your eyes may be open night and day toward this house [the Temple], the place concerning which You have said, "My name shall be there," that You may hearken to the prayer which Your servant offers. And hearken to the supplication of Your servant and of Your people Israel when they pray toward this place. Yes, may You hear in heaven, Your dwelling-place, and when You hear, may You forgive.
> —I Kings 8:28–30

The psalmist, too, pleads with God to:

> Give ear to my prayer, O God,
> And do not hide Yourself from my supplication.
> —Psalm 55:1

And upon hearing of the plight of those Jews who had returned from Babylonia to Jerusalem, Nehemiah offers up a prayer for them. He begins:

. . . Let Your ear be attentive and Your eye open to hear
the prayer of Your servant [Nehemiah] which I now pray
before You day and night for the people of Israel, Your
servants. . . . —Nehemiah 1:6

It is clear, then, that it is God and not man who decides whether
one's prayers are to be "heard."

Third, if God is to listen to the individual at all, then his prayers
must be offered under circumstances that will find favor with Him.
Says the psalmist:

Hear a just cause, O Lord; listen to my cry.
Give ear to my prayer from lips free of deceit.
From You let my vindication come.
Let Your eyes see the right.
If You search my heart. . . .
. . . You will find no wickedness in me. . . .
My steps have held fast to Your paths,
My feet have not slipped. —Psalm 17:1–5

And the prophet whom we call Second Isaiah asserts:

Thus says the Lord;
"Preserve justice and do righteousness
For soon My salvation will come
And My deliverance be revealed.
Happy is the person who does this. . . .
Who observes the Sabbath, not profaning it,
And restrains himself from doing any evil, . . .
And holds fast to My covenant.
I will bring them to My holy mountain [the Temple]
And make them rejoice in My house of prayer;
Their burnt-offerings and sacrifices
Will be accepted upon My altar. . . ."
—Isaiah 56:1–2, 6–7

Surely, said the authors of the Bible, God can be counted upon to
listen favorably to the prayer of one who comes before Him with
"clean hands and a pure heart" [Psalm 24:3–6].

And, finally, a fourth certainty: there is no doubt whatsoever
that God can grant any petition. . . .

A Matter of Faith

This belief runs through the entire Bible. It is found in the story of
Abraham's prayer to God for an heir [Genesis 15:2–6] and in Jacob's
prayer to be spared the vengeance of his brother Esau [Genesis

32:10–13]. It is with this firm belief in God's ability to answer prayer that one of the psalmists prays:

> Hear, O Lord, as I call with my voice,
> And be gracious to me and answer me. . . .
> Give me not up to the will of my adversaries,
> For false witnesses have risen against me,
> And they breathe out violence.
> I believe that I shall see the goodness of the Lord in the
> land of the living! —Psalm 27:7–13

And, says another psalmist:

> As for me, I will call upon God;
> And the Lord will save me.
> Evening and morning and at noon
> I utter my complaint and moan,
> And He will hear my voice.
> He will deliver my soul in safety from the battle that I
> wage,
> For many are arrayed against me.
> God will give ear and humble them. . . .
>   —Psalm 55:17–20

The faith expressed here is re-echoed in these words which the psalmist speaks in God's name:

> "Because he cleaves to Me in love, I will deliver him;
> I will protect him because he knows My name [Me].
> When he calls to Me I will answer him. . . ."
>   —Psalm 91:14–15

And when He so desires, God will indeed grant one's petitions:

> Out of my distress I called upon the Lord;
> The Lord answered me and set me free. —Psalm 118:5

Ezra acknowledges that God has acted favorably upon the hopes of the people for the rebuilding of the Temple. When the king of Babylonia decrees that the Temple should be restored, Ezra cries out:

> Blessed be the Lord, the God of our fathers, who put such
> a thing as this into the heart of the king to beautify the
> house of the Lord which is in Jerusalem, and who extended
> to me His kindness before the king and his counselors and
> before all the king's mighty officers. . . . —Ezra 7:27–28

Yes, if it is His will, God can act. Therefore one must have faith. Or, as the psalmist puts it:

Commit your way to the Lord;
Trust in Him, and He will act. —Psalm 37:5

The Effects of True Prayer

Though modern man does not expect God to change the natural order of the universe in his behalf or to interfere in general with people's freedom of action, he finds that with faith he can still count on God's help in response to his prayers.

Like the writers of the Bible, we, too, recognize that the will of God must remain supreme. He can choose to hear our prayers or not. And we must come before Him "with clean hands and a pure heart." Even then He may respond to our petitions by denying them.

But we also realize that instead of making any changes in the outward circumstances we may be facing, God can act upon us. If, for instance, we are confronted by certain problems, we may pray to Him for strength and wisdom to cope with them. Earnest, sincere prayer of this kind enables God to help us develop the courage and understanding we often need to overcome or even to live with our difficulties.

Although the authors of the Bible viewed God's response to prayer in quite different terms, they do provide an occasional hint of His acting upon the individual in response to his petition. For example, upon becoming the ruler of the Hebrew nation, King Solomon had a dream in which he prayed that God might grant him an understanding heart that he could more wisely rule over his people [I Kings 3:5–9]. So delighted was God with Solomon's prayer that He said to him:

> ". . . Because you have asked this thing, and have not asked for yourself long life, neither have you asked for yourself riches, nor the lives of your enemies, but have asked for yourself understanding to discern justice, behold I have done according to your word. . . ."
> —I Kings 3:11–12

And then, significantly, God goes on:

> "And I have also given you that which you have not asked, both riches and honor—so that no other king shall compare with you all your days." —I Kings 3:13

It was inevitable that Solomon, once having developed a heart capable of understanding his people, should come to enjoy riches and honor.

Or consider the case of the psalmist who suffered from deep feelings of guilt [Psalm 51:16]. He prayed:

> Create in me a clean heart, O God
> And renew a steadfast spirit within me. —Psalm 51:12

Prayer was the means by which he sought to become a more upright person. He believed that, if sincerely spoken and earnestly pursued, his prayer would find a response from God that would rid him of his anxiety.

The aim of both these prayers is clear. And by sincerely praying for self-improvement, we put ourselves into the position of meriting God's help.

Haven't we observed this principle at work within our own experience? Suppose, for instance, we yearn to have friends. We may not ask God to interfere with other people's lives and compel them to become our friends. Instead, if we pray to Him for the capacity to develop a more kindly, friendly disposition and then if we sincerely pursue this goal, we can achieve the kind of personality that wins us friends. In this way God truly answers our prayers.

Such prayer, the writers of the Bible knew, can do many things. It can help us to bear the heavy burdens that from time to time come upon all of us. For listen to one of the psalmists:

> In the day that I called, You did answer me;
> You encouraged me in my soul with strength.
> —Psalm 138:3

Or, as another puts it, "Cast your burden upon the Lord, and He will sustain you . . ." [Psalm 55:23–24]. Prayers of this nature aid us to develop the strength to face our problems, and in facing them, ultimately to solve them. In this way our prayers are answered.

Often, too, the inspiration of prayer can stir us to new heights. It can lift us above the pettinesses of people [Psalm 18:49]; it can urge us to greater perfection of ourselves [Psalm 27:11–14]; and it can encourage us to face and overcome our troubles [Psalm 22:10–27].

Different Kinds of Prayer

Thus far we have been discussing only one type of prayer, the kind that asks God to do various things for us. We call this "petitional" prayer.

However, prayer may take other forms depending upon our mood, and the Bible offers us a wide variety of examples. Here we shall consider just three of the more common types.

Prayers of "praise" are one type. These frequently arise from our sense of awe and gratitude as we look upon the vast universe and realize that God has created it all. So, in a mood of reverence for Him as the Creator, a psalmist says:

> The earth is the Lord's, and the fullness thereof;
> The world and they that dwell therein,
> For He has founded it upon the seas,
> And established it upon the floods. —Psalm 24:1–2

Another declares:

> When I behold Your heavens, the work of Your fingers,
> The moon and the stars, which You have established;
> What is man that You are mindful of him?
> And the son of man, that You think of him?
> Yet You have made him but little lower than the angels,
> And have crowned him with glory and honor.
> You have given him dominion over the works of Your hands;
> You have put all things under his feet,
> All sheep and oxen,
> And also the beasts of the field,
> The birds of the air, and the fish of the sea.
> O Lord, our Lord,
> How glorious is Your name in all the earth! —Psalm 8:4–10

Such prayers remind us of the blessings we enjoy at the hands of God. They keep us humble, thereby preventing us from becoming boastful or self-centered. We realize that life, the world, and all of its wonderful features are gifts of God. Hence, we are constantly moved to say with the psalmist:

> I will bless the Lord at all times;
> His praise shall continually be in my mouth.
> My soul makes its boast in the Lord. . . .
> O magnify the Lord with me,
> And let us exalt His name together! —Psalm 34:2–4

A second type of prayer, offered especially at times of joy, is that of "thanksgiving." For when we are happy, it is only natural to voice our feelings. On such occasions what is more appropriate than to thank God?

Thus, when despite our fears, things have turned out better than we expected, we can echo the prayer of one of the psalmists:

> I will give You [God] thanks with my whole heart,
> In the presence of the mighty will I sing praises unto
> You. . . .
> For . . . in the day that I called, You answered me;
> You encouraged me in my soul with strength.
>   —Psalm 138:1, 3

Or, in response to the glory of His creation and the wonder of Israel's history, we, too, can say:

> O give thanks unto the Lord, for He is good, . . .
> For His mercy endures forever. . . .
> To Him who alone has done great wonders, . . .
> To Him who by understanding made the heavens, . . .
> To Him who spread forth the earth above the waters, . . .
> To Him who made great lights, . . .
> The sun to rule by day, . . .
> The moon and stars to rule by night, . . .
> To Him who smote Egypt in their first-born, . . .
> And brought Israel out from among them. . . .
>   —Psalm 136:1, 4–11

Or, with still another psalmist, we can offer thanksgiving to God for strength in a time of trouble:

> You [God] did turn my mourning into dancing;
> You have removed my sackcloth, and girded me with gladness,
> That my soul might praise You and not be silent.
> O Lord my God, I will give thanks to You forever.
>   —Psalm 30:12–13

A third kind of prayer is that in which the individual seeks to come closer to God. These are sometimes called prayers of "trust" or "confidence." Through them we try to bring ourselves nearer to God by thinking of Him and finding joy in His presence. Under their influence our hearts glow with love of Him, and we feel refreshed and cleansed.

The Psalms, in particular, offer some of the best examples of prayers of trust or confidence. One of the most beloved is the Twenty-third Psalm which most of us know by heart, but here are several others:

> How precious is Your lovingkindness, O God!
> And the children of men take refuge in the shadow of Your wings.
> They are fully satisfied with the abundance of Your house,
> And You give them to drink of the river of Your pleasures.
> For with You is the fountain of life;
> In Your light do we see light. —Psalm 36:8–10

I lift up my eyes to the hills.
From whence does my help come?
My help comes from the Lord,
Who made heaven and earth.

He will not let your foot be moved,
He who keeps you will not slumber.
Behold, He who keeps Israel
Neither slumbers nor sleeps.

The Lord is your keeper;
The Lord is your shade on your right hand.
The sun shall not smite you by day,
Nor the moon by night.

The Lord will keep you from all evil;
He will keep your soul.
The Lord will guard your going out and your coming in
From this time forth and for evermore. —Psalm 121

The Lord is my light and my salvation; whom shall I fear?
The Lord is the stronghold of my life; of whom shall I be
afraid? —Psalm 27:1

How Prayer Helps

Though the writers of the Bible never dealt directly with the problem of man's freedom in relation to God's power to respond to prayer, the rabbis of the Talmud did. And they upheld God's power to act favorably upon certain kinds of petitional prayer.

They said God at any time can suspend a decision based upon His justice which would bring punishment upon man, and replace it by one based, instead, on His quality of mercy. But they, like the authors of the Bible, recognized that His will was supreme and that it alone determined the response to man's petitions. That is why many of our prayers that go back to talmudic times begin with the phrase, "May it be Your will, O Lord our God. . . ."

Yet those who wrote the Bible did establish the fact that, in accordance with His will, God hears and responds to prayer. And they succeeded in laying down the basic conditions necessary for prayer to be heard. Above all else, however, it is from them that we have inherited that deep sense of faith that prayer can help.

Recognizing the permanence of the physical and moral laws of God, we see how this is possible without disrupting the order of the universe or interfering with the freedom of others. For we know that God may also answer our prayers by acting upon us!

Thus, prayer which succeeds in creating appropriate changes in the individual becomes one of His ways of responding. By modifying our behavior and even remaking our character, God makes possible the very results for which we pray.

The faith that God can answer prayer gives man confidence for living even under the most trying circumstances. Jeremiah, facing constant danger for daring to speak unpopular truths to the people of Judah, drew courage from such faith. For inwardly he was moved by God's promise:

> ". . . If you utter what is precious, and not what is worth-less,
> You shall be as My mouth.
> They shall turn to you,
> But you shall not turn to them.
> And I will make you to this people a fortified wall of bronze;
> They will fight against you,
> But they shall not prevail over you,
> For I am with you to save you and deliver you,"
> Says the Lord. —Jeremiah 15:19–20

So, too, one of the writers of the Psalms declares:

> Whom have I in heaven but You?
> And there is nothing upon earth that I desire besides You.
> My flesh and my heart may fail,
> But God is the strength of my heart and my portion forever. —Psalm 73:25–26

In addition to providing us with courage, God accomplishes many other things through our prayers. Prayer can reinforce our conviction that life and the universe which He has created are basically good. It can refresh our spirits and cleanse us inwardly from feelings of guilt. It can bring us closer to God and strengthen our love for Him. It can encourage us to develop better, holier ways of living. And it can certainly help us avoid pride that inevitably leads to one's downfall [see Proverbs 16:18].

Do you recall the story of Daniel? This Jewish young man, we are told, was considered by the king of Babylonia to be one of the wisest people in the land. Yet Daniel knew that the real source of his wisdom lay not within himself. It was the gift of God; so, instead of becoming proud and boastful, Daniel remained humble. Undoubtedly it was prayer such as this that helped him:

> . . . Blessed be the name of God
> From everlasting even unto everlasting;
> For wisdom and might are His. . . .

I thank You and praise You,
O God of my fathers,
Who has given me wisdom and might. . . .
—Daniel 2:20, 23

Recognizing the many ways in which prayer can be of help, *The Guiding Principles of Reform Judaism* speaks of it in these terms:

> Prayer is the voice of religion, the language of faith and aspiration [longing]. It directs man's heart and mind Godward, voices the needs and hopes of the community, and reaches out with goals which invest [clothe] life with supreme value.

A Simple Question?

In their attitude toward the subject of prayer, the writers of the Bible, we see, reacted as men of religion, not as philosophers. Therefore they never once raised the question of whether the freedom God grants man prevents Him from responding to prayer.

Rather, they began with a deep faith that God responds to prayer and moved on from there to show some of the ways in which He acts.

This does not mean, however, that the writers of the Bible never dealt directly with religious problems. They did, and one of the questions they specifically tried to answer was why there is evil in the world. More particularly, they sought to know why God permits decent people to suffer. Haven't you yourself ever wondered about this?

Now on the surface this might sound like a simple question, but don't underestimate it. The authors of the Bible soon discovered that here they were dealing with one of man's most difficult problems. . . .

——————————— THINGS TO TALK OVER ———————————

1. In what ways does prayer help?

2. To what extent do you agree with the Bible's explanation as to why God does not always grant our requests?

3. Why can't we accept the beliefs of some of the biblical writers about miracle-producing prayer?

4. How do we account for the extensive use of the Book of Psalms in Jewish as well as Christian worship? ·

1. Would you agree with the way God answers prayer in the following passages: Exodus 15:22–25; Joshua 10:12–14; II Kings 1:1–10; Psalm 107:23–29?

2. What types of prayer do we find in: Psalm 9:1–5; 19:1–7; 59:1–6; 63:1–5; and 104:1–4?

3. In what ways does prayer seem to help people in these passages: Joshua 7:2–25; Judges 10:6–16; Psalm 37:5–10; Psalm 51:1–6?

4. What direct contribution have the following made to our own temple services: Exodus 15:11; Psalm 19:8–11, 15; Psalm 24:7–10; Psalm 121; Psalm 133:1?

——————————— FROM THE RABBIS' VIEWPOINT———————————

1. MIRACLES THROUGH PRAYER: See *Everyman's Talmud*, pp. 11–13, 294–295; and *A Rabbinic Anthology*, [560] p. 206, [580] pp. 214–216 [890–891] pp. 340–341, [984–990] pp. 371–375.

2. GOD AND PRAYER: See *Everyman's Talmud*, pp. 44, 52–53, 56, 87–89, 111; and *A Rabbinic Anthology*, [36–37] p. 18, [892–904] pp. 342–345, [907–912] pp. 345–346.

3. CONDITIONS FOR EFFECTIVE PRAYER: See *Everyman's Talmud*, pp. 84–93, 300–301; and *A Rabbinic Anthology*, [892–952] pp. 342–357.

————————————— OTHER THINGS TO READ —————————————

DOPPELT, FREDERIC A., *Dialogue with God*, Dorrance, Chap. 3: "Are Prayers Answered?" pp. 67–93; Chap. 4: "Why Prayers Fail," pp. 94–121; Chap. 5: "What Good Is It to Pray?" pp. 122–148.

FACKENHEIM, EMIL L., *Paths to Jewish Belief*, Behrman, Chap. 8: "Why Do We Pray?" pp. 97–106.

FREEHOF, SOLOMON B., *Preface to Scripture*, Union of American Hebrew Congregations, Chap. 4: "The Bible in Worship," pp. 34–41.

GITTELSOHN, ROLAND B., *Little Lower Than the Angels*, Union of American Hebrew Congregations, Chap. 13: "Why Pray?" pp. 216–235; Chap 14: "More About Prayer," pp. 236–258.

STEINBERG, MILTON, *Basic Judaism*, Harcourt, Brace, pp. 116–121.

WHY IS THERE EVIL
IN THE WORLD?

What's the Problem?

EVERY TIME WE HEAR A NEWS-CAST OR READ THE DAILY PAPER WE come face-to-face with the problem of evil in the world. That is because we are constantly running across items like these:

TORNADO SWEEPS THROUGH TINY SOUTHWESTERN TOWN

Twenty-seven Killed; Property Losses High

SIXTEEN MINERS TRAPPED AS EXPLOSION RIPS MINE

Rescuers Digging for Men in Wrecked Shaft

2 GUARDS SHOT DOWN AS BANDITS HIT CITY BANK

Robbers Kill Guards Who Protect Payroll

SCHOOL CHILDREN KILLED BY LARGE TRAILER TRUCK

Runaway Vehicle Hits Youngsters at Recess

| PLANE CRASH KILLS 74; | VESSEL STRIKES ICEBERG; |
| PILOT MISJUDGES SPEED | HOPE GONE FOR SURVIVORS |

| Four Survivors Tell | 108 Passengers and Crew |
| Tale of Air Tragedy | Die in North Atlantic |

Events like these are always distressing, but they are staggering when they involve relatives or friends. They cause us to wonder why such terrible things have to happen. And this, in turn, raises the whole question of why innocent people sometimes suffer.

This was no less perplexing to those who lived in Bible times. Like ourselves, they also believed that God is just and righteous [see, for example, Psalm 145:17], and that He rules over the world with lovingkindness and mercy [see, for example, Psalm 138:8]. They were likewise confident that God rewards the righteous and punishes the wicked [see, for example, Proverbs 10:3, 7; 11:8, 31].

Then why, they wondered, does He sometimes allow the wicked to prosper, or permit evil to befall the righteous? Similarly, with the various news items above, we may also ask why God should permit innocent children playing at school to be run down or bank guards performing their duty to be killed. Certainly these are difficult things to understand, and for religious people, in particular, they raise many serious questions.

Well, what did the authors of the Bible have to say about all this?

Is God Responsible for Evil?

In dealing with the whole problem, one of the first questions they had to face was whether God was responsible for the occurrence of evil. Because of their unique beliefs about God, the ancient Hebrew thinkers had a far more difficult task answering this than the peoples in neighboring lands.

Among the Greeks and Romans, responsibility for evil could be laid on the doorstep of many different gods. The finger of blame could be pointed at Zeus, Athene, Demeter, Apollo, or any of the rest. Furthermore, none of these deities was ever conceived of as wholly just or righteous. Out of simple jealousy, any one of them might decide to bring disaster upon a person for being too successful or too proud. For example, legend tells us that a Greek queen named Niobe was turned to stone by two of the gods merely because she boasted about the beauty of her children.

In the case of the Persians, evil was regarded as the work of a separate deity. They believed that there was not one God, but two, a concept that we call "dualism," from the Latin word *duo*, "two." One was Ahura Mazda; he was the god of light and goodness. The other, Ahriman, was the god of darkness and evil. The two were believed to be in constant conflict with one another. Because evil stemmed strictly from Ahriman, the people could absolve the god of goodness of any responsiblity for it.

Among the Greeks, there were two other possible answers. One was that there was no such thing as evil. The Stoics in particular took this position. Their leader, Epictetus, who lived during the first and second centuries of the Common Era, asserted, "The nature of evil does not exist in the universe," which is essentially the position of the Christian Scientist today. Others explained that what man observes as evil is really good as God sees it.

The second Greek attitude was the atheistic argument that because there was such evil in the world, there could not possibly be any God. A certain Greek poet of the fifth century B.C.E., Diagoras of Melos, expressed a typical point of view. He denied the existence of the gods because a wrong done to him remained unpunished. No deity, he maintained, would ever permit such a thing.

None of these solutions was possible to the authors of the Bible. That there could be no God was inconceivable. Indeed, only a fool would say that! [Psalm 53:2]. Nor could one deny the reality of evil, for this ran counter to their common-sense experience. They never doubted that pain and suffering were realities, as numerous passages in the Bible show [see, for example, Psalm 25:18 and Job 16:6]. Evil does exist. God Himself admits it when He brands Cain as a murderer [Genesis 4:9–12] or brings punishment upon His guilty people [see, for example, Zephaniah 3:5–6].

The notion that there might be a separate god of evil was also out of the question. Belief in only one God was far too deeply rooted. "Hear, O Israel, the Lord our God, the Lord is One," expressed their view [Deuteronomy 6:4]. "Before Me," one of the prophets states in the name of God, "there was no God formed; neither shall there be any after Me" [Isaiah 43:10]. Yes, God repeats, "I am the Lord, and there is no God besides Me" [Isaiah 45:5].

Nor, in view of the covenant between the Lord and the people of Israel, with all its insistence upon righteousness, could the ancient Hebrew thinkers accept the idea that God was neither good nor just. "The Lord is righteous in all His ways," one psalmist declares [Psalm 145:17]; "Good and upright is the Lord," maintains another [Psalm 25:8]. The prophet Isaiah has God say:

> ". . . I the Lord speak righteousness,
> I declare things that are right. . . ." —Isaiah 45:19

No, the idea that God was not wholly righteous, just, and good was something that the writers of the Bible could never bring themselves to believe. They observed the effects that worship of an evil god, Baal, had upon their neighbors, the Canaanites: it led quickly to human corruption, as the prophets pointed out [see, for example, Hosea 4:14, 17–19 and Jeremiah 19:5].

Consequently the authors of the Bible concluded that evil could originate from only one source, the single Source of everything, God. Typical are the following observations:

> . . . Shall evil befall a city
> And the Lord not have caused it? —Amos 3:6

> . . . Shall we receive good at the hand of God and shall we not receive evil? —Job 2:10

> Is it not from the mouth of the Most High,
> That good and evil come? —Lamentations 3:38

Once the authors of the Bible acknowledged that both evil and good come from God, they were forced to ask still another question: Why does He see fit to bring about all the troubles that beset mankind?

Evil, the Result of Wickedness

One recurrent theme that runs through the pages of the Bible is that misfortune is the inevitable consequence of wickedness. God repays the evil-doer for his deeds. "His own iniquities shall ensnare the wicked," one passage assures us [Proverbs 5:22]; "Whoever digs a pit [for someone else] shall fall in it [himself], and he that rolls a stone [against someone else], it shall return upon him," says another [Proverbs 26:27]. One psalmist puts it this way:

> Blessed is the man that has not walked in the counsel of the wicked,
> Nor stands in the way of sinners,
> Nor sits in the seat of scoffers. . . .
> In all that he does he prospers.

> Not so the wicked,
> For they are like the chaff which the wind drives away.
> Therefore the wicked will not stand up under judgment,
> Nor sinners in [comparison with] the congregation of the righteous,

For the Lord knows the way of the righteous;
But the way of the wicked will perish. —Psalm 1:1–6

Yes, God promises, "I will punish the world for its evil, and the wicked for their iniquity" [Isaiah 13:11].

Many tales told by the biblical writers emphasize this. For instance, you will recall that in the Creation story God commanded Adam and Eve not to eat the fruit of the Tree of Knowledge. But through the temptations of the serpent they disobeyed Him. As a result they were compelled to endure much suffering, including expulsion from the Garden of Eden and the necessity to work hard for their food [Genesis 3:16–24]. Much misfortune came to the first man and woman, therefore, because of their wickedness in rejecting God's command.

The same point is made in the story of the Flood. Why was it that the ancient people had to undergo destruction? The Bible tells us:

> . . . The Lord saw that the wickedness of man was great in the earth, and that all of the thoughts of his heart were evil all the time. . . . And the Lord said: "I will blot out man whom I have created from the face of the earth. . . ."
> —Genesis 6:5, 7

Hence rebellion against God by committing acts of wickedness led to the wholesale punishment of the human race.

Similarly, in the case of the twin cities of Sodom and Gomorrah. "The outcry against Sodom and Gomorrah is great and their sin is very grave," God tells Abraham [Genesis 18:20]. Therefore:

> The Lord rained on Sodom and Gomorrah brimstone and fire . . . out of heaven; and He overthrew those cities, and all the valley, and all the inhabitants of the cities, and whatever grew on the ground. —Genesis 19:24–25

Also, because of their sins, suffering came to the people of Israel as they made their way through the Wilderness. At Sinai, when Moses was at the top of the mountain receiving the commandments, the people grew restless and demanded a golden calf to worship. For rejecting the Lord and worshiping a false god, the people were severely punished. "The Lord sent a plague upon the people," we are told, "because they made the calf . . ." [Exodus 32:35].

A Not Fully Satisfactory Explanation

To a large extent, wickedness does lead to misfortune and suffering. The criminal, for instance, pays for his crime in many ways. His conscience may give him no rest; he can have no real friends or a normal, peaceful home life. And if he is found out, he must spend a good portion of his life behind bars.

Yet, as in our day, the biblical authors saw that the wicked were not always punished. One psalmist speaks unhappily of the great prosperity of the wicked [Psalm 73:3]. So do Jeremiah [Jeremiah 12:1] and Job [Job 21:7–15]. Koheleth observes that in many instances, the wicked seem to be enjoying what should justly belong to the righteous [Ecclesiastes 8:14].

Nor are the righteous always rewarded. Some, in fact, experience much suffering. The author of Psalm 7 cries to God that even though he has been righteous, his enemies are causing him great distress. "Oh that a full measure of evil would come upon the wicked," he finally bursts out, "and that You [God] would establish the righteous man who perishes in his righteousness" [Psalm 7:10]. Koheleth observes that he has seen the righteous perish whereas the wicked seem to be enjoying long life [Ecclesiastes 7:15]; and Job in his intense suffering also protests that he is innocent of any sin. Even God knows that, he says. Why, then, should he suffer, especially since the wicked seem to be prospering? [Job 12:6].

Now, those who wrote the Bible were not speaking of the petty complaints of people who are unhappy because they are not better off than their neighbors. Along with Koheleth, they knew that "one who loves money will not be satisfied with money; nor one who loves wealth, with gain" [Ecclesiastes 5:10]. There is no satisfying such people's desires. Nor would the ancient thinkers ever have commiserated with the person who is full of self-pity because he has only one car while his neighbor has two. Rather, they looked upon the possession of mere life itself as ample reason to thank God. Said one of the psalmists:

> I will praise the Lord as long as I live;
> I will sing praises unto my God while I have existence.
> —Psalm 146:2

When they spoke of evil, they meant genuine suffering—affliction, imprisonment, disgrace, pain, abject poverty, starvation, death.

Despite whatever evidence there was to the contrary, the authors of the Bible consistently held fast to the principle that evil-doing would be punished and righteousness rewarded. Typical of their attitude is this comment which Zophar, one of Job's friends, makes to him. Rebuking Job for insisting that suffering can come without some wickedness on his part, Zophar protests:

> You [Job] have said, "My doctrine is pure,
> And I am clean in God's eyes."
> But oh, that God would speak,
> And open His lips to you
> And that He would tell you the secrets of wisdom. . . .
> [You would] know then that God exacts less than your guilt deserves.
>
> If you set your heart aright,
> You will stretch out your hands toward Him.
> If iniquity is in your hand, put it far away,
> Let not wickedness dwell in your tents.
> Surely then you will lift up your face without blemish;
> You will be secure and will not fear.
> You will forget your misery. . . .
> And your life will be brighter than the noonday. . . .
> You will lie down and none will make you afraid;
> Many will seek your favor.
> But the eyes of the wicked will fail.
> All way of escape is lost to them,
> And their [only] hope is to breathe their last.
> —Job 11:4–6,13–20

The Hebrew thinkers knew that by and large Zophar was right. A great deal of human suffering *is* the result of evil-doing, and decent conduct generally brings rewarding consequences.

Still, the good fortune obviously enjoyed by some of the wicked, as well as the suffering endured by some of the innocent, called for further explanation. Belief in a just God, as the prophet Zephaniah maintained, demanded nothing less than perfect justice. "The Lord," he said, "will not do unrighteousness" [Zephaniah 3:5].

The Guilt of Others Causes Trouble

Several answers were found. One important answer declared that the suffering of the righteous was the result of the wickedness of the nation as a whole, or of its leaders, or of one's forefathers.

In our discussion of freedom of will and prayer, we have already seen how some of the biblical writers believed that the actions of the nation could affect the individual. We observed, for example, how God was said to have used the Assyrian nation for His own purposes [Isaiah 10:5–6]. But because Assyria thought it was their own might, rather than God's, which had won victory over Israel, Assyria was to be destroyed [Isaiah 10:18–19]. Hence the evil that was to befall each Assyrian was the consequence of his nation's sinfulness.

The biblical writers did not hesitate to pass the same kind of judgment upon their own people. Believing that God operated within the events of history by using the nations for His purposes, they held that the wickedness of the Hebrew people as a whole was responsible for the misfortune that often befell the individual.

Here is one example. Coming out of the Wilderness into the Promised Land, the children of Israel suffered greatly at the hands of the native peoples of Canaan. Why had this evil come upon them? This is the Bible's explanation:

> And the children of Israel did that which was evil in the sight of the Lord. . . . And they forsook the Lord, the God of their fathers. . . . And the anger of the Lord was kindled against Israel, and He delivered them into the hands of spoilers that despoiled them, and He gave them over into the hands of their enemies round about, so that they could no longer stand before their enemies. Wherever they went out, the hand of the Lord was against them for evil . . . and they were sorely distressed.
> —Judges 2:11–15

Other biblical writers pointed out that the people also encountered evil because of the unrighteous acts of some of their leaders. An illustration is the case of Manasseh, a later king of Judah. Concerning him, the Bible declares:

> And he did that which was evil in the sight of the Lord, according to the abominable practices of the nations whom the Lord drove out before the people of Israel. . . . And the Lord said by His servants the prophets, "Because Manasseh, king of Judah, has committed these abominations . . . and made Judah sin with his idols, therefore thus says the Lord, the God of Israel: Behold I am bringing upon Jerusalem and Judah such evil that the ears of everyone who hears of it will tingle. . . ."
> —II Kings 21:2–12

Another example is that of King Solomon and the wide-spread suffering he eventually caused. At the end of his reign, as you know, the nation underwent bitter civil strife. As a result, the Hebrew people were split into two kingdoms, Israel in the north and Judah to the south. Why did this happen, asks the Bible? Its answer was:

> And the Lord was angry with Solomon because his heart was turned away from the Lord, the God of Israel . . .

and he did not do what the Lord had commanded. Therefore the Lord said to Solomon: "Since this has been in your
mind and you have not kept My covenant and My statutes
which I have commanded you, I will surely tear the kingdom away from you. . . ." —I Kings 11:9–11

The guilt of one's forefathers may also be responsible. As we have
already noted, certain biblical writers promise that the people will
be punished for the sins of their forefathers [see, for example, Exodus 20:5; 34:7 and Numbers 14:18]. In a similar way they will
also enjoy the fruits of their ancestors' good deeds. Thus God tells
Jehu, the rebel captain of the Northern Kingdom's army, that he
has done well in destroying Queen Jezebel and uprooting the worship of her gods. Therefore, He promises him, "Your sons of the
fourth generation shall sit upon the throne of Israel" [II Kings
10:1–30].

These various explanations did not go unchallenged. The notion
that one might suffer because of the sins of others, whether it be
those of the nation as a whole or of one's forefathers, met with
some criticism from other biblical writers. In the tale involving the
destruction of the wicked cities of Sodom and Gomorrah, for instance, Abraham is pictured as protesting God's plan. "Will You
indeed sweep away the righteous with the wicked?" he argues with
Him. Abraham finally compels God to admit that He will not destroy
the cities if they contain at least ten righteous people [Genesis
18:20–32]. Moses and Aaron likewise object to God's intention to
destroy all the Hebrews in the Wilderness because of the sin of one
man, Korah [Numbers 16:22].

Opposition is heard from some of the later prophets as well.
Ezekiel, in particular, maintains that it is only the individual himself who must pay the penalty for his sins. "The person who sins,"
he insists, "[only] he shall die" [Ezekiel 18:4]. Then he goes on to
explain:

> You [the people of Israel] say, "Why should not the son
> suffer for the iniquity of the father?"
>
> "When the son has done what is lawful and right and has
> been careful to observe all My statutes, he shall surely live.
> Only the soul that sins shall die. The son shall not suffer
> for the iniquity of the father, nor the father suffer for the
> iniquity of the son; the righteousness of the righteous shall
> be upon himself, and the wickedness of the wicked shall
> be upon himself." —Ezekiel 18:19–20

Yet, while Ezekiel found it necessary to hold the individual responsible for his acts, the truth is that the deeds of others, some-

times those deeds done even in remote parts of the world, do affect us. In a globe as shrunken as ours, what happens in such places as Berlin, China, the Congo, and elsewhere, can have serious consequences for all of us. Similarly what each American does affects the conduct of the nation as a whole and the lives of millions, not only here but all over the world.

Ezekiel was not wrong in the stand he took, but then neither were those writers of the Bible who insisted that the actions of others can produce evil that affects the individual.

Just Be Patient . . .

Still many were not satisfied. They came upon some individuals whose suffering was obviously not the result of the sins of society. Even more glaring, however, was the example of the wicked who were enjoying prosperity. How could a just and righteous God permit such a thing!

We can well imagine some saying to themselves, "Here I am. I always try to obey God's laws and to be faithful to His covenant. I help the poor. I am considerate in all my actions. Yet I suffer while the wicked man prospers! Why should it be so?" (Psalms 71 and 86, for example, reflect this kind of thinking.)

As if in reply, here is the answer of one psalmist:

> Do not fret because of the wicked,
> And do not be envious of wrong-doers!
> For they will soon fade like the grass,
> And wither like the green herb.

> Trust in the Lord and do good;
> So you will dwell in the land and enjoy security.
> Take delight in the Lord,
> And He will give you the desires of your heart. . . .

> Be still before the Lord, and wait patiently for Him,
> Do not fret over him who prospers in his way,
> Over the man who carries out evil schemes!

> Refrain from anger, and forsake wrath!
> Do not fret; it tends only to evil.
> For the wicked shall be cut off,
> But those who wait for the Lord shall possess the land.

> Yet a little while and the wicked will be no more;
> Though you look well at his place he will not be there.
> But the humble shall possess the land,
> And delight themselves in abundant prosperity.

The wicked plots against the righteous
And gnashes his teeth at him;
But the Lord laughs at the wicked,
For He sees that his day is coming. . . .

Wait for the Lord and keep to His way,
And He will exalt you to possess the land;
You will look upon the destruction of the wicked. . . .
— Psalm 37: 1–13, 34

The answer, then, is to be found in the future. In just a little while, the psalmist tells us, God will take care of the wicked. His deep faith in God's righteousness and fairness assured him that justice would be done . . . eventually!

A similar answer is given in the Book of Lamentations. Those who wrote this little book apparently lived through several periods of terrible destruction, probably beginning with the Babylonian triumph over Judah in 586 B.C.E. The writing convinces us that they were personally familiar with disaster. The language is vivid and terrifying; you can almost hear the cries of the dying and the moans of those watching their country being turned into ruins.

Naturally the writers were tormented by such experiences. They wondered why these evils came upon them "for He [God] does not willingly afflict or grieve the sons of men" [Lamentations 3:33]. The answer, of course, is that the people have sinned [Lamentations 3:39, 42]. But once the people change their ways and turn to righteousness, God will certainly punish the wicked who oppress them. Indeed:

> You will pay them back, O Lord
> According to the work of their hands.
> You will give them heaviness of heart;
> Your curse will be upon them.
> You will pursue them in anger and destroy them
> From under the heavens of the Lord.
>   — Lamentations 3: 64–66

The prophet Jeremiah also questioned why the evil-doers who threatened his life [Jeremiah 11:21] continued to thrive. And so he turned to God with:

> You are righteous, O Lord,
> Even when I would complain to You;
> Yet will I reason with You:
> Why does the way of the wicked prosper?
> Why do all who are treacherous succeed? — Jeremiah 12:1

Here his faith in God's justice assures him that the prosperity of the wicked cannot last. For having raised the question, Jeremiah goes on to say:

> They [the wicked] have sown wheat and reaped thorns,
> They tire themselves out but profit nothing,
> They shall be ashamed of their harvests
> Because of the fierce anger of the Lord. —Jeremiah 12:13

Similarly, the prophet Habakkuk also inquires of the Lord:

> You [God] who have eyes too pure to behold evil
> And cannot look upon wrong,
> Why do You look upon those who do treacherous things
> And remain silent when the wicked swallows up
> The man that is more righteous than he? —Habakkuk 1:13

And the answer that he arrives at is that the wicked will certainly be repaid. Woe to all of them! [see Habakkuk 2:5–19]. Rest assured, he says, "the righteous shall live by his faith" [Habakkuk 2:4].

The answer of these and other biblical writers is clear. The righteous may suffer and the wicked prosper, but it is only for a time. Wait, be patient! Both will get what is justly due them.

A Blessing in Disguise

Though some were willing to wait for the Lord to act, others were not so content. They still could not see how, even for a short while, a just God could permit injustice to triumph, the wicked to be successful, and the righteous to suffer. We catch some of this impatience in these words spoken by a psalmist:

> Awake, why do You sleep, O Lord?
> Arouse Yourself! Do not cast us off forever!
> Why do You hide Your face?
> Why do You forget our affliction and oppression?
> For our soul is bowed down to the dust,
> Our body cleaves to the ground.
> Rise up, come to our help!
> Deliver us for Your mercy's sake! —Psalm 44:24–27

The fact that the Hebrew people now in Babylonian exile continued to suffer prompted Second Isaiah to come forward with still another explanation. Earlier, you will recall, we saw how he described Israel as the "Servant of the Lord" with a special mission to mankind. Now the prophet tells that, in addition to their own sins, it is this mission that has been responsible for the people's troubles and has made Israel:

> . . . Despised, and forsaken of men,
> A man of pains, and acquainted with sickness;
> As one from whom men hide their faces,
> He was despised, and we had no regard for him.
> —Isaiah 53:3

There is a connection between the misfortunes of the people, the prophet insists, and their role as the Servant of the Lord. It is necessary that Israel suffer as an example to the world. Its plight serves as a warning to the rest of mankind to follow God's ways. Consequently, in looking upon the evil that has befallen the Jews, the other peoples themselves say:

> Surely he [Israel] has borne our sufferings and carried our pains,
> Whereas we thought he had been stricken,
> Punished by God and afflicted [because of his own wickedness].
> He was wounded because of our transgressions,
> He was crushed because of our iniquities;
> He experienced the suffering which might lead to our welfare. . . . —Isaiah 53:4–5

Actually, we find many examples of this principle operating today. Driving along the highway, for instance, we may pass the scene of an accident. Affected by the sight of someone else's misfortune, we usually begin driving more cautiously. Similarly, upon observing the suffering of Israel, says Second Isaiah, the nations of the world will be moved to become more righteous. In this sense, suffering is really a sign of God's wider love for mankind, rather than "punishment" as such.

Other writers of the Bible also came to picture suffering as a form of God's "discipline." This was His way of improving the individual, they said. For God is very much like a human father who, in the best interests of his children, often trains them by means of correction. In fact, some of the biblical authors put it precisely this way. Here is one such statement:

> For whom the Lord loves He disciplines,
> As a father the son in whom he delights. —Proverbs 3:12

This explanation for suffering appears in other passages as well. The writer of the Book of Deuteronomy declares: "Know then in your heart that as a man disciplines his son, the Lord your God disciplines you" [Deuteronomy 8:5]. "Blessed is the man whom You chastise, O Lord," concludes a psalmist [Psalm 94:12]. Far from being a punishment, suffering should be regarded as an indication of God's special love. One should certainly not "despise the Lord's discipline" nor reject it [Proverbs 3:11].

Viewing suffering in this light is, of course, another possible answer to the problem. It is often true that suffering is "a blessing in disguise." Though a toothache is painful, the pain compels us to do something about an infection which otherwise might cause us to lose all our teeth. The loss of a loved one, painful as it is, tends to make us more considerate and loving of the other members of our family.

Our suffering then becomes a form of God's instruction by which we frequently discover things that we cannot find out any other way. "The reproofs of instruction," says the writer of Proverbs, "are the way to [a more virtuous] life" [Proverbs 6:23]. Indeed, all too often the only way some of us learn important lessons is through bitter experience.

A Final Answer

Despite all the explanations for the existence of evil, it was left to the author of the Book of Job to provide us with what, thus far, has remained the final answer.

The Book of Job, you remember, is presented in the form of a drama. Here, within the setting of a supposed contest between God and Satan (the meaning of this Hebrew word is "adversary"), Job's religious faith is tested. Everything he has is taken away from him, his possessions, his home, even his children. On top of this, he is afflicted with a terrible disease [Job 1–2:8].

It is then that we find Job sitting on the ground, scraping his itching skin with a piece of pottery and grieving over his situation. But what torments him most is why God has made him, a righteous man, suffer?

In the presence of three friends who have come to comfort him, Job gives voice to his anguish:

> Let the day perish when I was born,
> And the night when it was said: "It is a boy!"
> . . . Why did I not die at my birth? —Job 3:3, 11

His friends try to console him. Inevitably they find themselves also trying to explain the cause of his troubles. Note what they say and how Job answers them. (For brevity, the passages here have been condensed. However, you will certainly also want to read the original.)

ELIPHAZ: Your suffering has worn you out,
But haven't you confidence as a result of your faith in God?
Isn't your uprightness your hope?
Think now! What innocent man ever perished,
Or in what instance has the upright been destroyed?
People are punished for the evil they do,
And reap the consequences of their wrongdoing. [See Job 4:1–8.]

JOB: Surely I am entitled to kindness from a friend;
Make me understand where I have done evil.
[See Job 6:14, 24.]

BILDAD: How long will you say such things?
Does God pervert justice?
If your children sinned against Him,
Then He has made them pay the penalty.
And if you were completely pure and upright,
Surely He would see to it that you were prospering. [See Job 8:1–6.]

JOB: But I am blameless! Worse, I am sick of living.
For it is plain that God destroys both the innocent and the wicked indiscriminately.
When disaster brings sudden death,
He laughs at the ruin of the innocent!
If it is not He, then who is it? [See Job 9:21–24.]

ZOPHAR: You say, "My life is pure and I am clean in God's sight."
But oh if God would only tell you!
Then you would know that He is punishing you less than your guilt deserves. [See Job 11:4–6.]

JOB: I've heard enough from all of you.
I, too, know all of these answers.
It is with God that I want to speak
And argue my case with Him.
Even though He may kill me,
I would still argue my case before Him.
[See Job 13:1–3, 15.]

The reasons offered by his friends do not satisfy Job. For they have told him simply what he already knows. He agrees that punishment comes to evil-doers, and were he guilty, he would not be protesting. But the point is that Job really has *not* sinned; he *is* thoroughly righteous. To a man such as he, the argument that he is being punished for his sins, even secret ones, does not apply. His friends, then, are "sorry comforters" [Job 16:2].

Obviously only God alone can explain to Job why he has been so badly treated. Therefore he demands that God Himself answer him [Job 13:20–28].

In this tale, God finally responds from a whirlwind and says to Job:

> "Who are you to confuse My purposes with meaningless words?
> Stand up like a man and see if you can answer *My* questions—
> Where were you when I laid the foundations of the earth?
> Were you with Me when I determined how far the seas should extend?
> Have you brought forth each new day since you were born,
> Or caused the dawn to appear in the east?
> Have you entered the springs of the sea,
> Or walked in the deepest parts of the deep?
> Do you know the whereabouts of the gates of death?
> Are you aware of every feature of the earth's surface?
> Where is the way to the dwelling-place of light?
> And where is the place of origin of darkness, snow, hail, wind, and rain?
> Who brings the rain and causes the ground to produce grass?
> Can you set the stars in their places or release them?
> Or tell them where to shine upon earth?
>
> Surely you are able to do these things,
> Or else how can you find fault and argue with the Almighty?
> Before you do, first answer My questions."
> [See Job 38; 40:1–2.]

To which Job, taken aback, concedes:

> Who am I to answer You,
> I who am of so little account?
> It is true I have questioned,
> But I have nothing more to say. —Job 40:3–5

. Then God replies:

> "Well, then, how can you say that My ways are wrong,
> Or condemn Me in order to justify yourself?
> Are you in any fashion like God?
> Can you rule the world in majesty?
> Can you humble the proud, and put down the wicked?
> If you can, then you can deliver yourself out of your suffering.

> But look at you!
> You cannot even compare in strength with the hippopota-
> mus which I have made,
> Nor in ferociousness with the crocodile I have created!"
> [See Job 40:1–41:34.]

This, then, is God's answer. Job must realize that no human being, limited as he is in power, intelligence, and length of life, can hope to understand the workings of mighty, everlasting God. Man will always be unable to know why various things happen to him or to explain fully the reason for the existence of evil in the world. This, at last, is what Job recognizes. Now he admits:

> I know You can do everything,
> And that no purpose of Yours can be interfered with. . . .
> Alas, I have said things that I didn't understand,
> Things too difficult for me to know;
> Therefore I despise myself for my actions,
> And I repent for what I have done. [See Job 42:1–6.]

The drama is finished. Job has renewed his faith in God, though he cannot fully understand the why of evil and suffering in the world. It is enough for him to trust in God's wisdom and ultimate justice. All that matters is that through his suffering he has come to know God better, and this religious experience in turn has helped him bear his pain.

It is this, the author of the book is telling us, that is the only answer human beings will ever find to the problem of evil.

What Can We Do about It?

In struggling with the problem, the authors of the Bible did reach certain conclusions which, in spite of our human limitations, make it possible for us to do something about evil.

They made it clear that above all, misfortune comes about largely through the wickedness of both the individual and society. For instance, the terrible sins of Adolf Hitler, with the support of many of the German people, brought ruin and destruction upon millions. Ultimately, of course, their dreadful wrong-doing was severely punished. But as a consequence, millions of innocent people did suffer and die.

Perhaps, as some of the writers of the Bible might have explained, the innocent were forced to endure this in order that the rest of the world might recognize the evil of Nazism and take measures to root it out. Others might add that the catastrophe undoubtedly did serve to arouse world Jewry to a new sense of duty to its covenant and to awaken mankind to an awareness of the evil of which modern man is still capable. This all-too-tragic calamity was a sickening and sobering lesson to the human race. And from it may have already come certain developments of tremendous importance to the Jews and to mankind generally—the establishment of the State of Israel, the awakening of a new sense of maturity on the part of American Jewry, a greater sensitivity to human rights in many parts of the world including our own country, and the Genocide Convention of the United Nations aimed at outlawing mass extermination of people because of their religion and race.

We realize, of course, that this is little consolation to the six million Jews who perished, or to their bereaved families. The final answer here can only be that given by the author of Job—the affliction of the innocent is something beyond our understanding, but not beyond our trust in God. Nevertheless, we can certainly see that the basic cause was the wickedness of Hitler and his followers. Evil once let loose rarely stops with only the guilty. Sin and wickedness, like disease, are highly infectious. They bring pain to the innocent as well as the guilty.

But equally clear, too, is the fact that man is not entirely helpless to cope with the problem of evil. The writers of the Bible knew that righteous living was man's most potent weapon against permitting evil to take root and to flourish so that it eventually could destroy the innocent. If, for example, the German people had promptly recognized Hitler's wickedness as such and halted it right from the start, the Nazi atrocities and World War ii would never have occurred. Thus, the millions who perished would still be alive today. This, in essence, is what the Bible is really telling us.

Little wonder, therefore, that in the turmoil and disaster for the Jewish people after the close of the biblical period, the rabbis found good reason to lay ever greater stress upon the need for morality, especially on the part of Jewry. "If all Israel repented a single day," they said, "the Messiah would come [to usher in God's Kingdom]" [Jerusalem Talmud: Taanith 64a]. In the same way the tragedy of the Nineteen-Thirties and Forties and the evils abroad in the world today should spur us on to a more intensive pursuit of our Mission and the ultimate establishment of God's Kingdom on earth.

This is what Reform Judaism asks. For though it is still true that, as Job discovered, man cannot fully understand why evil exists, he must nevertheless do as much as he can, with God's guidance and help, to overcome it. First and foremost he must dedicate his life to the practice of righteousness. He should also work for the well-being of his fellow man. He can help bring the wicked to speedy justice. And he can make full use of his God-given abilities to safeguard people against all sorts of calamities, such as war, explosions, tornadoes, automobile accidents, disease, and the like. The dramatic example of Drs. Jonas Salk and Albert Sabin, who in our own time discovered how to protect people from polio, gives us every reason to believe that man can indeed prevent many other forms of suffering.

A Related Question

In arriving at their conclusions about the existence of evil, the authors of the Bible came face-to-face with still another problem. This was the question of the purpose of life.

Actually, as the author of Job and others reasoned, if people were destined to suffer pain and misfortune at the hands of God, why were they ever created in the first place?

Thus Job asks, "Why didn't I die at birth? Why is life given to someone who must suffer bitterly?" [Job 3:11, 20]. Similarly, in the midst of punishment in the stocks, the prophet Jeremiah exclaims:

> Cursed be the day
> On which I was born!
> The day when my mother bore me,
> Let it not be blessed!
> Why did I [ever] come forth from the womb
> To see toil and sorrow,
> And spend my days in shame? —Jeremiah 20:14, 18

The question of life's purpose, then, is something that arises directly out of the problem of evil. Naturally those who wrote the Bible wanted to know why God created man when life often brings him nothing but suffering. . . .

———————— THINGS TO TALK OVER ————————

1. To what extent do you agree with the Bible's reasons for the prosperity of the wicked?

2. From your own experience, to what degree are the Bible's explanations for the cause of evil true?

3. In what way is the Bible correct in its views about reward for righteousness and punishment for evil-doing?

4. As Jews, how must we react to the evils that exist in our present-day world?

──────────── SOME OTHER BIBLE PASSAGES TO CONSIDER ────────────

1. How would modern Judaism react to the way Koheleth deals with the problem of evil? See Ecclesiastes 3:16–22; 4:1–3; 7:13–14; 7:15–17; 9:1–3.

2. How would you answer the argument voiced by Elihu to Job? See Job 34:10–12; 37:23–24.

3. In what way does Ezekiel answer the problem of why evil befell the people of Israel? See Ezekiel 5:5–8; 18:29–32; 22:1–16.

4. According to the psalmist, how is the evil-doer to be compensated? Psalm 7:12–17; 11:4–6; 18:47–49; 31:18–19; 37:10–13; 92:7–8.

──────────── FROM THE RABBIS' VIEWPOINT ────────────

1. EVIL WITHIN MAN: See *Everyman's Talmud*, pp. 93–99; and *A Rabbinic Anthology*, [757–781] pp. 295–302.

2. THE SUFFERING OF THE RIGHTEOUS: See *Everyman's Talmud*, pp. 117–127; and *A Rabbinic Anthology*, Chap. 28, "On Sufferings," pp. 541–555.

3. REWARD AND PUNISHMENT: See *Everyman's Talmud*, pp. 117–127, 392–412; and *A Rabbinic Anthology*, [1618–1632] pp. 584–591, [1635–1636] p. 593.

──────────── OTHER THINGS TO READ ────────────

FACKENHEIM, EMIL L., *Paths to Jewish Belief*, Behrman, Chap. 5: "Why Does God Permit Evil?" pp. 59–71.

FREEHOF, SOLOMON B., *Book of Job—A Commentary*, Union of American Hebrew Congregations, "Introduction," pp. 3–33; pp. 235–239.

GITTELSOHN, ROLAND B., *Little Lower Than the Angels*, Union of American Hebrew Congregations, Chap. 16: "When Life Is Sad," pp. 282–300.

KOHLER, KAUFMANN, *Jewish Theology*, Macmillan, Chap. 29: "God and the Existence of Evil," pp. 176–179.

STEINBERG, MILTON, *Basic Judaism*, Harcourt, Brace, pp. 53–57.

$\mathscr{S}even$

IS THERE PURPOSE TO LIFE?

Why the Question?

HAVE YOU EVER WONDERED ABOUT THE PURPOSE OF LIFE?

Of course you have. Nearly everybody has at one time or another. For instance, we face the question when we choose an occupation. We know that, above all else, our vocation must give us a sense of worthwhileness to life.

The problem also arises when hardship or suffering occurs. It is then, like Job and Jeremiah, that one begins to ask, "Why was I ever born?" [see Job 3:1–16 and Jeremiah 20:14–18]. For what troubles us is not only our misfortune but our uncertainty about the very nature and purpose of life itself.

This is often a problem to people who, ironically, are well off. Having almost everything they need—money, clothes, fashionable homes, and all the latest conveniences—they sometimes find life no longer a challenge. In this they exemplify the story of the man who in his younger years yearned for an expensive automobile. When later in life he was able to afford it, he confessed to a friend that he now had nothing more to live for.

Obviously, prosperity does not necessarily make for happiness or zest for living. Nor does it automatically answer man's need for a purpose to life. In fact, the increasing abundance of material wealth in the Western world is even considered one of the reasons for the higher rate of suicide in such affluent countries as Sweden and the United States.

However, of all human experiences, probably none compels us to think more deeply about life's purpose than our awareness of the universe. For just consider some of the facts with which we are familiar. . . .

To begin with, we know that our earth is only one of nine major planets that revolve around the sun, some ninety-three million miles away from Earth. Together, these nine planets make up the Solar System, which science tells us is only a tiny part of the vast number of similar systems that form our particular galaxy—a formation of some ten thousand million stars, separated from each other by such vast distances that astronomers must measure them in "light years."

A light year is the distance over which light can travel in a year's time. To calculate this we multiply the speed of light (186,000 miles a second) by sixty seconds for each minute, then by sixty minutes in the hour, times twenty-four hours in the day and 365 days of the year. In very round numbers, a light year comes to nearly six million million miles. Astronomers estimate that the distance from our Solar System to the center of the Milky Way is about 30,000 light years. From one end of the Milky Way to the other is about 100,000 light years, or some 600,000,000,000,000,-000 miles!

But this isn't all. Farther out in space is a cluster of a dozen or so other galaxies to which it is now thought the Milky Way belongs. Each contains thousands of millions of systems, each with thousands of millions of its own stars. And beyond, there may be hundreds, thousands, or even millions of still other galaxies, for thus far man has only been able to reach out in space to a distance of about two thousand million light years. How far the universe extends beyond this is unknown, perhaps millions upon millions of light years in all directions!

Our minds simply cannot comprehend such a tremendous expanse; we are overwhelmed by the vastness of the universe! Maybe the life of one human being on earth isn't so important after all! Perhaps man is really of no great significance in the universe! Thoughts like these make us wonder all the more about human existence and exactly where man fits into the whole scheme of things.

And the more we wonder, the more insistent become our questions. Foremost among them is whether there really is any purpose to life.

One Man's Opinion

The writers of the Bible were as concerned as we with this question.

To be sure, they had none of our modern scientific knowledge. They believed that the earth was the center of the universe and that the space beyond it was quite limited. Above the earth was simply a "firmament" or canopy, a dome-shaped heaven into which the sun, moon, and stars were permanently set [see Genesis 1:1–18].

Nonetheless, their awareness of the wonder of the universe, along with many of their own personal experiences, compelled them to think about the purpose of man. This is the way one psalmist put it:

> When I behold Your [God's] heavens, the work of Your fingers,
> The moon and the stars which You have established,
> What is man . . . ? —Psalm 8:4–5

Despite all the centuries of struggle, hardship, and disaster, scarcely any of the writers of the Bible ever concluded that man really wasn't very important or that there wasn't any purpose to life.

The one exception is Koheleth, a person who, interestingly, seems to have been quite well-to-do. We can infer this from the fact that in his quest for wisdom, he appeared to be able to engage in nearly every kind of activity he desired—building and planting [Ecclesiastes 2:4–6], acquiring property and possessions [Ecclesiastes 2:7], pleasure-seeking [Ecclesiastes 2:8], and study [Ecclesiastes 7:23–25].

How did Koheleth arrive at his conclusions about the purposelessness of life? Partly, from observing that man wasn't too different from other creatures on earth. "All come from the dust," he asserts in Ecclesiastes 3:20. This same observation is given in another account of Creation. Man and the beasts were both formed by God from "the dust of the ground," it is recorded in Genesis 2:7, 19.

To Koheleth, human life does not seem to differ greatly from that of the animals. "They all draw the same breath," notes Koheleth, "and man enjoys no advantage over the beasts" [Ecclesiastes 3:19]. Why, originally God even sought a mate for man from among the animals [Genesis 2:20]. And one of Job's friends conceives of man as no better than a "worm" or "maggot" [Job 25:6].

Moreover, the final destiny of man and of all the other creatures appears to be the same. Echoing the observation of one of the psalmists that man "is like the beasts that perish" [Psalm 49:13,

21], Koheleth emphasizes that both man and beast must eventually return to the dust [Ecclesiastes 3:19–20].

Yes, in certain respects human life did not appear very significant to Koheleth. Even the psalmists were impelled to note:

. . . They [human beings] are like a dream,
Like grass which grows up in the morning.
In the morning it flourishes and grows up;
In the evening it is cut down and withers. —Psalm 90:5–6

As for man, his days are like grass,
He flourishes like a flower in the field;
For the wind passes over it, and it is gone,
And its place knows it no more. —Psalm 103:15–16

Man is like a breath,
His days are like a passing shadow. —Psalm 144:4

And as for the purpose of life, at times—particularly in times of tragedy—there seemed to be none. "My days are vanity [without meaning]," Job in his suffering complains [Job 7:16].

But it was left to Koheleth to pronounce the whole of human existence pointless. "Vanity of vanities, everything is vanity," he insists [Ecclesiastes 1:2]. All that man does is purposeless [Ecclesiastes 1:13–14]. There is no real reason for man to work [Ecclesiastes 2:22–23], or to pursue pleasure [Ecclesiastes 2:1], or even to seek wisdom [Ecclesiastes 1:13–18]. Therefore, he arrives at this pessimistic conclusion:

I considered the dead who are already dead as more fortunate than the living who are still alive; but better than both is he who has not yet been [born]. . . .
—Ecclesiastes 4:2–3

And, finding no fundamental purpose to life, Koheleth inevitably sinks into deep despair.

Fortunately for us, Judaism has always regarded the views of Koheleth as merely one man's opinion, worthy of consideration because they do contain a certain amount of truth, but mistaken in their conclusions. Hence they were rejected by practically all the other writers of the Bible.

Man, the Guardian of the Earth

It is true that the writers of the Bible recognized the minuteness of man as compared to the infinite magnitude of God and His universe.

Man, remarked one psalmist, is as short-lived as the grass and the flower; his body is nothing but dust. God, on the other hand, is "from everlasting to everlasting," and His "throne is established in the heavens" [Psalm 103:14–19]. The psalmist who described human existence as a "dream" spoke of God like this:

> Before the mountains were brought forth,
> Or You did ever form the earth and the world,
> Even from everlasting to everlasting, You are God. . . .
> A thousand years in Your sight
> Are but as yesterday when it is past,
> And as a watch [a few hours] of the night. —Psalm 90:2, 4

Yet man, insignificant as he is, was destined for a purpose. God created him for a reason—to be the guardian of His creation on earth!

This is stated in a number of biblical passages. For instance, in one account of Creation after man is placed on earth as the climax of the sixth day, the author tells us:

> And God blessed them [men and women]; and God said unto them: "Be fruitful and multiply, and replenish the earth and subdue it; and have dominion over the fish of the sea, the fowl of the air, and every living thing that creeps upon the earth." —Genesis 1:28

Looking about the universe and speculating about the role of man, one psalmist arrives at the same conclusion:

> You [God] have made him to have dominion over the works
> of Your hands;
> You have put all things under his feet:
> Sheep and oxen, all of them,
> Yes, and the beasts of the field,
> The fowl of the air, and the fish of the sea;
> Whatsoever passes through the paths of the seas.
> —Psalm 8:7–9

Still another declares:

> The heavens are the heavens of the Lord,
> But the earth He has given to the children of men.
> —Psalm 115:16

Even today, with the possibility of travel in space, man's chief responsibility seems destined to remain the guardianship of the planet Earth. The fact is, as we are increasingly coming to realize, the many perils of space-travel and the vast distances involved make it somewhat unlikely that man will ever get much beyond his own

Solar System. And from what we now know of the other planets in our own System, even if he reaches all of them, he may not find any too hospitable.

On the other hand, as the psalmists point out, the earth belongs to man. Everything connected with it has been entrusted to him, all living creatures, from plant-life to other human beings, its soil and seas, the mountains, even its atmosphere. And all the more in this age of atomic energy, satellites, and missiles do we appreciate man's responsibility for the earth's future. For it is completely within man's power to preserve and develop it, or utterly destroy it.

Man, the Reflection of God

In addition to serving as the guardian of the earth, man, various writers of the Bible declare, is also expected to reflect the nature and desires of his Maker. In contrast to Koheleth, who saw no difference between humans and beasts, these Bible writers insisted that man was unique. There was something of the godly within him!

Thus, the Book of Genesis points out that, unlike the situation when other forms of life were created, when it came time to shape human beings God said, "Let Us make man in Our image, after Our likeness" [Genesis 1:26]. (The use of "Us" and "Our" in such passages has been interpreted in two different ways. Some of the rabbis, in a rather fanciful explanation, said that before creating man God consulted with His angels. However, the majority of the commentators state that the plural pronoun represents what is commonly called "the plural of majesty," a form of speech used by rulers who customarily refer to themselves as "we." This is most appropriate since those who wrote the Bible thought of God as the Ruler of Israel and of the world, as we see in such passages as I Samuel 12:2 and Psalm 10:16.)

And immediately following this declaration of His intention:

> God created man in His own image, in the image of God He created him; male and female He created them.
> —Genesis 1:27

Although it was certainly true that the human being was mortal and the possessor of many traits in common with the animals, he was nevertheless distinctive. He alone possessed the capacity to be like his Creator in many ways. Consequently, concerning man, one psalmist was moved to write:

> You [God] have made him but little lower than the angels,
> You have crowned him with glory and honor. —Psalm 8:6

For many of the biblical authors, then, the fact that man was created in God's image and was "but little lower than the angels" meant that he was expected to project the qualities and desires of his Maker. Thus one of the biblical writers calls upon the people to be holy because the Lord their God is holy [Leviticus 19:2]. And because a just God is anxious for man to develop a just society, people are expected to attend to the welfare of the poor, the handicapped, the stranger, the laborer, and others. (Note especially the constant refrain of "I am the Lord" in passages like Leviticus 19:13–14 and 33–34.)

In a sense, God is like the sculptor whose talents are made visible in a statue. He may also be compared to a parent who sees his own character and desires reflected in the behavior of his children. God expects His qualities and purposes to be revealed through man, His prize creation. Hence, speaking of the people of Israel, one of the prophets has God state:

> "Everyone that is called by My name,
> And whom I have created for My glory,
> I have formed him; yes, I have made him." —Isaiah 43:7

In another passage God tells Moses, "I will be hallowed among the children of Israel" [Leviticus 22:32]. And to Aaron, the high priest, God says, "Through those that are near Me I will be sanctified, and before all the people I will be glorified" [Leviticus 10:3].

Above all, as Isaiah says, God's ways are to be reflected by proper conduct:

> The Lord of Hosts is exalted through [the people's practice of] justice,
> And God, the Holy One, is sanctified by [their practice of] righteousness. —Isaiah 5:16

Misconduct impairs God's glory in the sight of mankind. So, in accusing the people of Israel of various misdeeds, Amos states that they have profaned God's holy name [Amos 2:6–7]. Even the way in which man worships Him may detract from His glory. To carry on idolatrous rites, for example, is a profanation of His name [Leviticus 20:3].

Though these teachings were directed to the Jews, they applied no less to the rest of mankind. As the writers of the Bible saw it, a principal reason for man's existence is to glorify his Creator.

The Need to Work

To care for the earth and to reflect the ways of his Maker, man finds it necessary to carry on certain activities. These, in turn, provide him with still other purposes for living.

One, of course, is to work, and so important is this that it is prescribed in the Ten Commandments themselves. The Fourth Commandment tells us:

> *Six days shall you labor and do all your work,* but the seventh day is a sabbath to the Lord your God; on it you shall not do any manner of work. . . . —Exodus 20:9–10

To fulfil his purpose on earth man is required to work. In the first place, through his labor he reflects the example of his Creator. Just as the Lord labored to create the heavens and the earth, so human beings are expected to work at their tasks [see Genesis 2:1–3 and Exodus 20:8–11]. Indeed, says one of the prophets, people actually learn certain kinds of work from God Himself! For instance, He teaches the capable farmer how to plow [Isaiah 28:24–26] and how to reap [Isaiah 28:28–29].

Second, labor is necessary so that man may care not only for himself alone but also for the good earth that God has given him. Indeed, as the prophet Isaiah tells us, this planet itself was created that man might make the most of it:

> For thus says the Lord who created the heavens;
> He is God
> Who formed the earth and made it;
> He established it,
> He did not create it a waste.
> He formed it to be inhabited! . . .   —Isaiah 45:18

Consequently in the Creation story God promptly prescribes work for man. Immediately after forming Adam and Eve, He says to them, "Be fruitful and multiply, and replenish the earth and bring it under [your] control . . ." [Genesis 1:28]. Shortly thereafter the Bible reports, "And the Lord God took the man and put him in the Garden of Eden to till it and keep it" [Genesis 2:15].

It was only after man disobeyed God by eating from the Tree of Knowledge that work was made burdensome, and he was told, "By the sweat of your face shall you eat bread" [Genesis 3:19]. And until we are able, once more, to reestablish that ideal world of the Garden of Eden, where mankind can live in harmony with God and all His creation, we must not expect our tasks to be easy or always pleasant.

Even though work may sometimes be difficult, the necessity to work remains the very essence of man's life and serves as an important purpose for his existence. In fact, through fulfilling God's command to engage in labor, the human being comes to enjoy one of his most precious blessings. For how dreary life would be if there were absolutely nothing to do! That is why people who are temporarily out of work find each day sheer torture. We can certainly understand why one of the psalmists would say:

> When you eat the work of your hands,
> Happy will you be, and it will be well with you.
> —Psalm 128:2

The rewards of honest toil are great indeed. Not only does work enable us to occupy our days with useful, productive activity, but it is also a source of real satisfaction to most people, no matter what their job may be. So worthwhile is it that one of the writers of Proverbs was moved to say, "Do you see a man diligent in his work? He shall stand in the presence of kings!" [Proverbs 22:29].

Work, then, should not be regarded as a nuisance or a burden. Even Koheleth with his negative outlook upon life was compelled to admit:

> There is nothing better for a man than that he should eat and drink and find enjoyment in his toil. This also, I saw, is from the hand of God. —Ecclesiastes 2:24

> Behold, what I have seen to be good and fitting is to eat and drink and find enjoyment in all the toil with which one toils under the sun the few days of his life which God has given him, for this is his lot. Every man also to whom God has given wealth and possessions and power to enjoy them, and to accept his lot and find enjoyment in his toil—this is the gift of God. —Ecclesiastes 5:17–18

Man, the writers of the Bible understood, was created to work. It is one of his prime purposes in life, and through it he fulfils his responsibilities as the guardian of the earth and the reflector of his Creator.

Marriage and Family Life

But man is also expected to marry, father children, and establish a wholesome family life.

As guardian of the earth, he is to "be fruitful and multiply and replenish the earth" [Genesis 1:28]. It was for this reason that God created mankind both "male and female" [Genesis 1:27]. The Creation story also tells us what happened after Adam was created:

> And the Lord God said, "It is not good that man should be alone; I will make a help-mate fit for him." . . . And the Lord God caused a deep sleep to fall upon the man, and he slept; and He took one of his ribs, and closed up the place with flesh instead. And the rib which the Lord God had taken from man He made into woman, and brought her to the man. Then the man said, "This is now bone of my bone and flesh of my flesh. . . ." Therefore shall a man leave his father and mother and cleave unto his wife, and they shall become one flesh. —Genesis 2:18, 21–24

From this we see that marriage was established by God Himself, and the individual who carries out His will in this respect is sure to merit His blessing. "He who finds a wife finds a good thing," observes one of the biblical writers, "and he obtains favor from the Lord" [Proverbs 18:22].

In biblical times, as we note in the case of Isaac and Rebekah [Genesis 24], marriages were almost always arranged by the family. Nonetheless, the husband and wife were expected to love one another. One passage advises:

> . . . Rejoice in the wife of your youth. . . .
> Let her affection fill you at all times with delight,
> Be infatuated always with her love. —Proverbs 5:18–19

That love was essential to a happy marriage is also clear from the story of Jacob's courtship of Rachel. He loved her enough to agree to serve an additional seven years as her father's servant [Genesis 29:1–30].

This emphasis upon love is found in many other places in the Bible. For instance, we are told that Elkanah, the father of Samuel, loved his wife Hannah dearly [I Samuel 1:5]; and Michal, the daughter of King Saul, fell deeply in love with David and insisted upon marrying him [I Samuel 18:20, 28].

Moreover—and this may surprise you—nowhere in literature do we find more beautiful love poetry than in the Bible, notably in the Song of Songs. The title alone tells us that the composer of this book felt that love was the most wonderful music of all. For listen to him sing to his beloved:

> Oh that you would kiss me with the kisses of your mouth!
> For your love is better than wine. —Song of Songs 1:2

She, of course, is the only one in the world for him:

> Behold, you are beautiful, my love;
> You are so beautiful! . . .
> As a lily among the thorns,
> So is my love among women. —Song of Songs 1:16; 2:2

Her beauty and charm have captivated him:

> You have captured my heart, my dear one;
> You have captured my heart with one glance of your eyes,
> With one jewel of your necklace.
> How sweet is your love, my beloved, my bride!
> How much better is your love than wine! . . .
>   —Song of Songs 4:9–10

Happily, the maiden reciprocates his love. For she says:

> As an apple tree among the trees of the forest,
> So is my beloved among men.
> Under its shadow I delighted to sit,
> And its fruit was sweet to my taste. . . .
> My beloved is mine, and I am his. . . .
>   —Song of Songs 2:3, 16

Finally she turns to him with the deepest of longing and cries:

> Set me as a seal upon your heart,
> As a seal upon your arm,
> For love is strong as death. . . .
> Many waters cannot quench love,
> Neither can the floods drown it. . . .
>   —Song of Songs 8:6–7

As for family life, husband and wife are expected to remain true to one another. Faithlessness to one's marriage covenant is condemned as a crime against God Himself. One of the Ten Commandments warns against committing adultery [Exodus 20:13], and a second, against coveting the wife of another man [Exodus 20:14].

To insure happiness, husbands and wives are called upon to accept their many responsibilities. From the example of the Patriarchs we see that the husband is to provide for the family (as, according to Genesis 30:30, in the case of Jacob) and to protect them (as with Abraham who, in Genesis 24, makes certain that Isaac obtains a suitable wife). Through his personal conduct he is also to be the moral guide for his family [see, for instance, Proverbs 20:7].

The wife is to attend to her household duties, and in Bible times they were indeed many. Before the days of modern appliances, shopping centers, and supermarkets, the wife had much to do. The "good wife," as she is portrayed by one biblical book, possesses a great many domestic skills as well as traits of character:

> A good wife, who can find?
> She is worth far more than jewels.
> Her husband trusts in her and lacks nothing.
> She does him good and not harm all her life. . . .
> She rises while it is yet night
> And prepares food for her family. . . .
> With her own hands she plants a vineyard. . . .
> She puts her hand to the distaff,
> Her hands hold the spindle. . . .
> She makes coverlets;
> Her clothing is fine linen and purple. . . .
> She speaks with wisdom,
> And the teaching of kindness is upon her tongue.
> She attends well to her family,
> And does not eat the bread of idleness.
> Her children rise up and call her blessed,
> And her husband also praises her. —Proverbs 31:10–28

Marriage was expected to bring forth children whom various writers of the Bible consider the gift of God Himself. [See, for example, Genesis 33:5, Isaiah 8:18, and Psalm 127:3.] Parents are responsible for the proper upbringing of their offspring:

> Train a child in the way that he should go,
> And when he is grown he will not depart from it.
> —Proverbs 22:6

One important result of this training is respect for parents [Exodus 20:12; see also Proverbs 20:20 and 23:22].

Naturally, the rearing of children demands a wide range of moral instruction. Thus one finds within the Bible this advice from a father to his son:

> Trust in the Lord with all your heart,
> And lean not upon your own understanding [alone]. . . .
> My son, . . . be wise and use good judgment. . . .
> Do not withhold good from him who deserves it. . . .
> Do not plot evil [things] against your friend
> Who remains trustingly beside you. . . .
> Do not envy a person of violence,
> Nor choose any of his ways. . . .
> —Proverbs 3:5, 21, 27, 29, 31

Moreover, one's children are to be thoroughly educated in all phases of religious living:

> "And these words which I [God] command you this day
> shall be upon your heart, and you shall teach them [God's
> commandments] diligently to your children. . . ."
> —Deuteronomy 6:6–7

Through worthwhile family living, then, man achieves his high purpose for existence. Enjoying the love of his mate, producing and properly rearing his children, and carrying out his family responsibilities, man serves as both the guardian of the earth and the reflector of God's glory. Thereby he replenishes the human race with worthy descendants whose lives, like his own, testify to the holiness of the Lord.

This emphasis upon marriage and the family has remained distinctively Jewish. Even beyond the fulfilment of the divine purposes for man generally, the institution of marriage also came to represent to our people the carrying out of their covenant with God. In fact, this very covenant-relationship itself is often pictured as a "marriage." So Hosea speaks of God "betrothing" the people of Israel [Hosea 2:21–22], and Jeremiah condemns their wickedness in these terms:

> "Surely as a faithless wife leaves her husband,
> So have you been faithless to Me, O house of Israel,"
> Says the Lord. —Jeremiah 3:20

A marriage filled with mutual love and devotion between husband and wife mirrors the kind of relationship that God seeks with His own people. A marriage lacking such qualities is an affront to Him. And the children that issue from such a marriage can scarcely be expected to carry on Israel's role as God's Servant-people. Rather, says the psalmist, only:

> The children of Your [God's] servants shall dwell secure;
> And their posterity shall be established with You.
> —Psalm 102:29

The Pursuit of Knowledge

There are at least two other purposes to man's existence as the biblical authors see it, and both are based on God's demand and expectation that man lead a moral life. For only the righteous can satisfy God's objectives for mankind.

The story of the generation of the Flood, for example, confirms this. Observe what it tells us:

> And the Lord saw that the wickedness of man was great in the earth, and that every imagination of the thoughts of his heart was only evil continually. And the Lord God repented that He had made man on the earth, and it grieved Him at heart. And the Lord said, "I will blot out man whom I have created from the face of the earth . . . for I am sorry that I have made them." But Noah found favor in the sight of the Lord. . . . Noah in his generation was a righteous man and whole-hearted. . . . —Genesis 6:5–9

Obviously, as in the case of Noah, in order to carry out his functions as guardian of the earth and reflector of God's ways, man must live a life of righteousness.

But how can man come to know precisely what is expected of him? Various writers of the Bible advise him to study. The Book of Proverbs, for instance, begins by declaring that its purpose is to enable the individual:

> To know wisdom and instruction;
> To comprehend the words of understanding;
> To receive the discipline of wisdom,
> Justice, right, and equity. —Proverbs 1:2–3

"Accustom your ear to listen to wisdom, and incline your heart to understanding," another verse advises [Proverbs 2:2]. For, it goes on:

> . . . The Lord gives wisdom;
> From His mouth come knowledge and understanding;
> He stores up sound wisdom for the upright;
> He is a shield to those who walk in integrity.
> —Proverbs 2:6–7

And the purpose of one's learning?

> Then you will understand righteousness and justice,
> And equity, every good path;
> For wisdom will come into your heart,
> And knowledge will be pleasant to your soul;
> Discretion will watch over you;
> Understanding will guard you
> Delivering you from the way of evil. . . .
> [And from those] who rejoice in doing evil. . . .
> —Proverbs 2:9–14

Instruction, therefore, is as precious as life itself [Proverbs 4:13; 8:32–36].

The writers of the Psalms, too, stress the value of study. Blessed is the person, says one psalmist, whose:

And on His teachings he meditates day and night.
. . . Delight is in the Torah of the Lord,
—Psalm 1:2

For, declares another psalmist:

The Torah of the Lord is perfect, restoring the soul;
The testimony of the Lord is sure, making wise the simple;
The precepts of the Lord are right, rejoicing the heart;
The commandment of the Lord is pure, enlightening the
eyes;
The fear of the Lord is clean, enduring forever;
The ordinances of the Lord are true, and righteous alto-
gether.
More to be desired are they than gold, even much fine gold;
Sweeter also than honey and the drippings of the honey-
comb.
Moreover by them is your servant [that is, each individual]
warned;
In keeping them there is great reward. —Psalm 19:8–12

This emphasis on instruction and study may be found throughout
the Bible. Moses, for instance, considers the teaching of God's commandments to the people his major duty [Exodus 18:15–20]. The
people are expected to know God's words intimately [Deuteronomy
11:18] and impart them to their children in turn [Deuteronomy 6:7;
11:19]. "Lack of knowledge will destroy the people," asserts one
prophet [Hosea 4:6]. And in a later period, those who returned from
Babylonian exile to Palestine were promptly taught the "law of
God" by Ezra, Nehemiah, and others [Nehemiah 8].

Thus, the pursuit of knowledge leading to moral improvement
is deemed an important responsibility of living.

The Quest for Social Justice

But those who wrote the Bible did not stop here. They recognized
that man is a social creature and that moral improvement also involves the society in which he lives. Consequently, another of his
principal responsibilities is to insure the well-being of all people
through the establishment of a fair and just society. We call this
"social justice" or, more commonly today, "social action," striving
to achieve just treatment for all people in all classes of society.

"Hate evil and love good, and establish justice in the gate," demands Amos [Amos 5:15], and Micah declares:

It has been told you, O man, what is good,
And what the Lord requires of you—

> Only to do justice and to love mercy,
> And to walk humbly with your God. —Micah 6:8

Isaiah also insists:

> . . . Seek justice, relieve the oppressed,
> Judge the fatherless, plead for the widow. —Isaiah 1:17

As guardian of the earth, man is expected to produce a society in which all human beings may enjoy the fundamental blessings of life, a society in which:

> Every man shall sit under his vine and under his fig-tree,
> And none shall make them afraid. . . . —Micah 4:4

For, as various writers of the Bible insist, all men are God's children. The colored people of Ethiopia, says one prophet, are as much the children of God as the people of Israel [Amos 9:7]. And from the author of Malachi we hear:

> Have we not all one Father?
> Has not one God created us?
> Why do we deal treacherously, every man against his brother? . . . —Malachi 2:10

To help bring about a righteous social order contributes to man's true understanding of God. In fact, says Jeremiah, this is the way one comes to know God Himself:

> ". . . Did not your father . . . do justice and righteousness?
> Then it was well with him.
> He judged the cause of the poor and the needy;
> Then it was well.
> Is not this [the way] to know Me?" says the Lord.
>   —Jeremiah 22:15–16

There is much for man to do in the way of social action. Like Job, one must help the unfortunate:

> . . . I delivered the poor that cried,
> The fatherless also that had none to help him.
> The blessing of him who was about to perish came upon me;
> And I caused the widow's heart to sing for joy. . . .
> I was eyes to the blind,
> And feet to the lame.
> I was a father to the needy,
> And I searched out the cause of him whom I did not know.
>   —Job 29:12–16

Isaiah calls upon the people to:

> . . . Share your bread with the hungry,
> And bring the homeless poor into your house;
> When you see the naked, cover him. . . . —Isaiah 58:7

And the Book of Deuteronomy states:

> If there be among you a needy man . . . within any of
> your gates, . . . you shall not harden your heart nor shut
> your hand from your needy brother, but you shall surely
> lend him sufficient for his need. . . . For the poor shall
> never cease out of the land. Therefore I [God] command
> you saying, "You shall surely open your hand unto your
> poor and needy brother in your land."
> —Deuteronomy 15:7–8, 11

The pursuit of social righteousness also makes many other demands. Exploitation of people must be ended and slums abolished [Isaiah 42:22]. Laborers should receive fair treatment [Jeremiah 22:13]. Foreigners are entitled to every protection [Ezekiel 47:22–23; see also Leviticus 19:33–34 and Deuteronomy 10:19]. The equal administration of justice is essential [Deuteronomy 16:18–19], and good government is likewise a necessity. One of the psalmists prays:

> Give the king Your judgments, O God,
> And Your righteousness to the king's son;
> That he may judge Your people with righteousness,
> And Your poor with justice.
> Let the mountains bear prosperity for the people,
> And the hills, righteousness!
> May he defend the cause of the poor of the people,
> Give deliverance to the needy,
> And crush the oppressor. . . .
> In his days may righteousness flourish
> And peace abound, till the moon be no more!
> —Psalm 72:1–4, 7

Peace, too, is a blessing to be sought, and Isaiah looks forward to the time when:

> . . . The work of righteousness shall be peace,
> And the effect of righteousness, quietness and confidence
> forever;
> And my people will dwell in a peaceful habitation,
> In secure dwellings, and in quiet resting-places.
> —Isaiah 32:17–18

In general the demands made upon man are summed up in this statement:

> Justice, justice, shall you pursue, that you may live and inherit the land which the Lord your God gives you.
> —Deuteronomy 16:20

To the writers of the Bible, then, reflecting the ways of one's Maker and acting as a true guardian of the earth requires each person to be genuinely concerned with the needs of his fellow man. Truly, as one of the great biblical teachings states it, we must love our neighbors as ourselves [Leviticus 19:18]. We can never forget that one of the basic purposes to man's life is a never-ending effort to achieve universal justice through social action.

Wanted: Some Definitions

The Bible has a great deal to say about the purpose of human existence. Life, it seems, has two main objectives: man is to serve as the guardian of the earth and he must reflect the ways of his Creator.

He fulfils these objectives in numerous ways: by work, marriage and family life, moral improvement based upon knowledge of God's demands, and striving for a just social order. In all these ways human beings find ample incentive for living life to the full!

In performing these activities, people are constantly aided by religion. Religion directly helps men to understand the purposes of life. A skeptical person like Koheleth was unable to discover any real reason for human existence. On the other hand, individuals like the prophets found their incentive for courageous living in their deeply religious feelings, which compelled them to reflect the ways of God among their fellow men. Little wonder that the pursuit of justice for all people was one of their most important missions in life!

The authors of the Bible were thinking of mankind as a whole when they spoke of the purposes of human existence. However, for themselves and for their own people, they saw an additional purpose, an even heavier responsibility. Because of the Jewish people's covenant with God and their Mission, the Jews must be the outstanding example of what it means to be the guardian of the earth and the living reflection of the ways of the Almighty.

Therefore, as members of the household of Israel, we must always be mindful that our lives are filled with a special, added purpose: we must be the servants of God, continually striving to bring about His Kingdom on earth. This is why the rabbis speak of each Jew as "the partner of God" in the continuing work of creation. And this explains why in our worship we pray:

> . . . May we be co-workers with You [God] in the building of Your Kingdom which has been our vision and goal through the ages. —*Union Prayerbook*, Vol. I, p. 45

The teachings of our religion stress the purpose of life for mankind in general and for the Jew in particular. The writers of the Bible placed great emphasis upon the role of religion in life and the need for people to act in accordance with religious teachings and ideals—in other words, to be religious.

But what does it mean to "be religious"? Who is the religious person? Are you sure you know?

Again this is something that the writers of the Bible themselves had to define. . . .

--------- THINGS TO TALK OVER ---------

1. Why is having some purpose for living important to all of us?

2. In what ways do the Bible's answers to the question of life's purpose apply today?

3. From the biblical point of view, how does religion help us find purpose in life?

4. What would you say are our special functions as Servants of God in the modern world? What are some specific examples?

--------- SOME OTHER BIBLE PASSAGES TO CONSIDER ---------

1. Read the entire description of the "good wife" found in Proverbs 31:10–31. How would you rewrite this to apply to the modern woman?

2. From the biblical point of view, what are the obligations of the children in family life? See Leviticus 19:3; Deuteronomy 27:16; II Kings 2:23–24; Proverbs 1:8; 23:19–25.

3. How do the following illustrate man's purpose on earth: Isaiah 56:1–2; Psalm 40:5–11; Job 34:10–13, 21–30; 36:22–24?

4. Of what advantage is it to man to reflect the ways of God? See Genesis 18:19; II Kings 21:19–24; Isaiah 24:1–15; Psalm 119:1–8; Proverbs 10:29.

────────────── FROM THE RABBIS' VIEWPOINT ──────────────

1. MAN'S DUTY TO GOD: See *Everyman's Talmud*, pp. 72–75, 223–225; and *A Rabbinic Anthology*, [84–92] pp. 35–37, [230–232] pp. 86–87.

2. THE DUTY OF LABOR: See *Everyman's Talmud*, pp. 203–207; and *A Rabbinic Anthology*, [1219–1236] pp. 440–445.

3. MARRIAGE AND FAMILY LIFE: See *Everyman's Talmud*, pp. 171–175, 179–182; and *A Rabbinic Anthology*, Chap. 12, "The Family: [a] The Father and Mother," pp. 500–506, Chap. 13, "The Family: [b] The Wife," pp. 507–515, Chap. 14, "The Family: [c] Children," pp. 516–521.

────────────── OTHER THINGS TO READ ──────────────

FACKENHEIM, EMIL L., *Paths to Jewish Belief*, Behrman, Chap. 6: "What Is Man?" pp. 75–83.

GITTELSOHN, ROLAND B., *Little Lower Than the Angels*, Union of American Hebrew Congregations, Chap. 8: "God and You," pp. 115–139.

HEATON, E. W., *Everyday Life in Old Testament Times*, Batsford, Chap. 4: "Home Life," pp. 68–96.

LEVY, FELIX A., "Judaism and Marriage," No. 19, *Popular Studies in Judaism*, Union of American Hebrew Congregations.

STEINBERG, MILTON, *Basic Judaism*, Harcourt, Brace, Chap. 5: "The Good Life," pp. 59–90.

VORSPAN, ALBERT, and LIPMAN, EUGENE J., *Justice and Judaism*, Union of American Hebrew Congregations, Chap. 1: "Foundations," pp. 6–24.

Eight
WHO IS RELIGIOUS?

What's the Answer?

IF YOU WERE TO ASK YOUR FRIENDS TO NAME EXAMPLES OF PEOPLE whom they consider to be "religious," you would, without any doubt, get many different answers. Among them might be the following:

My choice is A—— because she believes so very deeply in God. I've never seen anyone quite so religious at heart. To her, God is always near and she has complete trust in Him.

To me, Mr. B—— is very religious. He never misses any of the services at temple, and he's constantly working for the congregation.

I consider Mrs. C—— the ideal religious person. She observes all the holidays faithfully, the candlelighting on Friday nights, the Passover seder, Chanuko, and all the rest.

There's no one more religious than D——. He won't eat a thing that isn't strictly kosher. He won't ride on the Sabbath; he won't even turn on the lights on Friday nights.

To Mr. E—— true religion means being charitable. There isn't a cause to which he doesn't contribute. He's always working for the United Jewish Appeal, the Community Chest, and many other drives. After all, isn't this the highest form of religion?

If religion has anything to do with ethics, then Mr. F—— is one of the most religious people I know. You can always depend on him for complete fair-dealing and honesty in business as well as in his private affairs.

Mrs. G—— is my idea of a religious person. Her religion consists of helping people. Whenever you're in trouble—sickness, a death in the family, anything—you can always count on her being right there to help.

When I think of someone religious I immediately think of H——. He spends a great deal of his time in Jewish study— Hebrew, the Bible, rabbinic literature, Jewish history, and the rest. He says that a Jew can't really be religious without studying.

Which is the best example? Is any one of these examples truly a "religious" person?

This isn't easy to answer. In so far as we can see, certainly each of the people mentioned is engaged in specific important religious *acts*. But is any one of them a truly "religious" person?

This leads to two more questions. First, is "being religious" something we can judge solely from outward appearances? In our various examples above, we have been considering principally *external* actions. Yet isn't there something more, something *inward* and unseen that is just as necessary?

And second, can we isolate one or even a few characteristics and say that these make a person "religious"? Doesn't the term "being religious" involve a combination of a great many things?

The answer to all these questions depends upon how we define the term "religious". . . .

A Problem in Bible Times, Too

Even in biblical times the definition of a religious person was no less a problem, although those who wrote the Bible never actually used the word "religious." The Hebrew language had no such word. Instead, the individual was spoken of as "upright" or "righteous," one who "feared the Lord" or "served God."

Nonetheless, the biblical authors had definite ideas about who was religious, and, as in our own day, various qualities were emphasized. Those who wrote from the standpoint of the priesthood stressed rituals and observances. The prophets underscored personal and social righteousness. Many of the psalmists gave importance to inner feelings of faith and trust in God. And others stressed the study of God's commandments as a means of gaining knowledge of His will. As a result, different kinds of individuals, possessing different characteristics, were often pictured as "religious."

To some biblical authors, the Nazirite, the person whose life was totally consecrated to God, exemplified the truly religious person. Thus, one Bible passage tells us:

> . . . When either a man or woman shall clearly take a vow, the vow of a Nazirite, to consecrate himself to the Lord, he shall abstain from wine and strong drink. . . . All the days of his vow of Naziriteship no razor shall come upon his head; until the days of his consecration to the Lord are fulfilled he shall be holy, he shall let the locks of the hair of his head grow long. All of the days that he consecrates himself to the Lord he shall not come near a dead body. . . . All of the days of his Naziriteship he is holy unto the Lord. —Numbers 6:2–8

To other Bible writers, the priest represented the truly religious person. He alone was entitled to approach the altar of the Lord [Numbers 18:7], and his life was consecrated to God's service [Leviticus 8:33]. So, in speaking of the priests, a passage in the Book of Exodus declares:

> ". . . You shall anoint him [Aaron] and sanctify him that he may minister unto Me [God] in the priest's office. And you shall bring his sons . . . and anoint them, as you did their father, that they may minister unto Me in the priest's office. And their appointment shall be for an everlasting priesthood throughout their generations."
> —Exodus 40:13–15

Some of the ancients looked upon the prophet as the prime example of a religious man. The prophet was not only consecrated to God [see, for example, the prophet's "consecration vision" in Isaiah 6:1–8], but he was also actually considered the Lord's spokesman [Deuteronomy 18:18]. He was believed to possess the "spirit of the

Lord" [Numbers 11:25], and in many places in the Bible the prophet is called a "man of God" [see, for example, I Samuel 2:27 and 9:6; I Kings 12:22 and 17:24; II Kings 8:4]. So highly were prophets regarded, that on one occasion Moses was said to have declared, "O that all of the Lord's people were prophets, that the Lord would put His spirit upon them!" [Numbers 11:29].

While they held Nazirites, priests, and prophets in very high regard, the writers of the Bible also esteemed many other individuals as "religious." As a matter of fact, they had praise for many ordinary people. For example, they called Noah a "righteous and whole-hearted man" who "walked with God" [Genesis 6:9], and Hannah, the mother of Samuel, was looked upon as a reverent, pious woman [I Samuel 2:20]. Of Othniel, one of the Judges, the Bible says, "The spirit of the Lord came upon him" [Judges 3:10]; and God was said to have promised Gideon, another Judge, that He would certainly be with him [Judges 6:16]. In I Kings 9:4, David is pictured as a religious man, and in II Chronicles 8:14 he is even called "the man of God."

Actually the writers of the Bible were in general agreement about who was religious, and their definition is perhaps summed up in this statement that appears in the final chapter of the Book of Ecclesiastes:

> The end of the matter, all having been heard, [is this]: fear
> God and keep His commandments, for this is the whole
> [obligation] of man. —Ecclesiastes 12:13

Here, as the authors of the Bible saw it, are the two basic characteristics of the religious person: he reveres God, and he does His will by keeping His commandments.

While this definition appears simple, it is not. To be truly religious, a person must carry out certain duties and responsibilities, and show in every aspect of his life his complete love, devotion, and fear of God. These actions were not left to the individual's whim or preference. Rather, as we shall now see, the authors of the Bible explained in detail precisely what they meant by reverence for God and keeping of His commandments.

The Necessity for Worship

In the view of the authors of the Bible, the first requirement for the truly religious person was faithfulness in carrying out all forms of worship.

As we have already noted, sacrifices had long been the most important element in Hebrew worship. Originally, sacrifices could be performed almost anywhere, but gradually only certain places were designated for the purpose. Thus we are told that for the tribes coming out of Egypt, sacrifices were to be offered near the "tabernacle" which housed the Ark [Exodus 29:42–44]. The forerunner of our own synagogue Ark, this ancient Ark was a portable wooden chest containing the "Law of God." It was considered very holy [Exodus 25:16]—so much so that, as we note from the following passage, its presence was counted upon to bring the people victory in battle:

> . . . Now Israel went out to battle against the Philistines . . . and Israel was defeated by the Philistines who slew about four thousand men on the field of battle. And when the troops returned to camp, the elders of Israel said, "Why has the Lord put us to rout today at the hands of the Philistines? Let us bring the Ark of the covenant of the Lord here . . . that He may come among us and save us from the power of our enemies." So the people . . . brought the Ark of the covenant of the Lord of hosts. . . . —I Samuel 4:1–4

In this instance, however, the people's hopes were not realized. Their army was defeated and the Ark itself was captured! [I Samuel 4:5–22]. Yet, as we see in I Samuel 5–6, the power of the Ark was so awesome that the Philistines finally had to return it to the people of Israel.

At a much later period, worship centered about the Jerusalem Temple, built by King Solomon [I Kings 6–7]. It was a magnificent building constructed of cedar, gold, ivory, and precious stones, and here the Ark was now kept [I Kings 8:1–9].

Although from time to time sacrifices continued to be offered elsewhere (for instance, at Beth-El, as we note from I Kings 12:29–33), regular worship was carried on in the Temple in Jerusalem. Public sacrifices were conducted there every morning and afternoon [Exodus 29:38–39] and on the Sabbath and the various holidays, such as Passover and Shovuos [Numbers 28:9–31]. Every individual was expected to contribute annually to the Temple's maintenance [Exodus 30:13; Nehemiah 10:33–34], and to go on a pilgrimage to the Temple at least three times a year to offer up his sacrifices in person [Exodus 23:14–17; 34:22–23]. Moreover, under certain circumstances, such as when a person made a vow to sacrifice to God, he was required to bring the offering there himself [I Samuel 1:11–27; Psalm 66:13–15].

Prayer was also part of worship. For instance, certain prayers were to be recited in connection with the offering of each person's first fruits and tithes, a tenth of his yearly gain [see Deuteronomy 26:1–10, 12–15]. In dedicating the Temple, King Solomon himself is reported to have prayed:

> May Your [God's] eyes be open toward this house night and day . . . and may You hearken to the supplication of Your servant and of Your people Israel when they shall pray toward this place. . . . —I Kings 8:29–30

To which God is said to have responded:

> ". . . I have heard your prayer and your supplication which you have made before Me. I have hallowed this house which you have built, to put My name there forever. My eyes and My heart shall be there perpetually." —I Kings 9:3

Among other things, then, the religious person was one who participated in Temple worship and offered the proper prayers and sacrifices. In these words of one of the psalmists we catch something of the spirit of devotion to the Temple that marked the religious man:

> One thing that I asked of the Lord, that will I seek after:
> That I may dwell in the house of the Lord all the days of my life,
> To behold the beauty of the Lord, and to visit early in His temple. . . .
> And I will offer in His tabernacle sacrifices with the trumpet-sound;
> I will sing, yes I will sing praises to the Lord.
> —Psalm 27:4, 6

The Performance of Ritual

In addition to sacrifices and Temple worship in general, reverence for God and obedience to His commands required the performance of various rituals.

A great many of these rituals were part of daily life in ancient times. Some grew out of very ancient concepts of "holiness" designed to protect the individual from becoming tainted with "uncleanness." Since God's people were to be holy in His sight, they had to take precautions to be ritually and morally pure. The people were commanded in the Book of Leviticus:

> ". . . I am the Lord your God who has set you apart from
> the [other] peoples. And you shall not walk in the customs
> of the nations that I am casting out before you, for they
> did all these [objectionable] things and therefore I ab-
> horred them. . . . You shall therefore make a distinction
> between the unclean bird and the clean; you shall not
> make yourselves abominable by beast or bird or anything
> with which the ground teems, which I have distinguished
> for you as unclean. You shall be holy to Me, for I the Lord
> am holy and have separated you from the [other] peoples
> that you should be Mine." —Leviticus 20:24–26

This necessity to be holy explains the many laws in the Bible per-
taining to dietary matters involving certain foods that can or cannot be eaten. Any animal that chews the cud and has a cloven hoof
is permissible [Leviticus 11:3]. However, many other creatures, including the pig, camel, ostrich, and lizard, are prohibited [see Leviticus 11:4–8, 13–23]. Moreover, eating the blood of any living thing
is strictly forbidden [Deuteronomy 12:23–25].

Every individual was also expected to purify himself of all forms
of religious "uncleanness." A man was religiously "unclean," for example, if he had certain diseases [see, for instance, Leviticus 14]
or if he came in contact with a corpse [Numbers 19:11–22]. Bathing, sacrifices, and other rites were prescribed to overcome all such
contamination.

As a sign of the Covenant between God and Israel the circumcision
of every male was likewise commanded. [See, for instance, Leviticus
12:3 and Joshua 5:2–7.] The practice was traced back to Abraham,
to whom God had said:

> "This is My covenant which you shall keep between Me
> and you and your descendants after you: every male
> among you shall be circumcised. . . . And he that is
> eight days old among you shall be circumcised. . . . Any
> uncircumcised male shall be cut off from his people, for he
> has broken My covenant." —Genesis 17:10–14

And in the years after the writing of the laws of the Bible the rabbis
added still other rituals to sanctify the life of the individual, rituals
of every male was likewise commanded. [See, for instance, Leviticus
such as a prescribed marriage ceremony or particular rites to be
carried on by mourners.

Obviously, therefore, a religious person was one who performed
all the rituals.

The Observance of Holy Days

Beyond performing all the rituals, a religious person faithfully commemorated the various sacred days that occurred throughout the cycle of the Jewish year.

The most sacred of all was the Sabbath, another symbol of the Covenant. Its paramount importance can be seen from the fact that it is the only observance mentioned in the Ten Commandments [Exodus 20:8–11].

Sabbath observance enabled the people to maintain the Covenant. Further, they were following the very example of God Himself, for He is reported to have said:

> ". . . You shall keep My Sabbaths, for this is a sign between Me and you throughout your generations, that you may know that I, the Lord, sanctify you. You shall keep the Sabbath, therefore, because it is holy to you. . . . Six days shall work be done, but the seventh day is a day of solemn rest, holy to the Lord. . . . It is a sign between Me and the children of Israel forever. For in six days the Lord made heaven and earth, and on the seventh day He rested from His work and was refreshed."
> —Exodus 31:13–17

The religious man was also obliged to celebrate the annual holy days. These commenced with the observance of the first day of the seventh month which in later times became known as Rosh Ha-shono. (See Ezekiel 40:1 which is the only place in the Bible where the term *Rosh Ha-shono,* used for "the beginning of the year," occurs. Interestingly, it gives the date as the "tenth day," our present Day of Atonement.) Concerning this holiday, one Bible passage states:

> . . . In the seventh month, in the first day of the month, shall be a solemn rest to you, a memorial proclaimed with the blast of horns, a holy convocation. You shall do no work but shall bring an offering made by fire unto the Lord.
> —Leviticus 23:24–25

Ten days later came the Day of Atonement when all the people asked God for forgiveness from their sins. On this day they were to refrain from work, "afflict their souls" (fast), and offer the appropriate sacrifices [Leviticus 23:27–32 and Numbers 29:7–11].

In contrast to these solemn days, there were the three great "pilgrim festivals," so named because they were holidays on which the people were bidden to come to the Temple in Jerusalem [Deuteronomy 16:16]. During these festivals, as on the other sacred days, work was prohibited, and special sacrifices required.

The first pilgrim festival known as the "Festival of Tabernacles" (Sukos) was a harvest celebration. It began four days after Yom Kippur and was observed for a week [Leviticus 23:34–36; Deuteronomy 16:13–15]. During this time, the people were enjoined to dwell in booths as a reminder, it was said, of their forefathers' experiences in the Wilderness [Leviticus 23:42–43]. An eighth day of the festival was also introduced to serve as a time of "solemn assembly" [Leviticus 23:36; Numbers 29:35–38].

The first month of spring, Nisan, saw the coming of the second great pilgrim festival, Passover, also known as the "Festival of Unleavened Bread." It was celebrated for seven days with the eating of matsos [Exodus 12:14–20; Leviticus 23:5–8]. This holiday, of course, commemorated the deliverance of the Hebrews from Egypt [Exodus 12:17].

Finally, seven weeks after Passover, came the third pilgrim festival, the "Festival of Weeks" (Shovuos), a time of thanksgiving for the wheat harvest [Leviticus 23:15–21; Numbers 28:26–31]. The holiday was also associated with the giving of the Law at Mount Sinai, probably because of the passage in Exodus 19:1 and its reference to the "third month" after leaving Egypt.

These three great festivals were not the only holidays observed in biblical times. Others included the "Festival of the New Moon," which came at the beginning of every month and was celebrated with special worship and Temple sacrifices [Numbers 28:11–15], and Purim, the "Festival of Lots" [Esther 9:20–28].

The religious person, then, was expected to observe all of these special days deemed holy to God.

The Practice of Righteousness

Worship, rituals, and holidays were designed to bring the individual closer to God and make him more faithful to the Covenant. But the heart of the Covenant was the practice of righteousness, the very essence of reverence for God and obedience to His commands.

This becomes clear in a number of prophetic passages which challenge the notion of those Jews who considered faithful worship, ritual, and holiday observance as their sole or most important way of demonstrating religious responsibility. Amos, for one, spoke out against this. As the people of the Northern Kingdom were in the midst of offering sacrifices at their temple in Beth-El, the prophet, speaking in God's name, thundered:

> "I hate, I despise your festivals,
> And I take no delight in your solemn assemblies.
> Yes, even though you offer Me your burnt offerings and grain offerings,
> I will not accept them;
> Neither will I regard the peace offerings of your fatted beasts.
> Take away from Me the noise of your hymns;
> I will not listen to the melody of your harps.
> But let justice roll down like waters,
> And righteousness like an ever-flowing stream."
> —Amos 5:21–24

Micah argued that all other forms of religious practice were of little value if the essential element—the conduct of the individual—was ignored:

> With what shall I come before the Lord,
> And bow myself before God on high?
> Shall I come before Him with burnt-offerings,
> With calves a year old?
> Will the Lord be pleased with thousands of rams,
> With ten thousand rivers of oil? . . .
> He has shown you, O man, what is good,
> And what the Lord requires of you:
> Only to do justly, and to love mercy,
> And to walk humbly with your God. —Micah 6:6–8

Still, many of the people believed that the Temple itself was so holy that worship there immediately won the favor of the Lord. Not so, insisted the prophets:

> Do not trust these deceptive words: "This is the temple of the Lord, the temple of the Lord, the temple of the Lord."
>
> Behold, you trust deceptive words to no avail. Will you steal, murder, commit adultery, swear falsely, sacrifice to Baal, and worship other gods . . . and then come and stand before Me in this house which is called by My name, and say, "We are delivered!"—only to go on doing these evil things? —Jeremiah 7:4, 8–10

The Temple, said the prophets, is no substitute for righteous living. Neither are sacrifices:

> ". . . Your burnt-offerings are not acceptable,
> Nor are your sacrifices pleasing to Me [God]."
> —Jeremiah 6:20

Nor is the observance of Sabbaths and holidays:

> "Bring no more vain offerings:
> Incense is an abomination to Me [God].
> New Moons and Sabbaths and the holding of religious gatherings—
> I cannot endure iniquity along with the solemn assembly.
> Your New Moons and your appointed festivals
> My soul hates;
> They have become a burden to Me,
> I am weary of bearing them." —Isaiah 1:13–14

The prophets were not objecting to religious observance as such. It certainly had an important role in Judaism. However, what the prophets wanted the people to realize was that religious observance could not replace obedience to God's moral and ethical demands.

Most of the other Bible writers shared their point of view. In chapter 19 of Leviticus, a book which reveals a strong priestly influence, ordinances to observe the Sabbath and to show reverence for the Temple stand side-by-side with commandments to love the stranger and practice true justice [Leviticus 19:30 and 33–36].

Certain rules of conduct were to be adhered to by all Jews. To begin with, faithfulness to the Ten Commandments [Exodus 20:2–14] was obligatory. But there was much more. Ezekiel, for example, saw the religious person as one who:

> . . . Does not oppress anyone, but restores to the debtor
> his pledge, commits no robbery, gives bread to the hungry,
> and covers the naked with clothing . . . keeps from com-
> mitting sin, and practices true justice between man and
> man. —Ezekiel 18:7–8

Note that "righteousness" here also includes charitable acts. In fact, ts'doko, "righteousness," is the very Hebrew word Jews still use for "charity."

Amos advised each person to "Hate evil, love good, and do justice . . ." [Amos 5:15]. One psalmist defined the religious person as:

> He who walks uprightly and does what is righteous,
> And speaks the truth in his heart;
> Who has no slander upon his tongue,
> And does no evil to a friend,
> Nor makes false charges against his neighbors;
> In whose eyes a wicked person is despised,
> But he honors those who have reverence for God;
> Who keeps his promises and does not change;
> He that does not lend his money on interest,
> Nor take bribes against the innocent. . . . —Psalm 15:2–5

Many other moral and ethical requirements are mentioned in the Bible. [For more examples see Exodus 22:20–27; Isaiah 1:16–17; and Jeremiah 7:5–10.] But as we have now seen, righteous conduct was considered an indispensable part of religious living.

The Necessity for Knowledge of God's Demands

Thus from the biblical point of view, to be religious required personal and social righteousness as well as worship, ritual, and holiday observance. But how can a Jew fulfil these requirements if he doesn't know exactly what they are and is not aware of the precise nature of God's demands? Therefore, one also required considerable knowledge of religious teachings.

Some of these teachings came directly from God Himself [Deuteronomy 4:36]. To one of the psalmists, God says:

> "I [God] will instruct you and teach you in the way you
> shall go;
> I will give [you] counsel. . . ." —Psalm 32:8

Another psalmist declares, "O God, you have taught me from my youth" [Psalm 71:17]. Among the prophets, Jeremiah also pictures God as giving the people instruction [Jeremiah 32:33].

The people may learn of God's demands in various additional ways. As we note from this advice given Moses by his father-in-law, the leaders were obliged to teach the people:

> And you shall teach them [the people] the statutes and the
> laws, and shall show them the way in which they must go.
> —Exodus 18:20

Another biblical passage reports that a priest was used by the King of Assyria to instruct the new settlers of Palestine "in the manner of the God of the land" [II Kings 17:24–28]. And as we have already seen, parents, too, were instructed to teach their children God's commandments [Deuteronomy 6:7].

Over and above all the ways of transmitting knowledge, the individual himself was also expected to study. In speaking of the religious person, one psalmist states:

> . . . His delight is in the teaching of the Lord,
> And on His Torah he meditates day and night. —Psalm 1:2

Another psalmist advises young people to study God's teachings so that they may not "forget His word" [Psalm 119:9–16]. A biblical passage elsewhere pictures God as telling Joshua:

This book of the Torah shall not depart out of your mouth,
but you shall meditate on it day and night, . . .
—Joshua 1:8

Note how the psalmist expresses his own need to study:

Oh how I love Your [God's] Torah!
It is my meditation all the day.
Your commandments make me wiser than my enemies,
For it is ever with me.
I have more understanding than all my teachers,
For Your testimonies [teachings] are my meditation.
I understand more than the aged,
Because I have kept Your teachings. . . .
How sweet are Your words to my taste,
Sweeter than honey to my mouth!
Through Your teachings I get understanding;
Therefore I hate every false way. —Psalm 119:97–104

Without such knowledge, the prophet Hosea insists, one cannot be acceptable to God:

My people are destroyed for lack of knowledge;
Because you have rejected knowledge
I [God] will also reject you, so that you shall no longer be
My priest.
Because you have forgotten the law of your God,
I will also forget your children. —Hosea 4:6

To be religious, therefore, meant that a Jew also had to possess substantial knowledge of God's demands. Some of this knowledge could be acquired by inspiration and instruction from others. But most of it had to be attained by personal study of His teachings as found in the sacred writings.

Religion of the Heart

From all of this it is clear what those who wrote the Bible meant by "fearing God" and "keeping His commandments." They meant acquiring knowledge of God's will and applying it through moral living and regular worship of Him through prayer and ritual.

But this was not all they meant. True reverence demanded something more. It required a constant inner awareness of Him. This is what the Bible calls "knowing God." The writer of Proverbs assures us that with the pursuit of genuine wisdom:

Then you will understand the fear of the Lord
And find the knowledge of God. —Proverbs 2:5

And in speaking to Hosea, God says:

> "I desire mercy and not sacrifice,
> The knowledge of God rather than burnt-offerings."
> —Hosea 6:6

"Knowing God" involves deep inner feelings. With it comes "fear" of Him, the awareness that "His eye is ever upon us" [see Psalm 33:18]—in other words, a sensitive conscience. It is this, observes the Book of Exodus, that keeps people from wrong-doing [Exodus 20:17]. It is basic, says the psalmist, because:

> The fear of the Lord is the beginning of wisdom,
> Good understanding have all those who practice it. . . .
> —Psalm 111:10

Related to the sense of awareness is the sense of awe that the religious person experiences in his thoughts of God. The Lord's greatness inspires the kind of emotion that moves one prophet to exclaim:

> There is none like You, O Lord,
> You are great, and Your name is great in might.
> Who would not stand in awe of You, O King of the nations?
> For this is Your due. . . . —Jeremiah 10:6–7

And a psalmist says:

> Great is the Lord and highly to be praised;
> He is awesome beyond all gods. . . .
> The Lord made the heavens.
> Honor and majesty are before Him,
> Strength and beauty are in His sanctuary. . . .
> O worship the Lord in the beauty of holiness;
> Tremble before Him all the earth! —Psalm 96:4–6, 9

In his awe of God, the individual feels humble. "I am only dust and ashes," cries Abraham as he pleads with God to spare the righteous of Sodom and Gomorrah [Genesis 18:27]. Jacob, in his prayer for help as his brother Esau approaches, expresses his deep humility when he says:

> . . . O God of my father Abraham, and God of my father Isaac, O Lord, who told me: Return to your country and your kinsmen, and I will do you good; I am not worthy of all the mercies and of all the truth which You have shown Your servant. . . . —Genesis 32:10–11

And one can be sure that God will certainly listen to the humble [Psalm 9:13; 10:17].

Feelings of gratitude to God likewise stir the reverent man. One psalmist gives voice to his sense of thankfulness in these words:

> I will give thanks to the Lord with my whole heart. . . .
> I will tell of all Your marvellous works. . . .
> I will be glad and exult in You;
> I will sing praises to Your name, O Most High!
> —Psalm 105:1–5

Revering God means putting one's complete trust in Him. The attitude is that expressed by Job amidst all his suffering, "Though He [God] slay me, yet will I trust in Him" [Job 13:15]. Yes, "Put your trust in the Lord," advises a psalmist [Psalm 4:6] and then you will be able to say:

> In peace I will both lie down and sleep;
> For You, O Lord, make me dwell in safety. —Psalm 4:9

For the religious man:

> . . . Is not afraid of evil tidings;
> His heart is firm, trusting in the Lord. —Psalm 112:7

Beyond even this, however, our knowledge of God, gained through fear and awe of Him as well as gratitude and trust, must ultimately lead to abiding love for Him. Here again God may be compared to a father whose guidance and authority the child respects. With experience, the child also comes to trust his father and to be grateful to him for all he provides. In the process, awe, respect, trust, and appreciation merge into an all-embracing feeling we call "love."

To know the Lord in this very deep sense is to love Him. Thus, immediately following the Sh'ma, with its emphasis upon the nature of Israel's God, we are told, "And you shall love the Lord your God with all your heart, with all your soul, and with all your might" [Deuteronomy 6:5].

Love of Him is stressed throughout the Bible. "Love the Lord, all you godly people!" exclaims one psalmist [Psalm 31:24]. Similarly, Joshua commands the people of Israel to love God as well as observe His commandments [Joshua 22:5]. Another passage declares that God tests His people to determine whether they truly love Him with all their heart [Deuteronomy 13:5].

Love of Him includes even those things associated with His worship. Thus, one psalmist expresses his deep devotion to the Temple, God's house [Psalm 26:8], and another describes his great affection for the Lord's Torah [Psalm 119:97–104].

The inner feelings of the human being, then, are of great importance in God's sight. This is confirmed in I Samuel 16:1–13, in the illuminating story about the prophet Samuel who was ordered by God to find a suitable successor for King Saul. At His command Samuel goes to the house of Jesse and asks that all his sons appear before him. As the first son approaches, Samuel is convinced that because of his powerful physique he is the one to be selected. But God warns him:

> Do not look at his appearance or the height of his stature, because I have rejected him; for the Lord sees not as man sees. Man looks at the outward appearance, but the Lord looks within the heart. —I Samuel 16:7

And truly it is from deep within oneself that true religious feeling must come.

Seeking Atonement for One's Sins

As the writers of the Bible saw it, then, there were two major requirements for leading a truly religious life: reverence for God and obedience to His commands. To fulfil these requirements, a person had to:

1. Participate in worship
2. Perform rituals
3. Observe holy days
4. Practice righteousness
5. Acquire knowledge of God's demands
6. Love God and have complete faith in Him

But being realistic, the writers of the Bible also knew the shortcomings of human beings. Few people, they realized, find it possible to live up to all of these requirements. Knowingly or unknowingly, many fail, and thus they become guilty of sin.

The Hebrew word for "sin"—*chet*—most often used by the writers of the Bible has the root meaning of "missing the mark," as when an archer misses the target. This is the very Hebrew word that appears in the following passage:

> All this people, even seven hundred chosen men, were left-handed; every one could sling stones at a hair's-breadth and not *miss*. —Judges 20:16

To sin, therefore, means missing the mark by failing to live fully up to the demands of the religious life.

Because God's requirements are so exacting and people are only human, it is rare that anyone can go through life without sinning at some time or other. As one of the friends of Job put it:

> Shall mortal man be [completely] just before God?
> Shall a man be [absolutely] pure before his Maker?
> —Job 4:17

Others also recognized the difficulty of leading the completely religious life. The prayer of King Solomon at the dedication of the Temple states that "there is no person who does not sin" [I Kings 8:46], and Koheleth observes:

> Surely there is not a righteous man on earth who [always] does good and never sins. —Ecclesiastes 7:20

Similarly Proverbs declares:

> Who can say, "I have made my heart clean; I am pure from my sin"? —Proverbs 20:9

Consequently, people require some way of "atonement," of making amends and obtaining God's forgiveness for their shortcomings.

The authors of the Bible provided for this. To begin with, they prescribed certain sin and guilt offerings [see, for instance, Leviticus 1:4], various cleansing rituals such as sprinkling and bathing [see, for instance, Numbers 19:7–9], and a special day, the Day of Atonement. Originally the ritual of atonement even included an actual scapegoat to carry away the sins of the people [Leviticus 16].

But complete atonement calls for much more beyond rituals. The individual is expected to be genuinely sorry for his unworthy acts. The writers of the Psalms, in particular, emphasized this. One wrote:

> The Lord is near to those that are of a broken heart,
> And saves those who are of a contrite [remorseful] spirit.
> —Psalm 34:19

Another prayed:

> Be gracious to me, O God, according to Your mercy. . . .
> Wash me thoroughly from my iniquity,
> And cleanse me from my sin.
> For I know my transgressions;
> And my sin is ever before me.

Against You, You only, have I sinned,
And done that which is evil in Your sight. . . .
—Psalm 51:3–6

To atone, one is also required to confess his guilt. Thus a passage in the Book of Proverbs says:

He who conceals his transgressions will not prosper,
But he who confesses and forsakes them will obtain mercy.
—Proverbs 28:13

One psalmist who sought atonement reports:

I acknowledged my sin to You [God],
And I did not hide my iniquity;
I said, "I will confess my transgressions to the Lord,"
And then You did forgive the guilt of my sin. —Psalm 32:5

If a person has committed certain specific wrongs against another, atonement demands suitable recompense, as the following selection clearly indicates:

If anyone sins and commits a breach of faith against the Lord by deceiving his neighbor in a matter of deposit or security, or through robbery, or if he has oppressed his neighbor, or has found what was lost and lied about it, swearing falsely, . . . he shall restore what he took by robbery, or what he got by oppression or the deposit which was left with him, or the lost thing which he found, or anything about which he has sworn falsely. He shall restore it in full, and shall add a fifth to it, and give it to him to whom it belongs, on the day of his guilt-offering. . . . *Then* the priest shall make atonement for him before the Lord and he shall be forgiven for any of the things which one may do and thereby become guilty.
—Leviticus 5:21–26

Abandoning one's undesirable ways, as Isaiah tells us, is still another requirement for atonement:

Let the wicked forsake his [evil] way,
And the man of iniquity his [evil] thoughts,
And let him return unto the Lord, and He will have compassion upon him,
And to our God, for He will abundantly pardon.
—Isaiah 55:7

Another prophet declares:

. . . Repent and turn yourselves away from all your transgressions so that they shall not be a stumblingblock of iniquity to you. Cast away from you all your transgressions in which you have transgressed, and make yourselves a new heart and a new spirit. . . . —Ezekiel 18:30–31

Prayer and fasting are also part of true repentance:

"Yet even now," says the Lord,
"Return to Me with all your heart,
With fasting, with weeping, and with mourning;
And rend your hearts, not your garments . . ."
—Joel 2:12–13

We are told that those who returned from exile to Palestine sought atonement for their sins by fasting, confession, and prayer [Nehemiah 9:1–3].

Charitable acts are likewise effective in obtaining God's forgiveness. Isaiah proclaims in God's name:

Is this not the fast that I have chosen?
To loose the bonds of wickedness, . . .
To let the oppressed go free,
And to break every yoke?
Is it not to share your bread with the hungry,
And bring the homeless poor into your house;
When you see the naked, to cover him,
And not to hide yourself from your own flesh?
—Isaiah 58:6–7

And Daniel is said to have advised the King of Babylonia, "Break off your sins by giving charity, and your iniquities by showing mercy to the poor" [Daniel 4:24].

Readiness to atone for one's sins, as we can see, therefore, is another quality of the religious man. Of such a person, the Bible says:

Happy is he whose transgression is forgiven, whose sin is pardoned.
Happy is the man whom the Lord considers to have no iniquity,
And in whose spirit there is no deceit. —Psalm 32:1–2

Different . . . Yet the Same

From the standpoint of the Bible, we now know who is the religious person. He is, as the Book of Ecclesiastes puts it, the one who "fears God and keeps His commandments."

To begin with, he possesses considerable knowledge of God's demands. Within him are deep feelings of love, awe, and reverence for God and complete trust in Him. He fulfils his religious obligations by faithfully carrying on worship, ritual, and holiday observance. In all of his actions he seeks to be completely moral and ethical; and wherever he falls short of doing God's will, he is ready to atone and seek His forgiveness. Although various writers of the Bible put special emphasis upon one or another of these requirements, it is clear that to be truly religious, the individual must fulfil all of them.

Does our modern definition of the religious person really differ very much from the ancient definition?

It is true that in the centuries following the writing of the Bible, the rabbis altered and added details they considered essential to religious living. They strengthened the Jews' obligation to study, pray, and practice benevolence, and they widened the area of moral responsibility. For instance, they stressed the need to forgive the wrongs done to us, and they increased the number of safeguards protecting animals and all other living creatures.

It is also true that in our own time, too, we have made certain changes in ritual, worship, and holiday observance. No longer, for example, does Reform Judaism compel the observance of the dietary laws or the performance of religious purification through ritual baths. Our mode of keeping the Sabbath is also considerably different from that of Bible times.

Yet, despite differences in detail, our definition of a truly religious person has not really changed. For to be genuinely religious, must we not have a deep reverence and love for God and extensive knowledge of His demands? Must we not carry on the worship, ritual, and holiday observances appropriate to our times? Must we not live moral and ethical lives? And where we fail, must we not atone for our sin? The answer to all these questions is yes.

The truly religious Reform Jew knows this, and acts accordingly every day of his life.

On to the Subject of Death

At this point, we are ready to consider another subject.

Like the others we have already explored, there is still another reality that every human being has to face.

We refer to the subject of death. As one of the psalmists asked, "What man can live and never see death?" [Psalm 89:49].

But why must we die? And after death, what happens to us?

These are questions which you can be sure were of utmost concern to the writers of the Bible. . . .

1. In view of the Bible's definition, whom would you call a religious Reform Jew?

2. In what ways and why would the definition of a religious person differ in the case of an Orthodox and a Reform Jew?

3. To what degree is the Bible's emphasis upon religious study still valid today?

4. How would you answer someone who said he could be a good religious Jew by being merely ethical and charitable?

──────── SOME OTHER BIBLE PASSAGES TO CONSIDER ────────

1. To what extent does the psalmist consider regular worship necessary in Judaism? See Psalm 5:2–4; 48:10; 71:14–16; 81:2–5; 92:2–4.

2. What are some of the rituals prescribed by the Bible that we continue to carry on today? See Leviticus 23:24; 23:39–43; Numbers 9:10–11; Nehemiah 8:1–8.

3. What are some of the objects originating in Bible times that are found in modern synagogues? See Exodus 25:31–40; 26:31–34; Leviticus 24:2–4; Nehemiah 9:3.

4. Why, according to the Bible, is knowledge so important to the proper worship of God? See Deuteronomy 31:9–13; Isaiah 11:2–4; 53:11; Hosea 4:1–3; Proverbs 11:9.

──────── FROM THE RABBIS' VIEWPOINT ────────

1. THE DUTY OF RELIGIOUS PRACTICE: See *Everyman's Talmud*, pp. 87–93, 157–167; and *A Rabbinic Anthology*, [459–486] pp. 175–182, [507–524] pp. 191–196, [898] p. 343.

2. THE PURSUIT OF RIGHTEOUSNESS: See *Everyman's Talmud*, pp. 195–202, 225–252; and *A Rabbinic Anthology*, [531–539] pp. 197–200, [542] p. 200, Chap. 15, "Justice, Honesty, Truth in Oaths," pp. 382–411.

3. FAITH IN GOD: See *Everyman's Talmud*, pp. 84–87, 223–225; and *A Rabbinic Anthology*, [541] p. 200, [877–886] pp. 334–338.

—————————————— OTHER THINGS TO READ ——————————————

FREEHOF, SOLOMON B., *Preface to Scripture*, Union of American Hebrew Congregations, Chap. 4: "The Bible in Worship," pp. 34–41.

GITTELSOHN, ROLAND B., *Little Lower Than the Angels*, Union of American Hebrew Congregations, Chap. 10: "What Is Religion?" pp. 159–176.

HEATON, E. W., *Everyday Life In Old Testament Times*, Batsford, pp. 213–232.

SCHWARTZMAN, SYLVAN D., *Reform Judaism in the Making*, Union of American Hebrew Congregations, Chap. 14: "Reform's Present Principles," pp. 134–142.

SILVERMAN, WILLIAM B., *The Still, Small Voice*, Behrman, Chap. 10: "The Still, Small Voice, " pp. 196–218.

$\mathcal{N}ine$

IS DEATH THE END?

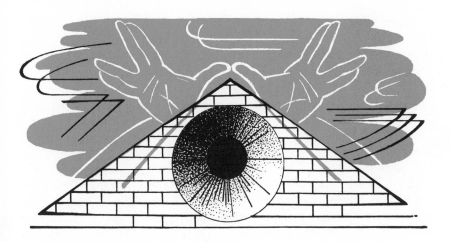

An Old, Old Belief

THE BELIEF THAT PEOPLE LIVE ON AFTER DEATH IN ONE FORM OR another is very old.

As far back as 100,000 years ago, the Neanderthal man may have believed in an afterlife. Archaeologists have found traces of food items and flint implements along with the remains of Neanderthal man. These suggest that man's very ancient ancestors may have been making provision for some existence after death.

The practice of burial itself started some 30,000 years ago. By 15,000 B.C.E. in Europe, corpses were often painted with a red dye and interred with ornaments, tools, and weapons, strongly pointing to a concern for their afterlife. In the State of Israel, caves dating from this same period yield evidence of similar types of burial.

Certainly, by five thousand years ago, the beliefs of the Egyptians in an afterlife were already highly developed. They preserved the bodies of their dead in mummified form through a skilful process of embalming, and placed them in tombs, of which the pyramids were a more elaborate type reserved for the pharaohs. Buried with them were containers of food and water, ointments, jewelry, and even furniture. A special "book of the dead" containing instructions for charms and incantations to assist them in attaining a happy afterlife was placed directly in the coffin. Sometimes even a fully-outfitted boat was sealed in the tombs of very high personages to enable their spirits to sail across the mysterious Eastern Sea and join the sun-god.

Belief in life after death has continued down to our time. All the great religions of mankind, Judaism included, teach that death does not completely put an end to man's existence. Some religions, such as Catholicism, Islam, and certain forms of Protestantism, maintain that there is a heaven and a hell to which the dead eventually go. Two of the great Far Eastern faiths, Hinduism and Buddhism, believe that after death the individual undergoes a "rebirth" and takes on some new form of existence—human, animal, a plant, a blade of grass, a stone, or some other object.

There are many people who are convinced that communication with the dead is possible, a belief known as "spiritualism." In most cases the alleged response of the dead through mediums and seances has proven to be a fraud. Nevertheless, many think that there is something to spiritualism, among them the late Sir Arthur Conan Doyle, creator of Sherlock Holmes, the brilliant English detective. And today there is even a branch of psychology that devotes itself to the investigation of all sorts of spiritualistic phenomena.

Belief in spiritualism is also very ancient. In fact, one account of a spiritualistic experience occurs right within the pages of the Bible itself.

A Prediction From the Grave

In I Samuel 28 we are told that King Saul, with the aid of a medium, the "Witch of Endor," succeeded in calling up a prophet from his grave to obtain a prediction about an important event.

Saul, it seems, was facing a crucial battle with his old enemy, the Philistines, and because their army seemed so overwhelmingly superior, he feared the outcome. Following the practice of his day, he promptly consulted various seers and dream-interpreters to find out what he should do to be victorious. This time, strangely, he could get no answer. In desperation he instructed his servants:

> "Seek out for me a woman who is a medium [one able to communicate with the dead] that I may go to her and inquire of her." And his servants said to him, "Behold, there is a medium at En-dor." —I Samuel 28 : 7

Carefully disguised, Saul went to her and asked her to bring up the spirit of the prophet Samuel, who had recently died. The woman refused because she said that King Saul had ordered all mediums to be driven out of the land. The King reassured her that she would not be punished and again he told her to bring up Samuel's spirit.

The woman consented, and in a short while she uttered a loud cry. The Bible describes in detail what followed:

> ". . . What do you see?" the King asked her.
> The woman said to Saul, "I see a godlike being coming up out of the earth."
> He said to her, "What is his appearance?"
> And she said, "An old man is coming up, and he is wrapped in a robe."
> Saul knew that it was Samuel, and he bowed with his face to the ground and prostrated himself.
> Then Samuel said to Saul, "Why have you disturbed me by bringing me up?"
> Saul answered, "I am in great distress because the Philistines are warring against me, and God has turned away from me and no longer answers me by means of seers or dreams. Therefore I have summoned you to tell me what I should do."
> And Samuel said, "Why then do you ask me since the Lord has turned against you and become your enemy? . . . The Lord will give Israel, together with you, into the hand of the Philistines, and tomorrow you and your sons shall be with me. . . ." —I Samuel 28:13–19

So convinced was King Saul that the prophet had come back from the grave to predict his defeat that he:

> . . . Fell at once full length upon the ground, filled with fear because of the words of Samuel; and there was no strength in him. . . . —I Samuel 28:20

His will to fight gone, it was inevitable that Saul and his men should be defeated. Therefore a few chapters later we learn:

> Now the Philistines fought against Israel; and the men of Israel fled before the Philistines, and fell slain on Mount Gilboa. . . . And Saul died, and his three sons, and his armor-bearer, and all his men on the same day together. —I Samuel 31:1, 6

Thus in biblical times, even as today, there were those who practiced spiritualism.

Why the Bible Objects

Although this tale is included in the Bible, there was strong and sustained objection on the part of the writers of the Bible to all forms of spiritualism and sorcery. "You shall not permit a sorceress to live," says the Book of Exodus [22:17]; "Do not turn to mediums or wizards," commands Leviticus [19:31]. These and many other passages condemn such practices [see Leviticus 20:6, 27; Deuteronomy 18:10–12; II Kings 9:22; and Jeremiah 27:9].

Why this great opposition? Because, to the writers of the Bible, sorcery and spiritualism were forms of rank paganism. They were part of "the abomination of the heathen nations" [Deuteronomy 18:9–12], directly associated with the practice of idolatry [see II Chronicles 33:6–7]. Hence, engaging in such practices was faithlessness to God.

But even when divorced from idol-worship, sorcery and spiritualism, in effect, denied the power and authority of God. To know the future or to alter the fate of the individual is the province of God, not some human diviner. Therefore, says Micah:

> . . . The soothsayers shall be put to shame,
> And the diviners confounded;
> Yes, they shall all cover their upper lip [be mournful],
> For there shall be no answer from God. —Micah 3:7

By believing in such practices, says the prophet Isaiah, the people reject God:

> . . . When they say unto you, "Consult the mediums and
> the wizards who chirp and mutter," should not a people
> consult their God . . . for the [authentic] teaching and
> testimony? —Isaiah 8:19–20

For, in comparison with the Lord, what power do mediums, diviners, astrologers, and the like possess? This is the way the prophet mocks the people:

> Stand fast in your [various forms of] enchantments and your
> many sorceries
> With which you have labored from your youth;
> Perhaps you may be able to be successful,
> Perhaps you may inspire terror [in others].
> You are worn out with your many consultations [of wizards];
> Now let the astrologers, the star-gazers,
> Those who prognosticate by means of each new moon,

Stand up and save you
From the things that will come upon you.
Behold, they themselves are like stubble,
The fire consumes them;
They cannot [even] save themselves
From the power of the flame, . . .
Such to you are those with whom you have labored, . . .
They wander about, each in his own direction;
There is no one who can save you. —Isaiah 47:12–15

Spiritualism and all other forms of divination and sorcery, then, are not merely useless. They are an affront to God Himself for they are a denial of faith in Him. That is why the authors of the Bible, in common with all religious people, so strongly object to them.

Is Life Good?

But there is still another reason why consultation of the spirits of the dead never took root in the Jewish religion: the main focus in Judaism has always been on life and the living.

"Shall people consult the dead on behalf of the living?" Isaiah scornfully asks his listeners [Isaiah 8:19]. Why, says Koheleth, "A living dog is better than a dead lion, for the dead know nothing," and only as long as a person is alive can he count on any future [Ecclesiastes 9:4–5]. The psalmists agree that the dead can no longer fulfil God's purposes [Psalm 6:6; 88:12–13; 115:17–18]; and, as King Hezekiah admitted after his recovery from a serious illness, only the living are able to praise God [Isaiah 38:18–19].

But what about life? Is it really good?

As the writers of the Bible saw it, life is very precious. Man must of course expect some suffering and hardship, for that is part of living. And, as in the case of Job, there may be times when we too may be moved to cry out in anguish, "I loathe my life, I do not want to live" [Job 7:16].

Man must also expect to experience a continuous struggle against the evil urge within himself. He faces the temptations of strong drink [Proverbs 23:29–35], sex [Proverbs 6:24–29], and innumerable forms of wickedness [see, for example, Proverbs 6:16–19]. Indeed, as the writer of Proverbs notes, "Many are the devices in the heart of man!" [Proverbs 19:21].

Yet, despite suffering and struggles, life as the gift of God is fundamentally good. This the psalmist recognizes when he praises God for saving him:

> . . . I will render thanksgiving offerings to You [God]
> For You have delivered me from death,
> Yes, my feet from falling
> That I may walk before God in the light of life.
> —Psalm 56:14

God Himself wants people to live [Ezekiel 33:10–12]. His greatest blessing to man is long life [Genesis 24:1; Psalm 21:4–6; 91:16]. The overwhelming interest of many of the psalmists is that God should spare their lives [see, for example, Psalm 16:10–11; 86:13; and 116:3–6].

But the real goodness of life lies in fulfilling God's purposes through obedience to His will. "You shall keep My statutes and My ordinances," God instructs the people of Israel, "which by so doing a person shall live" [Leviticus 18:5]. Indeed, God informs Moses:

> ". . . Man does not live by bread alone, but man lives by everything that proceeds out of the mouth of the Lord."
> —Deuteronomy 8:3

And, adds the psalmist:

> What person is there who desires life,
> And yearns for many days in which he may enjoy good?
> Keep your tongue from evil,
> And your lips from speaking deceit.
> Depart from evil and do good;
> Seek peace and pursue it. —Psalm 34:13–15

What makes life good is man's ability to choose to be faithful to God and His ways [see Psalm 73:28]. For then he has not only fulfilled the desires of His Creator but, in the eyes of those who wrote the Bible, he has earned one of life's chief rewards, a good reputation. For, they declared:

> A good name is better than precious ointment. . . .
> —Ecclesiastes 7:1

> A good name is to be chosen rather than great riches,
> And loving favor [from God and man] is better than silver or gold. —Proverbs 22:1

The Finality of Death

As for death, the writers of the Bible had no doubt whatever that it was final. Death could not be wished away; nor, once it had occurred, could anyone do anything to reverse it.

In the entire Bible, there are only two exceptions. One is the revival of a dead child by Elijah in I Kings 17; the other, by Elisha in II Kings 4. However, these, like similar acts ascribed to Jesus in the New Testament [for example, Matthew 9:23–26; Luke 7:11–15; and John 11:28–44], were clearly regarded as extraordinary. They were viewed as miracles, singular deeds performed through the will of almighty God Himself, and completely out of the ordinary.

Apart from these two exceptions, the consistent attitude taken by the biblical writers was that there was no recourse from death. The best illustration of their thinking is the story told in II Samuel 12 about King David and his ailing son.

David is described as fasting and praying in the hope that God might spare the boy's life. However, once the child was dead, the King arose and went about his normal affairs. His servants were shocked at this change in behavior, since they had witnessed his strenuous fasting and weeping during the child's illness. David told his servants:

> . . . While the child was yet alive, I fasted and wept; for I said: "Who knows whether the Lord will not be gracious to me, that the child may live? But now that he is dead, why should I fast? Can I bring him back again? I shall go to him, but he will not return to me." —II Samuel 12:22–23

As David pointed out, once death came, it had to be accepted. This did not mean there was no grief or mourning; the Bible cites many examples of a deep sense of sorrow over the loss of a loved one. Jacob, for instance, grieved greatly for Joseph whom he believed dead, and we are told that he:

> . . . Mourned for his son many days. All his sons and all his daughters rose up to comfort him, but he refused to be comforted. . . . So [he] wept for him. —Genesis 37:34–35

We feel David's overwhelming grief, too, at the death of another son, Absalom, who was killed in a revolt against him:

> And the king was very deeply moved, and he went up to the chamber over the gate and wept. And as he wept he said: "O, my son Absalom, my son, my son Absalom! Would I had died instead of you, O Absalom, my son, my son!" —II Samuel 19:1

Sorrow was expressed in various ways: by weeping [II Samuel 3:32], by beating one's breast [Isaiah 32:12], tearing one's garments [II Samuel 3:31], fasting [I Samuel 31:13], and wearing sackcloth [Genesis 37:34]. Friends would also come to comfort the mourners [Job 2:11–13]. However, the people were warned against carrying grief to excess. For example, cutting one's flesh to express sorrow, a practice carried on by other peoples, was strictly forbidden [Leviticus 19:28].

The body of the deceased was placed upon a bed (that is the Hebrew word in II Samuel 3:31) with care and respect and carried to its burial place the same day. The bier was accompanied by those who mourned [II Samuel 3:31] and there was lamentation at the graveside [I Kings 13:30]. Afterward the mourners would fast [II Samuel 3:35]. Then neighbors and friends would prepare food and a "cup of consolation" for the mourners [see Jeremiah 16:7 and Ezekiel 24:17–18].

The customary period of mourning was seven days. Thus Joseph mourned seven days for his father [Genesis 50:10], and David and his followers fasted seven days following the burial of Saul and his sons [I Samuel 31:13]. For a great leader like Moses, however, the people were said to have "wept and mourned" thirty days [Deuteronomy 34:7–8]; for Aaron, too, they mourned for thirty days [Numbers 20:29].

Why Humans Die

While the writers of the Bible considered death to be final, they did give some thought to basic questions connected with death. One question they pondered was, why is it necessary for a person to die?

Death, they finally decided, was the natural and inevitable end of life, as God Himself had created it. "Dust you are and unto dust you shall return," the first man was told by God [Genesis 3:19]. "What man is there that lives on and shall not see death?" asked a psalmist [Psalm 89:49]. King David was reminded, "We must all die, and are as water spilled on the ground which cannot be gathered up again" [II Samuel 14:14]. Later, on his deathbed, David told his son Solomon, "I am about to go the way of all the earth" [I Kings 2:1–2].

Similarly, the author of Job states:

> All flesh shall perish together,
> And man shall return unto dust.   —Job 34:15

And in another passage, he observes:

> Man that is born of a woman
> Is of few days and full of trouble.

> He comes forth like a flower, then he withers;
> He flees like a shadow, and does not remain. —Job 14:1–2

Two other ideas are touched on briefly in the Bible. They flash on and off very quickly and are never developed fully anywhere in the Bible. The first occurs in connection with the tale of the "Tree of Life" in the Garden of Eden. It suggests that man once had the opportunity to live forever but neglected to take advantage of it [Genesis 3:22–24]. The second arises when certain individuals— Enoch, in Genesis 5:24, and Elijah, in II Kings 2:1—were said to have been "taken by God." This curious phrasing suggests that they somehow escaped dying. However, this may only be a more poetic way of saying that they died.

Neither of these ideas is pursued further. For all practical purposes, the writers of the Bible were convinced that since God had so established it, death was inevitable for everyone.

The Timing of Death

The biblical authors also pondered the timing of death and who, in the final analysis, determined this.

Here there was general agreement that the individual himself was responsible for the length of his stay upon earth. Doing God's will extended one's life, whereas wickedness and rebellion against Him shortened it. Thus, one writer says:

> The fear of the Lord prolongs [one's] days;
> But the years of the wicked shall be shortened.
> —Proverbs 10:27

And another declares:

> . . . I know that it will be well with them that fear God
> . . . but it will not be well with the wicked, neither will he
> prolong his days, which are as a shadow, because he does
> not fear God. —Ecclesiastes 8:12–13

The "way of life and death," said different writers, was open to each person and the choice was plainly his [Deuteronomy 30:19–20; Jeremiah 21:8]. Carrying out God's law was a way of prolonging life [Leviticus 18:4–5; Ezekiel 20:11]. "If you will walk in My ways to keep My statutes and My commandments," God tells Solomon, "then I will lengthen your days" [I Kings 3:14]. The wicked, on the other hand, court death. As one prophet appeals to the people:

. . . Turn away, turn away from your evil ways, for why
will you die, O house of Israel? —Ezekiel 33:11

The writers of the Bible did not doubt that it was God Himself
who ultimately decided when the individual would die. A passage in
Deuteronomy has God declare:

> See now that I, even I, am He
> And there is no god beside Me;
> I kill and I give life;
> I wound and I heal;
> And there is none that can deliver out of My hand.
> —Deuteronomy 32:39

When Job learned of the death of his children, he immediately exclaimed, "The Lord gave and the Lord has taken away; blessed be
the name of the Lord" [Job 1:21]. On another occasion Job declares:

> . . . His [man's] days are determined,
> And the number of his months lies with You [God],
> And You have appointed his bounds that he cannot pass.
> —Job 14:5

Yet, probably wanting to spare God the unpleasant duty, some
biblical writers said that He employed an "angel of death" to carry
out His decrees. In the majority of instances, he is called simply
"the angel of the Lord" [in II Samuel 24:15–17, for example]; in
one passage, he is called "the destroyer" [Exodus 12:23]. Nevertheless, in each instance death is part of the design of life as God has
created it, and therefore He is ultimately responsible for it.

Recognizing this, the writers of the Bible faced their own inevitable fate by seeking to make the most of life as God would want
it. They prayed:

> So teach us to number our days
> That we may get a heart of wisdom. . . .
> Satisfy us in the morning with Your [God's] steadfast love,
> That we may rejoice and be glad all our days. . . .
> Let the favor of the Lord our God be upon us,
> And may You establish the work of our hands,
> Yes, the work of our hands, establish it. —Psalm 90:12–17

And as the end of their lives drew near, they continued to voice their
trust in God:

> Yes, even though I walk through the valley of the shadow
> of death,
> I fear no evil,

> For You are with me;
> Your rod and Your staff,
> They comfort me. —Psalm 23:4

In this sense, death for the Jew was seen simply as a natural, normal part of his dedicated way of life.

What Is Death?

As the writers of the Bible conceived of it, death was the departure of the "breath of life." For all living beings possessed God-given "breath," or "spirit."

Thus, in the story of the creation of man we are told:

> Then the Lord God formed man of the dust of the ground and breathed into his nostrils *the breath of life* so that man became a living being. —Genesis 2:7

Similarly, in connection with the coming of the great Flood, God is said to declare:

> ". . . Behold I will bring a flood of waters upon the earth to destroy all flesh in which there is *the breath of life* from under heaven; everything that is on earth shall die."
> —Genesis 6:17

This "breath of life" was inseparably connected with the life-blood of the living [Genesis 9:4]. Consequently, the latter was regarded as especially sacred and man was sternly forbidden to eat it. In fact the people were told:

> "If anyone of the house of Israel or [among] the strangers that dwell among them eats any blood, I [God] will set My face against that person who eats blood, and cut him off from among his people. For the life of the flesh is in the blood; . . ." —Leviticus 17:10–11

With the departure of the breath of life, the individual dies. In the following passage Job is saying in effect, "As long as I am alive I will speak only the truth," but note how he puts it:

> As long as my breath is within me
> And the spirit of God is in my nostrils,
> My lips will not speak falsehood, . . . —Job 27:3–4

Indeed, God who has implanted the breath of life in all living things withdraws it at the moment of death. So Job declares:

If He [God] should take back man's spirit and breath,
All flesh would perish together
And man would return to the dust. —Job 34:14–15

Once the breath of life leaves, the psalmist observes, the life-functions cease and the body starts to disintegrate:

When his [man's] breath leaves, he returns to the dust,
On that very day his thoughts perish. —Psalm 146:4

And the writer of the final chapter of Ecclesiastes confirms this with:

The dust returns to the earth as it was,
And the spirit returns to God who gave it.
—Ecclesiastes 12:7

After Death, What?

What was the individual's fate after death? This was another question the writers of the Bible pondered, and eventually they reached a common conclusion. As we shall see later on, however, certain new ideas arose toward the end of the biblical period, about the third or second century B.C.E.

The writers of the Bible generally agreed that after life the individual sank into oblivion in a place known as "Sh'ol," commonly translated as the "pit" or "netherworld." Thus, when Jacob learned of the apparent death of his beloved son Joseph, he refused to be comforted but insisted that he himself would go down in mourning to Sh'ol (this is what the Hebrew of Genesis 37:35 says). Later, when Joseph, now governor of Egypt, demanded that his brothers bring Benjamin, the youngest brother, back to Egypt with them, their father Jacob refused. Said he:

. . . My son shall not go down with you; for his brother [Joseph] is dead, and he only is left. If harm should befall him on the journey that you are to make, you would bring down my gray hairs with sorrow to Sh'ol. —Genesis 42:38

"What man can live and never see death?" asks a psalmist. "Who can deliver his soul from the power of Sh'ol?" Everyone goes down to Sh'ol at the end and there is no other hope for man [Job 14:7–19].

Sh'ol was universally considered to be a pit deep within the earth to which all the dead went [see Psalm 88:7]. It was a place of complete silence [Psalm 115:17], a region of darkness and forgetfulness [Psalm 88:13]. Some said not even God could be found there [Isaiah 38:10–11], but others insisted, to the contrary, that He was everywhere, including the netherworld [Psalm 139:8; Job 26:6].

Existence in Sh'ol was vague and shadowy. No longer in bodily form [Psalm 49:15], the dead were essentially like shadows, and are often referred to as "shades" [see Job 26:5–6; Psalm 88:11; Proverbs 9:18]. Moreover there was no possibility for the living to have any further contact with them.

All in all, the biblical picture of Sh'ol is a dismal one. The psalmist who compared his misery to the condition of the dead there has left us this description from his own imagination:

> . . . My soul is full of troubles,
> And my life draws near to Sh'ol.
> I am counted among those who go down to the Pit;
> I am a man who has no strength,
> Like one forsaken among the dead,
> Like the slain that lie in the grave,
> Like those whom You [God] remember no more,
> For they are cut off from Your hand.
> You have put me in the depths of the Pit,
> In the regions dark and deep. —Psalm 88:4–7

The Promise of Resurrection

Some of the last prophets and writers of the Bible introduced a new conception of man's fate after death. They advanced the idea that the dead might be "resurrected," that is, brought to life again in bodily form.

Scholars believe that the notion of resurrection grew out of the hope that the nation of Israel would one day be reconstituted. The prophet Ezekiel likened his exiled people to a collection of dry bones which God restores to life. Here is his own description of what he saw in his vision:

> The hand of the Lord was upon me, and the Lord carried me out in a spirit and set me down in the midst of the valley; it was full of bones. And He led me round among them; and behold there were very many in the valley; and lo, they were very dry.
> And He said to me, "Son of man, can these bones live?"
> And I answered, "O Lord God, You [alone] know."
> Again He said to me, "Prophesy to these bones, and say to them, O dry bones, hear the word of the Lord. Thus says the Lord God to these bones: Behold I will cause breath to enter into you, and you shall live. And I will lay sinews upon you, and will cause flesh to come upon you, and cover you

> with skin, and put breath into you, and you shall live; and
> you shall know that I am the Lord."
> So I prophesied as I was commanded; and as I prophesied
> there was a noise, and behold a rattling; and the bones
> came together, bone to its bone. And as I looked, there
> were sinews on them, and flesh had come upon them, and
> skin had covered them; but there was no breath in them.
> Then He said to me, "Prophesy to the breath, prophesy, son
> of man, and say to the breath: Thus says the Lord God:
> Come from the four winds, O breath, and breathe upon
> these slain, that they may live."
> So I prophesied as He commanded me, and the breath
> came into them, and they lived, and stood upon their feet,
> an exceedingly great multitude. —Ezekiel 37:1–10

And shortly after, the prophet hears God promise Israel:

> . . . "Behold I will open your graves, and raise you from
> your graves, O My people; and I will bring you home
> into the land of Israel. And you shall know that I am the
> Lord when I open your graves and raise you from your
> graves, O My people. And I will put My spirit within you,
> and you shall live, . . ." —Ezekiel 37:12–14

What Ezekiel is speaking of here is clearly the restoration of *national* life to the Jewish exiles in Babylonian exile. There are some, however, who believe that the prophet may also have been thinking of individual resurrection.

A passage in the Book of Isaiah likewise appears to hold out hope for the resurrection of the people of Israel. In it the prophet promises the suffering people:

> Your dead shall live, their bodies shall rise.
> Awake and sing, those who dwell in the dust!
> For Your [God's] dew is a dew of light,
> And the earth shall bring the shades to life. —Isaiah 26:19

And in yet another passage, Isaiah seems to go beyond this first promise, and foretells ultimate resurrection of *all* people. For he prophesies:

> He [God] will swallow up death forever,
> And the Lord God will wipe away tears from all faces,
> And the reproach of His people He will take away from
> all the earth;
> For the Lord has spoken. —Isaiah 25:8

Only in the Book of Daniel do we find the resurrection of the dead definitely promised. The author of this book predicts that at the end of the reign of a certain evil king, the angel Michael will arise:

> And many of them that sleep in the dust of the earth will awake, . . . —Daniel 12:2

Thus, late in the biblical period arose the belief among a few writers that there was more of an afterlife than the shadowy existence of Sh'ol. As yet, however, belief in the eventual restoration of the dead to renewed bodily form does not appear to have been widespread.

It is only in the period of the rabbis that teachings of the immortality of the soul and the eventual resurrection of the dead became accepted Jewish belief. The soul, they taught, is part of God's spirit that gives life to the body and lives on with Him when man dies. And if he is deserving, with the coming of the Messianic Age, his body will be resurrected for eternal life in a blissful hereafter called "the world-to-come."

Reward and Punishment After Death

With their conception of Sh'ol, the writers of the Bible could scarcely have held out any hope of reward after death. Nor could there be any punishment.

Thus the psalmist asks:

> Do You [God] work wonders for the dead?
> Do the shades rise up to praise You?
> Is Your steadfast love declared in the grave?
> Or Your faithfulness in the region of abandonment?
> Are Your wonders known in the [place of] darkness?
> And Your saving help in the land of forgetfulness?
> —Psalm 88:11–12

The answer is obviously no. In death, there is nothing.

Therefore, any punishment for the wicked or reward for the righteous is to be experienced during their own lifetimes. The wicked, as we have already seen, are to be consigned to an earlier death [see also Psalm 9:17–18], and God may extend the life of the righteous [see Psalm 86:13]. But eventually, as Koheleth observes, they share a common end:

> . . . One fate comes to all, to the righteous and the wicked, to the good and the evil, to the clean and the unclean, to him who sacrifices and him who does not sacrifice. As is the good man, so is the sinner; and he who swears is as he who shuns an oath. This is an evil in all that is done under the sun, that one fate comes to all. . . .
> —Ecclesiastes 9:2–3

Only one contrary opinion is found in the entire Bible, and again it appears in the Book of Daniel. There, in connection with the resurrection of the dead, the writer asserts:

> And many of them that sleep in the dust of the earth shall awake, some to everlasting life, and some to shame and everlasting contempt. And those who are wise shall shine like the brightness of the firmament; and those who turn many to righteousness, like the stars forever and ever.
> —Daniel 12:2–3

With only this single exception, the writers of the Bible held fast to their belief that all men shared a similar fate after death. People receive reward and punishment during their lifetime; after death, there are no rewards, no punishments, nothing. In Sh'ol, all shades are alike; the good cannot be distinguished from the evil, nor can any be singled out for special treatment.

The appearance of the Book of Daniel with its belief in resurrection and its concept of reward and punishment after death reveals that Judaism was groping toward something more hopeful than a shadowy afterlife in Sh'ol. A more positive belief ultimately came with the teachings of the rabbis in the centuries after the Bible was set down.

Building upon the biblical hope of a Messianic Age, the rabbinic sages in the first few centuries of the Common Era offered man the promise of a life in the hereafter through both resurrection of the body and immortality, the continuing life of his "soul." This thinking opened the way for the introduction into Judaism of a wide range of beliefs concerning life after death, including the reward of eternal life for the righteous.

Questions . . . About the Bible Itself

In emphasizing life and living, modern Judaism follows the pattern of thinking set by the writers of the Bible. Although the ancients dealt with the subject of death, it is plain that they considered life far more important.

They viewed death as the natural end of all living creatures as God created them. No man could escape it, but through righteous living, one might be able to prolong his days on earth. To be privileged to live a long life, therefore, was another of man's great rewards.

Yet when God determined it, the breath of life would depart, giving way to death. The living would grieve. The dead would receive proper burial with care and respect, and would be sincerely mourned. Though a man's mortal remains returned to dust, somehow his being persisted in the oblivion of a shadowy netherworld. Only the writer of the Book of Daniel held out hope for rewards and punishments for the righteous and the wicked in the afterlife, and promised an ultimate resurrection for all.

So emphatically did the Bible stress the importance of life and living that our Jewish religion never became infected by the unhealthy and negative preoccupation with death that characterized the religions of so many other ancient peoples. Our Bible contains no hint, for example, of the morbid interest in life after death that so concerned the Egyptians. None of the elaborate myths and rites built up around the subject of death among so many of the other peoples of the ancient Near East ever sprang up in Judaism.

Thus the Jewish Bible never became a "book of the dead." On the contrary, with its positive emphasis on the good life, it served as a "book of the living" *for the living.*

No wonder, then, that generation after generation has cherished the Bible. People have been poring over it for more than 2,000 years now, and the more they have studied it, the more questions they have asked. Who, for instance, wrote the Bible? How did it become a "holy" book? How has it been preserved and passed down to us through the centuries?

In more recent times, modern Bible readers have been asking yet another question: How *true* is the Bible? People in our enlightened society are confused about whether they can really believe what they read in the Bible, particularly the stories of creation, miracles, angels, and the like.

No doubt these are questions that have occurred to you, too. Well, what are the answers? Would you like to know?

Let's begin with the question, Who wrote the Bible? . . .

———————— THINGS TO TALK OVER ————————

1. To what extent do your own beliefs about death and the afterlife agree with those of the Bible?

2. How do you explain the great emphasis of Judaism upon life, not death?

3. In what ways are present-day Jewish practices connected with death related to those of Bible days?

4. How has Christianity been influenced by the teachings of the Book of Daniel?

───────── SOME OTHER BIBLE PASSAGES TO CONSIDER ─────────

1. In what respect does the example of the Patriarchs illustrate the attitudes of the writers of the Bible toward death? See Genesis 23; 35:16–20; 37:31–35; 49:28–50:13.

2. What does the Bible regard as some undesirable practices associated with death? See Leviticus 19:28; 21:1–5; Deuteronomy 14:1; Jeremiah 16:6; Psalm 106:28.

3. What other mourning customs among the Hebrews does the Bible mention? See Genesis 38:14; Joshua 7:6; Jeremiah 16:6–8; Ezekiel 24:17.

4. How, according to the Bible, may one's life be lengthened? See Deuteronomy 30:20; Psalm 21:2–8; 91:14–16; Proverbs 4:1–13, 20–27; 10:27.

───────────── FROM THE RABBIS' VIEWPOINT ─────────────

1. THE NATURE OF HUMAN LIFE: See *Everyman's Talmud*, pp. 72–78, 81–84, 101–102; and *A Rabbinic Anthology*, [227–232] pp. 86–88, [1484–1486] pp. 528–529.

2. DEATH: See *Everyman's Talmud*, pp. 61, 78–81, 113–114; and *A Rabbinic Anthology*, [1518] p. 542, [1546–1547] pp. 551–552, [1553] p. 554, [1612–1613] pp. 580–581.

3. THE HEREAFTER: See *Everyman's Talmud*, pp. 378–412; and *A Rabbinic Anthology*, [1614–1661] pp. 582–607.

───────────── OTHER THINGS TO READ ─────────────

FACKENHEIM, EMIL L., *Paths to Jewish Belief*, Behrman, Chap. 9: "Are Men Immortal?" pp. 107–114.

GITTELSOHN, ROLAND B., *Little Lower Than the Angels*, Union of American Hebrew Congregations, Chap. 17: "What Happens to Us When We Die?" pp. 301–324.

MATTUCK, ISRAEL, "Immortality in Judaism," No. 21, *Popular Studies in Judaism*, Union of American Hebrew Congregations.

SILVER, ABBA HILLEL, *Where Judaism Differed*, Macmillan, Chap. 15: "That Death Is Better Than Life," pp. 265–284.

STEINBERG, MILTON, *Basic Judaism*, Harcourt, Brace, Chap. 10: "World to Come," pp. 159–170.

$\mathcal{T}en$

WHO WROTE THE BIBLE?

A Major Problem

IF YOU WERE ON A TELEVISION QUIZ SHOW AND YOU WERE ASKED who wrote *Julius Caesar*, *The Merchant of Venice*, and *Macbeth*, what would you answer? William Shakespeare, of course.

Don't be too sure! Do you know that there are some scholars who claim that William Shakespeare never wrote his own plays? They're convinced that the real author was Francis Bacon, a well-known writer and scientist who lived around the same time. A great many more think that certain of Shakespeare's dramas, such as *Macbeth* and *Henry VIII*, were written in collaboration with others. And practically everyone agrees that Shakespeare took many of his plots from existing materials.

Now if there is this kind of debate over Shakespeare's works, which were written almost 400 years ago, you can begin to understand why there is far more uncertainty about who wrote the Bible. Our Bible is at least five times *older* than Shakespeare's plays. Moreover, our Bible isn't a *single* book, but a whole collection of thirty-nine different books. Now you can appreciate why the problem of authorship is so complex.

Part of our difficulty arises because the Bible tells us nothing about who wrote certain books, such as Judges, Kings, Chronicles,

183

and Lamentations. Even where the Bible provides a hint about an author—for example, a book like Joshua bears the name of an individual; in a book like Song of Songs the first verse declares that it is the work of King Solomon—we still can't accept this hint at face value. We know, for instance, that Joshua could not possibly have written the entire book bearing his name. Why? How could he have written the concluding verses actually describing his own death? [see Joshua 24:29–31].

Our problem is made even more difficult because the Bible was written in ancient times and, like all ancient literature generally, it is unsigned. In those days it was not the custom for authors to set down their names. Also, the ancients had no system of copyrights. Further, in many cases, stories had been handed down for centuries by word of mouth, so that no one remembered who the original author really was.

Ancient writers often believed that their work had been inspired by the thinking of some earlier hero. Therefore, they gave credit to their hero not only for inspiration, but also for the authorship. To have their work appear more authoritative, some ancient writers deliberately affixed the name of a highly regarded earlier figure, or else gave their material an older historical setting. Many scholars believe this is what happened in the case of the Books of Esther and Daniel, for example.

Sometimes, too, for the sake of economy, authors would make use of the extra blank pages of an existing scroll. Consequently, the author of this already existing work received credit for the new material as well. This may have happened in the case of the Second Isaiah. His work was added on to that of the original Isaiah who lived some two centuries earlier.

This begins to give you some idea of why it is so difficult to answer the question, "Who wrote the Bible?"

A Closer Look at the Torah Section

The Bible, as we have seen, is a collection of thirty-nine books. To get a little closer to an answer to our question, we must look at the various biblical books themselves. And here, because of the very special way in which the first five books of the Bible were written, we shall concentrate on them.

If you are using the Jewish Publication Society translation of the Bible, you will note that it presents a list of the Bible books in the order they appear, and then it divides the Bible into three main sections. The first main section is titled "The Law"; it is more commonly known as the "Torah" or the "Five Books of Moses." Another name for it is the *Chumosh*, from the Hebrew word for "five." Still another frequently heard name is the "Pentateuch" which comes from the Greek words, "five books." The two other main sections which we will consider later on are "The Prophets" and "The Writings."

Returning to the Torah section, we find that the titles of all but one of its five books come from the Greek into which the Hebrew Bible was first translated. Actually these names are simply one-word descriptions of the contents. Genesis, the title of the first book, means "the beginning." The book tells what happened in the period from the creation of the world to the death of Joseph in Egypt. In Genesis we observe man's progress from Adam to Noah, and afterward we go into the history of the three Patriarchs, Abraham, Isaac, and Jacob.

Exodus, "the departure," is the second book of the Torah. It opens with an account of the oppression of the Hebrew slaves in Egypt and describes their eventual deliverance by God, through the work of Moses and his brother Aaron. After their rescue from the pursuing Egyptians through the miracle of the Red Sea, the people begin their journey through the Wilderness. In the course of their wanderings they receive the Ten Commandments at Mount Sinai. Exodus closes with an account of the building of the tabernacle for the worship of the God, whom the children of Israel have now promised to serve.

The third book, Leviticus, takes its name from the Greek word for "priestly legislation," because it is concerned with numerous laws dealing with the proper worship of the Deity. Leviticus deals with the service of the priesthood, sacrificial rites and offerings, ritual cleanliness, and personal holiness. Here we find the story of the consecration of Aaron and his sons as the priests, and the listing of many kinds of ritual and ceremonial obligations.

The fourth book, Numbers (the only one even today with an English title), takes its name from the fact that it opens with a numbering, or a census taken in the Wilderness. It describes some of the difficulties encountered by the Hebrews in the Wilderness. These include lack of food and water, rebellions against Moses, defeats by the Canaanite settlers of Palestine, and the deaths of Aaron and Miriam, the brother and sister of Moses. In Numbers, too, we find a variety of laws dealing with such matters as lepers, Levites, and holiday observances.

Finally, Deuteronomy, "the repetition of the law," reviews the experiences of the Hebrews from the time of Mount Sinai to the moment they are preparing to enter into the Promised Land. The book sets forth much religious and social legislation which the people are expected to obey as part of their covenant with God. Deuteronomy concludes with the appointment of Joshua as leader and the death of Moses.

Taken as a whole, these five books appear to be telling a single, connected story. They start with the beginning of the world and carry the spiritual development of man though the experiences of the Patriarchs and their descendants, the people of Israel. And they end as the Hebrew tribes, now under the leadership of Joshua, prepare to cross the Jordan River into the "Promised Land."

Did Moses Write the Whole Torah?

Jewish tradition insists that it was Moses himself who wrote the Torah. In fact, this is indicated in various places in the five books, themselves. Here are two examples:

> And the Lord said to Moses: "Write this [the account of the defeat of the Amalekites] as a memorial in a book and recite it in the ears of Joshua. . . ." —Exodus 17:14

> These are the stages of the people of Israel when they went forth out of the land of Egypt by their hosts under the leadership of Moses and Aaron. Moses wrote down their starting places, stage by stage, at the command of the Lord. . . . —Numbers 33:1–2

In some instances it is claimed that Moses himself composed the material, as in Deuteronomy 31:22 where we read:

> So Moses wrote this song [found in the following chapter] the same day, and taught it to the people of Israel.

In other instances, it is God who wrote and transmitted the Torah to the people through Moses. One example of this claim appears in Exodus 24:12:

> The Lord said to Moses, "Come up to Me on the mountain and wait there, and I will give you the tablets of stone with the teaching [the Hebrew says 'Torah'] and the commandment which I have written for their [the people's] instruction."

According to the Bible, however, Moses is finally considered to be the author of the Torah. That is what we conclude from the following passage in Deuteronomy:

> When Moses finished writing the words of this teaching
> [the Hebrew says "this Torah"] in a book, to the very end, he
> commanded the Levites who carried the ark of the cove-
> nant of the Lord, "Take this book of the Torah and put
> it alongside the ark of the covenant of the Lord your
> God. . . ." —Deuteronomy 31:24–26

Eventually, difficulties arose over this. By the time the Talmud was
completed, around 500 C.E., some of the rabbis were questioning
certain biblical passages. One passage in particular which made
Moses' authorship of the *complete* Torah appear impossible was the
concluding section of the Book of Deuteronomy. For there we read:

> So Moses the servant of the Lord died there in the land of
> Moab, according to the word of the Lord. And he was
> buried in the valley in the land of Moab. . . . And Moses
> was a hundred and twenty years old when he died; his
> eye was not dim, nor his natural force diminished. And the
> children of Israel wept for Moses in the plains of Moab
> thirty days, until the days of weeping and mourning for
> Moses were ended. —Deuteronomy 34:5–8

Obviously, Moses couldn't possibly have written a description of his
own death or the mourning that took place after it. Therefore the
rabbis of the Talmud were compelled to say that Joshua, not Moses,
composed the last portion of Deuteronomy.

Over the centuries that followed, various individuals also questioned the Mosaic authorship of other portions of the Torah. One,
for instance, was the great rabbinic scholar, Abraham ibn Ezra, who
lived in Spain in the twelfth century. Among other things, he
pointed out that it was not possible for Moses to have written this
verse from the book of Genesis:

> And Abraham called the name of that place [where he had
> taken Isaac to be sacrificed] Adonai-yireh ["God sees"]; as it
> is said *to this day*: "In the mountain where the Lord is
> seen." —Genesis 22:14

Ibn Ezra knew that Mount Moriah, which is referred to earlier in
the same chapter [Genesis 22:2], was the site of the Temple in
Jerusalem. II Chronicles 3:1 tells us that. Hence the phrase, "as
it is said to this day: 'In the mountain where the Lord is seen,'"
was actually a reference to the Temple. How could Moses have
written this, asked Ibn Ezra? He lived nearly 400 years before
David captured Jerusalem [II Samuel 5:7] or Solomon built the
Temple! [I Kings 6:9].

Another verse Ibn Ezra called attention to was Genesis 36:31

which says: "And these are the kings that reigned in the land of Edom, before any king reigned over the children of Israel." The period of the Hebrew kings, of course, came long after Moses' death. Therefore he could not possibly have written this either.

Such problems as these made it more and more difficult to accept the tradition that Moses had written the whole Torah.

Some Other Difficulties

As time passed, others began to deny that the Torah as a whole was written by any single individual. One of these was Baruch Spinoza, the great seventeenth century philosopher. What disturbed him were the many contradictions and repetitions that he found in the Five Books of Moses.

As one example, Genesis gives two different versions of the creation of woman. In Genesis 2:21–22 we find the description of how God made Adam fall into a deep sleep and took one of his ribs from which He formed Eve. Yet the previous chapter already states: "And God created man in His own image, in the image of God, He created him; *male and female* He created them" [Genesis 1:27]. Obviously there is a contradiction here.

Another example occurs in the story of Noah and the Flood. Genesis 7:12 says that "the rain was upon the earth forty days and forty nights." However, just a few lines later the text says, "And the waters remained upon the earth *a hundred and fifty days*" [Genesis 7:24]. In the same story, we also find that at first, Noah is commanded to bring into the ark two of every kind of animal [Genesis 6:19]. However, shortly afterward God commands him to take seven males and seven females of certain kinds of animals [Genesis 7:2].

These are not the only contradictions and inconsistencies we observe. In fleeing from his brother Esau, who wanted to kill him, Jacob is reported in one passage to have gone to the city of Haran [Genesis 27:43], and in another, to Paddan-aram [Genesis 28:2]. In one passage we read that the merchants to whom Joseph was sold by his brothers were Midianites [Genesis 37:36]; in another they are called Ishmaelites [Genesis 39:1]. In Exodus 2:18, Moses' father-in-law is named Reuel; in Exodus 3:1, Jethro; in Exodus 4:18 he is Jeser; and in Numbers 10:29 he suddenly becomes Hobab. There are many other instances of this kind of thing.

Repetitions of certain biblical incidents also posed problems for Spinoza and other scholars. A good example of such a repetition is an experience that both Abraham and Isaac were said to have undergone. If you will read Genesis 20:1–14 and 26:1–11 you will find almost the same story involving the two Patriarchs, their wives, and King Abimelech.

Little wonder, therefore, that some began to doubt that Moses or any other single individual could have written the entire Torah.

The Rise of Scientific Biblical Study

Jean Astruc, a French Catholic physician, made a fascinating discovery in the eighteenth century which earned him a place in history as the father of the scientific study of the Bible.

In carefully examining the Book of Genesis, Astruc found that various passages employed different Hebrew names for God. One was the word, "Elohim." Another was a name using the letters J-H-V-H which was probably pronounced "Jahveh," but which the Christians mistakenly read as "Jehovah." (Actually the letter "J" is the Hebrew "yod," pronounced like the English letter "Y." So this name for God is really "Yahveh." But with the rise of German biblical scholarship, the J-letter was used since it is pronounced as a "Y" in German. This usage was then carried over into English by early British Bible scholars.)

Since the two names for God, "Elohim" and "J-H-V-H," were not used interchangeably, Astruc found that when he separated the passages containing each name, he had two parallel accounts of certain biblical stories. Thus, as we observe from the following chart, he was able to isolate two different versions of the creation of woman and the Flood story:

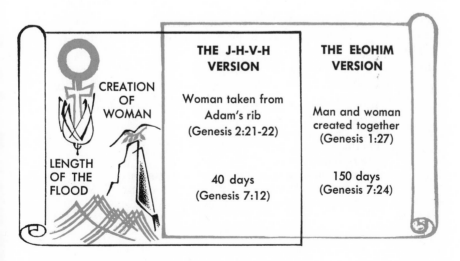

	THE J-H-V-H VERSION	THE EŁOHIM VERSION
CREATION OF WOMAN	Woman taken from Adam's rib (Genesis 2:21-22)	Man and woman created together (Genesis 1:27)
LENGTH OF THE FLOOD	40 days (Genesis 7:12)	150 days (Genesis 7:24)

To Astruc this explained many of the contradictions in the Bible. It also led him to conclude that the Five Books of Moses were actually different collections of material that had been skilfully woven together.

The work of Astruc and of scholars who came after gave rise to the scientific study of the Bible as a literary document with a history of its own, a discipline known as "Biblical Criticism." Instead of viewing the Torah in the traditional sense, as a collection of writings produced by God through Moses, Astruc and later scholars began to study it as material written by many different people over a long period of time.

Today, as the result of some two hundred years of scientific biblical scholarship, we can be certain that not only the Torah section but the whole Bible is a series of writings created and edited by a great many persons over a period of nearly two thousand years.

The Work of Biblical Scholarship

How has biblical scholarship been able to arrive at this conclusion? To a large extent, by carefully examining the text and contents of the Bible itself.

The language of the Bible is a good starting point. The Bible is written in Hebrew, but certain passages are written in Aramaic. This language, similar to Hebrew and using Hebrew characters, was not spoken by Jews generally until around the year 400 B.C.E., at the earliest. The Book of Daniel contains a good bit of Aramaic. We can be sure, therefore, that all the Aramaic passages were written fairly "late" in Jewish history—that is, after 400 B.C.E.

History provides more clues. Through their knowledge of the details of biblical history, scholars are able to relate various statements to particular periods during which they were most probably written. They are often able to date passages in different books by the very circumstances the passages describe.

As an example, let us look at these first six verses of Psalm 137:

> By the rivers of Babylon,
> There we sat; yes, we wept
> When we remembered Zion.
> On the willows there
> We hung up our harps.
> For there our captors demanded of us songs,
> And our tormentors asked of us mirth, saying,
> "Sing us one of the songs of Zion!"

How shall we sing the Lord's song in a foreign land?
If I forget you, O Jerusalem,
Let my right hand wither!
Let my tongue cleave to the roof of my mouth,
If I do not remember you,
If I do not set Jerusalem
Above my highest joy!

We know that beginning in 586 B.C.E. many of the people of the Southern Kingdom of Judah were taken captive to Babylonia. These verses had to be written around this time, for they express the heart-breaking sadness of one of the exiles who went through the actual experience. If this is so, then the Psalm could not have been composed, as tradition maintains, by King David who lived around the year 1000 B.C.E.

Another tool of the biblical scientist is archaeology. As more and more discoveries are made, the findings are proving to be extremely valuable in helping us understand the Bible. Excavations of many ancient cities and historical sites in the State of Israel and the whole Near East have provided us with much new information about the history of biblical times, the circumstances of the people's lives, the dates of events, and the locations of particular places. For example, through the development of a careful system of dating fragments of pottery found in excavations of biblical sites, William F. Albright of Johns Hopkins University has been able to provide us with a highly accurate chronology of ancient events. And thanks to his explorations of the Negev, the southern part of the State of Israel, Dr. Nelson Glueck, president of the Hebrew Union College-Jewish Institute of Religion, has now given us a much better description of the wanderings of the Hebrews in the Wilderness.

Similarly, the discovery and deciphering of ancient inscriptions and documents have helped us to understand obscure sections of the Hebrew text and enabled scholars to prepare more accurate translations of difficult biblical words and passages. Ancient inscriptions have also thrown much light on the life and times of the Hebrew people themselves. For example, from the Lachish letters, written on pieces of pottery by a Judean commander of a nearby military outpost, we have the account of an actual eyewitness to the Babylonian invasion of his country at the beginning of the sixth century B.C.E. [see II Kings 25:1–10]. And the Nuzi clay tablets discovered in northern Mesopotamia, which date back to the time of our Patriarchs, shed light on many of the practices of the Patriarchs, such as the sale of Esau's birthright [Genesis 25:27–34] and Isaac's deathbed blessing [Genesis 27].

Some Things Shared in Common

One fact most clearly revealed by archaeology is that the writers of the Bible lived and shared in the culture that was common to the ancient Near East.

Certainly most of us today realize that much in our own civilization has come from "borrowing" from other peoples. The English language, for example, contains thousands and thousands of words that come directly from other tongues. The ideas and literature of many nations and ages form the foundation of a great deal of our own American culture.

This borrowing also took place in ancient times. Like us, the writers of the Bible made use of the common culture of their time. We know this because many instances of language, incident, law, and practice found in the Bible are similar to instances discovered among other peoples of the ancient Middle East by archaeologists.

The Hebrew writers, however, did not simply reproduce what they borrowed. Rather, they gave it their own distinctive interpretation. We can see this more clearly if we contrast the following story, law, and hymn discovered among the neighbors of the Hebrew people with certain material from the Hebrew Bible.

A Story: A number of years ago, the fragment of an ancient clay tablet was uncovered in the rich soil near the Tigris and Euphrates Rivers of ancient Babylonia, now the country of Iraq. At first the writing on the tablet was unknown, but when it was finally deciphered, the writing was a story, an account of a flood similar to the one described in Genesis 6–8. The hero of the story was a man named Ziugiddu who was informed by the gods that they had decided to send a flood "to destroy the seed of mankind." Ziugiddu was saved from the ravages of the deluge which lasted for seven days and seven nights. Finally Utu, the sun-god, came and brought his light over the land, ending the flood.

This was written around the year 2000 b.c.e., and archaeologists have found two other versions written in later times. Both the later versions contain descriptions of the building of a vessel (an ark?), the destruction of mankind, and the way in which the vessel comes to rest on a mountaintop. Apparently, a tradition of a great flood was shared widely among the peoples of the ancient Middle East.

But the biblical version is certainly not the same as the Babylonian. The principal difference lies in the reasons for the Flood and the deliverance of Noah. The Bible changes the whole meaning and purpose of the story. The idea behind the Bible tale now is the justice of God in punishing the wicked and upholding the righteous. The Flood comes, not from the whim of some deity, but from the righteous character of the Lord Himself who demands righteousness from man. And Noah is saved, not because he is a favorite hero, but, as the Bible tells us, because:

> . . . Noah was a righteous man, blameless in his genera-
> tion; Noah walked with God. —Genesis 6:9

A Law: About the year 1700 B.C.E., there was a ruler of ancient Babylonia named Hammurabi. He had a code of his laws inscribed upon a great black stone which was then set up in an important temple so that his subjects might come to know them well.

At the beginning of this century, Hammurabi's stone pillar was discovered by archaeologists, and translated. Some of Hammurabi's laws sounded familiar, and when scholars looked into the Torah, they found many similarities. If you check the following quotation, you will find it almost identical with Leviticus 24:19–20:

> If a man harm his neighbor, as he has done so will it be
> done to him: wound for wound, eye for eye, tooth for
> tooth; as he has harmed a man, so will it be done to him.

Other parts of Hammurabi's Code likewise bear a very close resemblance to various laws of the Bible. But there are also some differences, very important differences. Here, for example, is one of Hammurabi's laws which surely would have been rejected by the writers of the Bible:

> If a man accuses another of practising sorcery upon him,
> but has not proved it, he against whom the charge of
> sorcery is made shall go to the sacred river. After plunging
> into it, if the sacred river overpowers him, his accuser shall
> take possession of his house. If, however, the sacred river
> shows him to be innocent and he is unharmed, he who
> charged him with sorcery shall be killed. He who plunged
> into the sacred river shall take the house of his accuser.

Compare this with the statements in Exodus 22:18 and Deuteronomy 18:10–12 which condemn all forms of witchcraft.

The most significant difference between the Babylonian Code and the Hebrew Bible is this: at both the beginning and end of his code, Hammurabi takes full credit for the laws. The writers of the Bible ascribe their laws to God!

A Hymn: Around 1370 B.C.E., Amenophis IV became the pharaoh of Egypt. Adopting the name of Akhen-Aton or Ikhnaton, "Aton's man," he proclaimed that the sun, Aton, was the only god of the land. He tried to win over the people to his beliefs but he did not have too much success. In fact, after his death the Egyptians quickly reverted to the worship of their old deities.

However, during his lifetime he did stimulate many new religious writings. Among them was a hymn to the sun-god that was discovered in the Egyptian sands a number of years ago. Here are some lines from this "Hymn in Praise of Aton":

> You appear beautifully on the horizon of heaven,
> O living Aton, the first who lives . . .
> You have filled every land with your beauty . . .
> How much is there that you have made,
> And that is hidden from me,
> O sole god, to whom none is to be likened!
> You did create the world according to your desire,
> While you were alone. . . .
>
> The world is in your hand
> According as you have made them.
> When you rise, they live;
> When you set, they die . . .
> You made the world for your son,
> Who came forth from your body,
> The king of Upper and Lower Egypt. . . .

Now open your Bible to Psalm 104 and compare the two. Yes, you will find some similarities, but the differences are far more striking. The Egyptian hymn has little of the rich poetic beauty of the Hebrew Psalm. Of deeper significance, however, is the fact that the sun here is described as the only god, whereas in the Psalm the sun is merely one of the heavenly bodies under God's control. Again, the Egyptian hymn speaks of the king as a kind of god himself, coming forth directly from the sun, but nowhere in the entire Bible is man considered as anything but mortal. In view of the Hebrews' strict belief in the one God who is the supreme Ruler of the universe, the deification of any human ruler would be inconceivable!

Yes, those who wrote the Bible were influenced by the cultures of their neighbors. But here the matter ends. For whatever ideas they may have borrowed, the authors of the Bible gave them new meaning and purpose through the genius of their own religious outlook.

How the Torah Was Written

Making use of all of the tools of biblical research, then, and putting their knowledge together like pieces of a giant jigsaw puzzle, scholars can tell us how, in general, the different books of the Bible came to be written. While they differ over details, by and large they are in substantial agreement about the question of authorship. Here is their conception of who wrote the Torah section.

Over long centuries, perhaps beginning as early as 2000 B.C.E., the various Hebrew tribes began building up a tradition of legends, anecdotes, historical experiences, laws, poetry, and other material. Some of this they drew from the common culture of the Near East and they reshaped it according to their own needs and beliefs. Much of it, too, may well have originated with the Patriarchs themselves and Moses.

All this material was passed on from generation to generation by word of mouth. It was recounted at tribal campfires and taught by fathers to sons. Even at this early period, some of the material may already have been put into written form. Ample archaeological evidence supports the fact that writing was already practiced in Mesopotamia, Egypt, and Canaan during the age of the Patriarchs. Furthermore, studies have led a growing number of scholars today to regard the oral traditions coming out of very early times as highly reliable.

About 1000 B.C.E., with the founding of the Hebrew kingdom, there began a systematic collection of all this material, and this continued for several centuries. The projects of gathering and assembling the material were carried out by various groups of people who evidently shared a common point of view. We often speak of them as "schools" of writers and editors. The earliest we call J, after the name of the Deity, J-H-V-H, that appears in the writings of this first "school." The work of the J school was probably completed about 850 B.C.E.

The process of gathering material and editing older collections went on. From around 750 to 650 B.C.E., the people of the E school —so called because of the name "Elohim" that they used for the Deity—developed their material, also based on old traditions. In later times, other editors combined the work of the E school with what had been produced by the J school. In some passages they substituted the E version for what they found in J; in others, they combined the two separate accounts. We have already seen examples of the combined accounts in the stories of the creation of woman and the Flood.

Next came the writers of the D school. The name comes from the Book of Deuteronomy, much of which had been prepared by the year 621 B.C.E. In the writings of the D school we find an emphasis upon keeping the commandments of the Lord so that the people may enjoy prosperity. The work of the D editors was finally completed around 550 B.C.E.

The last great school of writers and editors was P, so named because the material has a "priestly" point of view. Most of the Book of Leviticus is the work of this school. By 400 B.C.E., the P school had also succeeded in adding a great deal of material to the already existing collections of J, E, and D. Many scholars believe, for example, that the P school introduced into the story of Abraham's life most of the details regarding the practice of circumcision found in Genesis 17:9–14. The P school is also considered to be responsible for inserting into the account of the Wilderness period many of the laws dealing with the duties and privileges of the priesthood, such as we find in Numbers 18.

Although other gifted individuals, scholars, and thinkers undoubtedly contributed to the development of the Torah section as we now have it, these four schools seem to be responsible for most of its contents. On the following page, in summary-form, are the principal stages by which the Torah is thought to have come into existence. Thus, by about the year 400 B.C.E., the work of producing the Five Books of Moses was virtually finished.

Some Important Conclusions

What, in brief, have we discovered thus far about the authorship of the Torah? Here are four important conclusions:

1. Although tradition maintains that Moses was the author of nearly all the first five books of the Bible, we can be sure that the Torah is the work of many other hands. Much of it may indeed go back to the Patriarchs and to Moses through the transmission of oral and written traditions. However, the contributions of many other individuals and groups of later times are also clearly evident.

Since the Torah is the work of many thinkers and writers, what benefits do we see in this "multiple authorship"? The Torah, as it now stands, more adequately reflects the true values and teachings of Judaism as a whole than would the work of any single individual, no matter how gifted. In the process of sifting and resifting, writing and rewriting, extreme positions were bound to be modified by the experiences, judgments, and beliefs of successive generations of thinkers. Thus, wisdom prevailed. No extreme positions—such as the rigid practices of the Nazirites, for example—were ever established as the norm for Judaism.

HOW THE TORAH CAME TO BE WRITTEN

(According to Many Scholars)

SCHOOLS	DATE	INFORMATION ABOUT THE SCHOOL
J	To About 850 B.C.E.	The J school gets its name from the first letter of J-H-V-H, the name its writers used for the Deity. They were the first to begin the collection of much oral and probably some written material.
E	From About 750-650 B.C.E.	The writers of the E school are so named because they used the word "Elohim" for the Deity. Not only did they make use of ancient traditions of their own but they incorporated these into the older J account to form one common collection.
D	From About 621-550 B.C.E.	It is from the title of the Book of Deuteronomy that the writers of the D school get their name. Not only did they compose the bulk of this book but they also edited and added to the already existing collection of J and E. The D school emphasized the keeping of God's commandments so that people would enjoy His favor.
P	From About 500-400 B.C.E.	P reflects the "priestly" point of view, from which it gets its name. Making use of oral and written sources of their own, these writers were particularly interested in regulations concerning the sacrifices and priesthood. Not only did they compose the bulk of the Book of Leviticus but they also edited and added to the collections of J, E, and D as well.

2. The Torah was not produced during a single lifetime or even during several lifetimes. Rather, it contains material gathered, written, and edited over a span of more than one thousand years. Therefore, the Torah reflects differences in historical conditions, points of view, and emphases. We see how the priestly writers, for example, showed greater concern for ritual matters than the Deuteronomists who put their main stress on obedience to God's ethical and moral demands. Now we can understand why at times we find varying or contradictory statements in the Torah.

Despite all this, the Torah is a unified work. Its underlying unity is based upon a common agreement shared by all its authors about God's role in the life of His people and the expression of His will toward them. This common outlook serves to tie together even the occasional divergent points of view. This basic unified approach undoubtedly enabled generation after generation, for so many centuries, to see the five books of the Torah as a complete unity.

3. Producing the Torah was a continuing process of gathering, compiling, writing, revising, and editing. Sometimes material from different sources was woven into the whole. Often facts from contemporary experience were introduced into ancient material, or earlier traditions were drawn in to support later positions.

The mass of material underwent successive editings and revisions to reflect a continuing expansion and refinement of religious beliefs in the light of changing circumstances. We saw how the Hebrews' God-concept was modified from the anthropomorphic to the more spiritual, and we also noticed how ideas were adapted as the Jewish people gradually changed their way of life from the nomadic to the agricultural. The Torah reveals how the Jewish religion never became static. It was a growing, dynamic faith, continuously groping for greater understanding of God and His will.

4. The Five Books of Moses are the work of human beings. Like human beings of all periods in history, these men were affected by their traditions, the common culture of their world, their loyalties and their animosities, their environment, their outlook and philosophy.

Nonetheless, judged by normal human standards, these writers of the Torah were not ordinary people. They never tried to conceal human weaknesses or shortcomings, for example, even when these were blemishes on their own heroes. Thus they freely told how Jacob and his mother conspired to gain the blessing of Isaac [Genesis 27:1–29]; they did not hide Aaron's participation in the creation and worship of the Golden Calf [Exodus 22:1–6]; nor did they refrain from condemning their own people when their conduct warranted it, as when the Hebrews longed to return to the "flesh-pots" of Egypt [Exodus 16:1–3] or when their greed for quail overcame them [Numbers 11:31–34].

This frankness was deliberate. The writers of the Torah were moved by something far greater than national pride. Their people, they believed, had a destiny beyond that of ordinary nationhood. Bound to God in an eternal covenant, Israel was a people to be trained and disciplined for an ever-higher way of religious living. Therefore, as the Jewish thinkers and writers transmitted their traditions and were influenced by the events of their own times, they were able to maintain a perspective of a sublime goal. The life of their people involved much more than economics or politics. It was a divine challenge, the opportunity for a whole people to direct their normal human activities toward the higher purposes of their Creator. And it is this conception of life, human yet godly, which is set forth in the whole of their writing.

Although the other two major sections of the Bible—the Prophets and the Writings—were prepared in a considerably different fashion, we shall see that the conclusions we have reached regarding the Five Books of Moses generally apply to them as well.

Wanted: More Answers

Thus far we have focussed our attention upon only the first section of the Bible, the Torah or the Five Books of Moses. Yet, in terms of the number of pages, the Torah is only one-quarter of the total Hebrew Scriptures, and it contains only five of the Bible's thirty-nine books.

What about the other thirty-four? Who wrote them? How were they added to our Holy Scriptures? And how was the Bible as a whole completed? These are some of the questions we shall have to investigate.

Something else we may wonder about is how this collection of books came to be looked upon as "holy."

Let's consider what answers biblical scholarship has for us here. . . .

——————— THINGS TO TALK OVER ———————

1. In what ways have the findings of biblical scholarship influenced Reform views toward traditional Jewish practices and beliefs?

2. How does the fact that the Torah was not written exclusively by Moses affect its value for people today?

3. Why do Traditionalists find it necessary to defend the Mosaic author-ship of the Torah?

4. In what ways does the Torah section show the uniqueness of its authors?

──────────── SOME OTHER BIBLE PASSAGES TO CONSIDER ────────

1. To what extent did the writers of the Bible consider Moses the author of the Torah? (Note that where the word "law" appears in the follow- ing selections, the Hebrew has "Torah.") See Joshua 8:31; 23:6; I Kings 2:3; II Kings 23:25; Malachi 3:22.

2. Examine the following verses carefully. How do they serve to con-firm the views of modern scholars about the authorship of the Bible? Genesis 12:6; 36:31; Numbers 21:14; Deuteronomy 1:1. Also compare Exodus 4:20 and 18:2–3.

3. How do we know from the Bible itself that passages in the Aramaic language come from later periods in biblical history? See II Kings 18:13–35; Isaiah 36; Daniel 2:1–4; Ezra 4:7.

4. To what extent did the authors and editors of the Five Books of Moses show a higher sense of purpose for the people of Israel? See Genesis 12:1–9; Exodus 32; Leviticus 26:3–13; Numbers 22:2–24:13; Deuteronomy 28:1–14.

──────────────── FROM THE RABBIS' VIEWPOINT ──────────────

1. THE NATURE OF THE TORAH: See *Everyman's Talmud,* pp. xvi, 30–31, 131–132, 149, 154; and *A Rabbinic Anthology,* pp. lxv–lxxii, [315] pp. 119–120, [408] p. 150, [426] p. 157, [454–458] pp. 170–173.

2. AUTHORSHIP OF THE TORAH: See *Everyman's Talmud,* pp. 150, 154; and *A Rabbinic Anthology,* [364] p. 135, [422] p. 157, [426] pp. 157–158, [431] pp. 159–160, [436] p. 163, [450] pp. 168–169, [1655] pp. 604–605.

3. THE TEXT OF THE TORAH: See *Everyman's Talmud,* pp. 130, 141–142; and *A Rabbinic Anthology,* pp. lxii–lxv.

──────────────── OTHER THINGS TO READ ──────────────────

ALBRIGHT, WILLIAM F., *From the Stone Age to Christianity,* Doubleday, pp. 249–272.

FREEHOF, SOLOMON B., *Preface to Scripture,* Union of American Hebrew Congregations, Chap. 6: "Modern Bible Study," pp. 51–64.

GLUECK, NELSON, *Rivers in the Desert*, Farrar, Straus and Cudahy.

GOLDMAN, SOLOMON, *The Book of Books—An Introduction*, Harper, Chap. 4: "Biblical Criticism," pp. 39–67; Chap. 5: "The Dawn of Conscience," pp. 68–103.

HYATT, J. PHILIP, "The Writing of an Old Testament Book," pp. 22–31, in Ernest G. Wright and David N. Freedman, *The Biblical Archaeologist Reader*, Doubleday.

STEINBERG, MILTON, *Basic Judaism*, Harcourt, Brace, Section 3: "Torah," pp. 18–30.

$\mathcal{E}leven$

HOW THE BIBLE
WAS COMPLETED

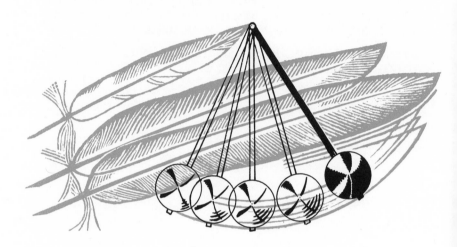

Bibles and Bibles

HAVE YOU EVER LOOKED AT THE "OLD TESTAMENT" PORTIONS OF THE
Protestant and Catholic Bibles? If so, you know that they're not
the same as our Hebrew Scriptures.

What are some of the differences?

The first difference you notice is in the number of books each
contains. The Hebrew Scriptures, you recall, is made up of 39. The
Old Testament of the Protestant Bible contains the same 39. But
the Catholic Old Testament contains seven extra books, making a
total of 46. Among these extras are such books as Judith, the Wisdom of Solomon, I and II Maccabees, and others not found in either
the Hebrew Scriptures or the Authorized Version of the Protestant
Church.

A second difference is the order of the books. In the Hebrew
Scriptures, for instance, the Book of Ruth appears in the final
section, known as "The Writings." But in both the Protestant and
Catholic Old Testaments, Ruth is found among the prophetic
works, just before the two Books of Samuel. And whereas our
Bible ends with the second Book of Chronicles, the Protestant

version closes with Malachi. The Catholic Old Testament ends with II Maccabees, a work that doesn't even appear in our Scriptures.

In the Catholic and Protestant Old Testaments, too, certain of the books have different names. The Catholic Bible calls the Book of Ezra, "I Esdras," and Nehemiah, "II Esdras." For the Song of Songs, both the Protestant and Catholic versions use the title "Song of Solomon."

Finally, neither of the Christian versions has the three separate divisions that we find in the Hebrew Bible. There is only the one Old Testament section as a whole.

You may wonder how these differences came about. The answer lies in the story of how the Bible was completed. To understand this, however, we must first find out how, after the Torah was completed, the other sections came into being.

What the Second Section Contains

If we examine the table of contents of our Bible, we find that all the books are grouped within these three major categories:

1. The Law ("Torah," or the "Five Books of Moses")
2. The Prophets
3. The Holy Writings (or just "Writings").

If we take the initials of the Hebrew words for each section—T from *Torah*, N from *Nevi-im* (Prophets), and CH, another form of the Hebrew letter K, from *K'suvim* (Writings)—we can understand how the Bible as a whole came to be called the *Tanach*.

In the second major section, "The Prophets," we find a total of 21 books, traditionally arranged in two parts. One is customarily called "The Former Prophets," the other "The Latter Prophets." These in turn are further subdivided on the basis of the size of the books into "The Major Prophets" and "The Minor Prophets." The chart on the following page shows at a glance the way these various books are grouped.

The first group, "The Former Prophets," consists of six books. The narrative opens as the Hebrew tribes, now under the leadership of Joshua, cross the Jordan River and move into the land of Canaan. The story continues with the conquest of the country under military leaders called "Judges" and the eventual establishment of a united kingdom under Saul, David, and Solomon. Then, after Solomon's death, comes the history of the divided kingdom. The story ends with the destruction, first, of the Northern Kingdom of Israel, and

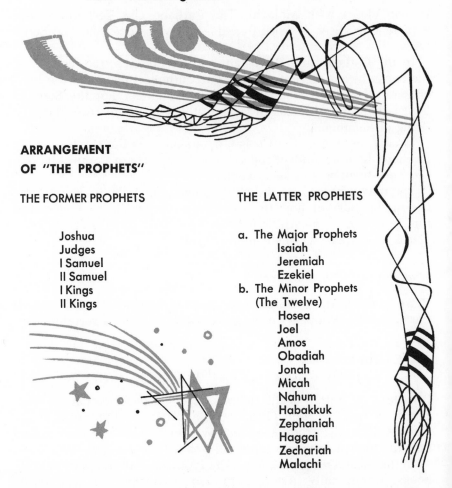

**ARRANGEMENT
OF "THE PROPHETS"**

THE FORMER PROPHETS

Joshua
Judges
I Samuel
II Samuel
I Kings
II Kings

THE LATTER PROPHETS

a. The Major Prophets
   Isaiah
   Jeremiah
   Ezekiel
b. The Minor Prophets
   (The Twelve)
   Hosea
   Joel
   Amos
   Obadiah
   Jonah
   Micah
   Nahum
   Habakkuk
   Zephaniah
   Haggai
   Zechariah
   Malachi

then, of the Kingdom of Judah to the south. In this group of books we meet some of the most famous biblical personalities— Joshua, Samson, Samuel, Saul, David, Solomon, Elijah, Elisha, and many others.

The second group, "The Latter Prophets," consists of fifteen separate books which present the teachings of the prophets of Israel. These begin with the three "Major Prophets," Isaiah, Jeremiah, and Ezekiel, and conclude with the twelve books of the "Minor Prophets." They are called "minor" only because the books are so short.

In this portion, we are introduced to the messages of inspired men who, beginning around the middle of the eighth century B.C.E., preached what they believed to be God's word to the people of both the countries of Israel and of Judah. As we have noted, the prophets emphasized generally that He expected the people to obey

His commandments and practice justice and righteousness. If the people refused, their nations would be destroyed and they would be taken into captivity. For as the one God of the universe, He was fully capable of using the great empires of the times to carry out His judgments.

When these predictions finally came true, the prophets sought to comfort the people. They promised that after the people had been purified through their sufferings, they would eventually be restored to the Land of Israel.

The Final Section: "The Writings"

The last main division of the Bible, "The Writings," contains thirteen books grouped as follows:

ARRANGEMENT OF "THE WRITINGS"

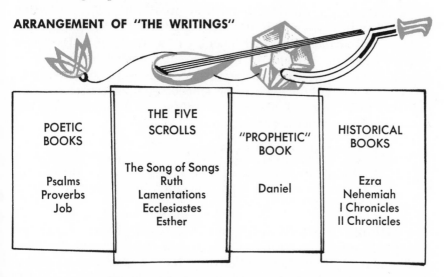

POETIC BOOKS	THE FIVE SCROLLS	"PROPHETIC" BOOK	HISTORICAL BOOKS
Psalms Proverbs Job	The Song of Songs Ruth Lamentations Ecclesiastes Esther	Daniel	Ezra Nehemiah I Chronicles II Chronicles

The first three works—Psalms, Proverbs, and Job—are known as "poetic books" because they are written almost entirely in poetic form. Psalms is a compilation of some of man's greatest inspirational literature. The Psalms express the doubts and hopes, the faith, yearnings, and prayers of its deeply religious authors. We can easily understand why much of the liturgy of both Judaism and Christianity is based upon this book.

Proverbs contains numerous maxims, adages, and sayings about the best way to live. The book advises men to cultivate wisdom, morality, and faith in God. The Book of Job tells the story of how

Satan, with God's consent, tested Job to learn if he was really as righteous as he appeared. In the course of his trials, Job sought to discover why the righteous suffer.

The next series of books is "The Five Scrolls," so named because traditionally each is read in the synagogue in scroll-form on one of the Jewish holidays. At Purim, the Book of Esther, telling of the Jews' triumph over Haman, is read from the "megillah," or "Scroll of Esther." Ecclesiastes, which deals with the question of the real purpose of life, is read on Sukos; the beautiful love poetry of the Song of Songs, on Passover. On Shovuos we read the story of Ruth, the Moabite woman who became a Jewess and, ultimately, the ancestress of King David himself. The Book of Lamentations, as its name indicates, contains "laments" over the destruction of Jerusalem. It is recited on the ninth day of the Hebrew month of Ab (during July or August) because it was on this day, tradition holds (despite the different date given in II Kings 25:8–9), that the First and the Second Jerusalem Temples were destroyed.

The one so-called "prophetic" book in the Writings is Daniel. It offers an exciting account of how a great Jewish hero was saved from a den of lions, and how his three friends were delivered from a fiery furnace without even being singed. This, of course, is testimony to their strong faith in God. In fact, the author even has Nebuchadrezzar, the King of Babylonia, exclaim:

> How great are His [God's] signs,
> How mighty His wonders!
> His kingdom is an everlasting kingdom,
> And His dominion is from generation to generation!
> —Daniel 3:33

The Writings conclude with four "historical" books. Ezra and Nehemiah, originally a single book, tell of the return of the Jews to the Land of Israel after the Babylonian exile of 586 B.C.E. and of their many trials in trying to rebuild the desolate country. I and II Chronicles, also originally one book, retell the history of the Jews from the beginning of mankind to the reign of Cyrus, the Persian conqueror of Babylonia, who, in 538 B.C.E., decreed that the Jews might return to their homeland.

Tradition and the Authorship of the Bible

Tradition had no doubts that Moses was the author of the Torah section. Tradition had positive, clear-cut answers, too, about the authors of the rest of the Bible.

Tradition held that in many instances, such as the books in the Prophetic section, the answers were perfectly plain. The books had been composed by those whose names they bore. Thus, said tradition, Joshua was the author of his own book, Samuel of his two, and all the other prophets produced their own works. Out of the total thirty-nine books of the Bible, then, tradition felt there could be no question about the authorship of twenty.

What about the remaining nineteen? All of these, said tradition, were written either by particular prophets or by others who possessed the "prophetic spirit." So, in addition to writing the Torah, Moses was also supposed to have written the Book of Job. The prophet Samuel, according to tradition, wrote not only his own books, but Judges and Ruth as well. The prophet Jeremiah composed I and II Kings and Lamentations; and Ezra, the Books of Nehemiah and I and II Chronicles. King David with the aid of ten "elders," including Adam, Abraham, and Moses, wrote the Book of Psalms; King Solomon produced Proverbs, the Song of Songs, and Ecclesiastes; and Mordecai, the heroine's cousin, wrote the Book of Esther. Tradition also admitted that certain books, such as Proverbs, Esther, and Daniel, underwent some editing by persons other than their authors.

At the same time tradition has always maintained that the writing of not only the Torah but also the rest of the Bible was motivated by the spirit of God. This contention is not difficult to understand when you think about how great writers find inspiration to write masterpieces. Fundamentally, each writer of the Bible was moved by His spirit, as the Bible specifically states in connection with the prophet Isaiah. For while speaking his message Isaiah tells the people:

> Now the Lord God has sent me, and [inspired with me with] His spirit.—Isaiah 48:16

What Modern Scholarship Says

We firmly believe that the Bible is an inspired work. Yet our conclusions about the authorship of the Prophets and Writings differ in many instances from those of tradition. That is because we accept the validity of many of the findings of modern biblical scholarship regarding all three sections of the Bible. While scholars may disagree about details, they do hold certain opinions in common about the authorship of the books in the Prophets and Writings.

On the following page is a chart summarizing the findings of

WHO WROTE THE PROPHETIC BOOKS?

(According to Many Scholars)

SECTION AND BOOK	THE TRADITIONAL VIEW	THE VIEW OF MODERN SCHOLARSHIP
Former Prophets:		
Joshua	Joshua (except for the concluding verses)	The D school who used material from J and E
Judges	Samuel	The D school who used material from J and E
I and II Samuel	Samuel	The D school who used earlier sources, possibly from J and E
I and II Kings	Jeremiah	The D school who used existing histories and legends
Latter Prophets:		
Major		
Isaiah	Isaiah	Isaiah, at least 2 other anonymous prophets, and editors
Jeremiah	Jeremiah	Jeremiah, other writers, and editors
Ezekiel	Ezekiel	Ezekiel and editors
Minor		
Hosea	Hosea	Hosea and editors
Joel	Joel	Joel and editors
Amos	Amos	Amos and editors
Obadiah	Obadiah	Obadiah, another writer, and editors
Jonah	Jonah	A literary work by an unknown author
Micah	Micah	Micah, other writers, and editors
Nahum	Nahum	Nahum, other writers, and editors
Habakkuk	Habakkuk	Habakkuk, other writers, and editors
Zephaniah	Zephaniah	Zephaniah, other writers, and editors
Haggai	Haggai	Haggai and editors
Zechariah	Zechariah	Zechariah, other writers, and editors
Malachi	Malachi	Unknown author and editors

WHO WROTE THE WRITINGS?
(According to Many Scholars)

SECTION AND BOOK	THE TRADITIONAL VIEW	THE VIEW OF MODERN SCHOLARSHIP
Poetical Books		
Psalms	David and ten "elders"	Many authors of religious poems, and editors
Proverbs	Solomon and editors	Many authors of folk wisdom, and editors
Job	Moses	An unknown author who used folk material, and editors
Five Scrolls		
Song of Songs	Solomon	Many authors of love poems, and editors
Ruth	Samuel	A literary work by an unknown author
Lamentations	Jeremiah	Many authors of dirges, and editors
Ecclesiastes	Solomon	An unknown author and editors
Esther	Mordecai and editors	A literary work by an unknown author
"Prophetic"		
Daniel	Daniel and editors	A literary work by one or more authors who made use of folk tales
Historical		
Ezra	Ezra	Later elements of the P school, called "The Chronicler"
Nehemiah	Ezra	Later elements of the P school, called "The Chronicler"
I Chronicles II Chronicles	Ezra	Later elements of the P school, called "The Chronicler"

biblical scholars and comparing them with the views of tradition. From this chart we see that modern scholarship has reached two main conclusions about the authorship of the prophetic books. First, as with the Torah section, the Former Prophets also seem to have been produced by various schools of writers. Scholars believe that the Deuteronomic school, using material similar to that of J and E in the Torah, are chiefly responsible for writing most of Joshua, Judges, Samuel, and Kings.

Second, although the books we call the Latter Prophets do show signs of considerable editing, they do seem in the main to have been written by the men whose names they bear. There are just two exceptions. One is the Book of Isaiah, which most scholars agree is the work of at least three distinct prophets who lived at different times. The other is the Book of Jonah which is a literary work produced by some unknown writer.

The situation regarding the Writings, however, is quite different, as we can see from the chart on page 209. Here we note that the books comprising this section of the Bible fall into three main categories. They are (1) collections of material written over a long period of time that were gathered and edited into a single book, like Psalms, Proverbs, and the Song of Songs; or (2) literary works by unknown authors, such as the Books of Ruth, Esther, and Daniel; or (3) the so-called "historical" works of Ezra, Nehemiah, and I and II Chronicles. Scholars have given to the authors of this last group of books the common name of "The Chronicler" because they all held similar views, resembling those of the P school.

Interestingly enough, we cannot be sure of the name of a single author of any of the books making up the Writings section.

Some Similar Conclusions

Despite the fact that we seem to have much more definite information about who wrote the Latter Prophets and very little about those who wrote the books of the Writings section, we find that in general our conclusions about the authorship of the Torah also apply to the other sections as well.

There is a major difference, of course, in the process by which the books in the Prophets and Writings sections came to be written. Only the books contained in the Earlier Prophets—Joshua, Judges, I and II Samuel, and I and II Kings—and the so-called "historical books" of the Writings section—Ezra, Nehemiah, and I and II Chronicles—are the products of "schools." All the rest are the works principally of individual writers. Thus, the Book of Isaiah is chiefly a compilation of the writings of several prophets, and the Psalms, a compendium of poetic prayers of individuals. The Books of Jonah and Esther are both, fundamentally, the literary works of individual authors.

Yet, with these exceptions, the Prophets and Writings sections of the Bible do share four characteristics of the Torah:

1. The books in the Prophets and the Writings reflect the work of many hands—authors, compilers, and editors. As such, then, they represent more than the views of a single individual. In their final form, they show the thinking of Judaism as a whole.

A striking example is the Book of Ecclesiastes. Its author, who was called Koheleth, was quite pessimistic, you will remember, about the purpose and value of life. "Vanity of vanities," he declared, "everything is in vain [Ecclesiastes 1:2]. Therefore his advice was:

> Go, eat your bread with enjoyment,
> And drink your wine with a merry heart,
> For God has already approved [decided] what you do.
> —Ecclesiastes 9:7

But note the more hopeful conclusion which a later writer appended to the Book of Ecclesiastes:

> [This is] the end of the matter; all has been heard. [The conclusion is:] fear God and keep His commandments, for this is the whole duty of man. For God will bring every deed into judgment, [even] every secret thing, whether good or evil. —Ecclesiastes 12:13–14

Thus, although Koheleth was free to give expression to his own point of view, a later writer added on the judgment of normative Judaism. Here this anonymous author reaffirmed the essential purpose and value of life as the Jewish religion saw them, correcting the extreme, more pessimistic outlook of Koheleth.

2. Like the Torah section, the Prophets and Writings took shape over an extended period of time and therefore often reveal differences in emphasis. Compare, for example, the point of view of "The Chronicler" who strongly opposes intermarriage [see Ezra 9:12–10:17 and Nehemiah 13:23–30] with that of the author of the Book of Ruth who praises a Moabitess [see Ruth 1; 4:11–22].

Yet, despite conflicting views, there is the same underlying unity to these sections that we found in the Torah. Throughout the books of these two sections, we see a consistent effort to interpret the will of God for His people. This effort serves to unify the varying points of view. While the books may contain differences in interpretations of His will, they nevertheless reveal an underlying quest for the holy life—a quest that motivates every writer.

3. Producing the books in the Prophets and the Writings sections, like the effort in producing the books of the Torah, was also a process of compiling, writing, revising, and editing over a long period of time. The Books of Proverbs and Lamentations represent a collection of material gathered over an extended period, and the Books of Joshua and Judges show evidence of much editorial work. But this is inevitable in the case of a religion like Judaism which continued to grow as its followers underwent new experiences and sought to interpret them in the light of an ever-higher conception of God and His will.

4. As is the case with the books of the Torah, those of the Prophets and Writings were also written by enormously gifted and inspired humans. No ordinary people could have written the magnificent works of the Major Prophets, for example, or the Books of Psalms and Job. They are literary masterpieces in their own right. And they have moved the minds and stirred the spirits of every generation of mankind in the entire civilization of the world for well over two thousand years. These Bible authors were rare individuals indeed: their ancient insights have applied to men down to, and including, our own age. From these talented men has come our sense of higher purpose to living in accordance with God's will for Israel and all mankind.

The Completion of the Torah

It is one thing to attempt to find out who wrote the Bible. It is another to discover how all the books were finally gathered together into the three great collections we have today. That is a story in itself.

Scholars believe generally that the three major sections—the Torah, Prophets, and Writings—were completed in precisely that order. Hence, to know when the Bible as a whole came into being, we must look into the development of each section.

The Bible itself provides a clue about the completion of the Torah section. We can be sure that the process was well under way by the year 621 B.C.E., because of this section in II Kings 22:

> Josiah was eight years old when he began to reign [over Judah], and he reigned thirty-one years in Jerusalem. . . .

In the eighteenth year of King Josiah, the king sent Shaphan . . . to the house of the Lord [the Temple], saying, "Go up to Hilkiah the high priest, that he may reckon the amount of money that has been brought into the house of the Lord . . . and collected from the people. And let it be turned over to the workmen who . . . are repairing the house of the Lord, that is, to the carpenters, builders, masons, as well as for the purchase of timber and stone for repairing the building. . . ."

And Hilkiah the high priest said to Shaphan the [king's] secretary [when he arrived at the Temple]: "I have found the book of the law [Torah] in the house of the Lord." And Hilkiah gave the book to Shaphan who read it.

. . . Then Shaphan the secretary told the king, "Hilkiah the priest has given me a book." And Shaphan read it before the king.

And when the king heard the words of the book of the law [Torah] he rent his clothes. And the king commanded . . . "Go [to one of the prophets], inquire of the Lord for me and for the people and for all Judah concerning the words of this book that has been found, for great is the wrath of the Lord that is kindled against us because our fathers have not obeyed the words of this book, to do according to all that is written concerning us." —II Kings 22:1–13

What was this book of the Torah? From its description, scholars believe it must have been a considerable portion of Deuteronomy, the fifth book of the Bible. Therefore, we know that by the year 621 B.C.E., when this event is usually dated, a definite Torah section was already developing.

And in the following speech by Jeremiah denouncing the people of Judah, we can see that the Torah was also beginning to be looked upon as the sacred "word of the Lord":

> How can you say, "We are wise,
> And the Torah of the Lord is with us"?
> Behold the false pen of the scribes
> Has made it a lie.
> The wise men shall be put to shame,
> They shall be dismayed and taken.
> Lo, they have rejected the word of the Lord,
> And what wisdom is in them? —Jeremiah 8:8–9

At the same time, it is generally believed that the work of producing the Torah was not completed before the time of Ezra and Nehemiah. Both these men, you will recall, labored with those who re-

turned from Babylonian exile to Palestine. Look at this statement
from the Book of Nehemiah:

> On the second day the heads of the fathers' houses of all
> the people, with the priests and Levites, came together to
> Ezra the scribe in order to study the words of the Torah.
> And they found it written in the Torah that the Lord had
> commanded by Moses that the people of Israel should dwell
> in booths during the feast of the seventh month [Sukos],
> and that they should publish and proclaim in all their
> towns and in Jerusalem, "Go out to the hills and bring
> branches of olive, wild olive, myrtle, palm, and other leafy
> trees to make booths, as it is written."
>
> So the people went out and brought them and made booths
> for themselves, each on his roof and in their courts, and in
> the courts of the house of God, and in the square at the
> Water Gate and in the square of the Gate of Ephraim. And
> all the assembly of those who had returned from the cap-
> tivity made booths and dwelt in booths; for from the days
> of Joshua, the son of Nun, to that day the people of Israel
> had not done so. And there was very great rejoicing.
>
> And day by day, from the first day to the last day, he read
> from the book of the Torah of God. They kept the feast
> seven days; and on the eighth day there was a solemn as-
> sembly, according to the ordinance. —Nehemiah 8:13–18

This seems to imply that until around 450 B.C.E., when Ezra gave
a public reading of the "Torah," neither the priests nor the people
knew how to celebrate the Sukos festival. But if the entire Torah
had been in existence before this, surely they would have had
ample information from Leviticus 23:39–43. Therefore, many
scholars reason that the Torah could only have been finished
somewhat around this time or shortly after.

When this happened is not at all definite, but we do have a clue.
Around 400 B.C.E., we think, a dispute broke out between the Jews
who had returned from Babylonia, and the Samaritans, the people
who then occupied the northern part of Palestine. We read of this
conflict in Nehemiah, beginning with 3:33. [See also Ezra 9:1–2;
10:2, 11.] Although rebuffed by the returning exiles, the Samaritans
continued to look upon themselves as Jews and to carry on various
Jewish practices.

There is still a very small community of their descendants living
today in the State of Jordan. A few dozen remaining Samaritans are
found in the State of Israel. Significantly, the only Scriptures which
they accept as sacred is the present Torah section. This leads many
scholars to conclude that the Torah as a whole must have already
been in existence around the year 400 B.C.E.

The Completion of the Prophetic Section

The material that went into the Prophetic books was also gathered over a long period of time. Actually, some of it, such as portions of Joshua and Judges, may be as old as any material in the Torah itself.

On the other hand, some of the contents of the Latter Prophets —especially certain additions to the Book of Isaiah—and several writings of the Minor Prophets, may have come from as late as the fourth or even third century B.C.E. However, we can be reasonably sure that by the year 200 B.C.E., the Prophetic section was practically in the form we have today.

How do we know this? We surmise it from the fact that the Book of Daniel, a "prophetic" book, appears among the Writings, and not the Prophets, where it logically belongs.

In a number of ways Daniel appears to be very much like one of the prophets. Like Jeremiah he is rescued from danger [Daniel 3:19–28], and he has visions from God in which he predicts future happenings. For instance, he foresees that the empire of Alexander the Great, the Greek conqueror of the Persians, will be divided up among his four successors [see Daniel 11:2–4].

Yet this book was not included within the Prophets section. Evidently, say many scholars, this is because it was written *after* the Prophets section had already been completed. And since the date generally given for the composition of the Book of Daniel is sometime around 170 B.C.E., the Prophetic section must have been finished before then, or roughly around the year 200 B.C.E.

Another piece of evidence also tends to support this conclusion. It comes from one of the extra books found in the Catholic Old Testament, the one called "Ecclesiasticus" (not the same as the Ecclesiastes of our Bible). This was written by a Jewish school teacher named Ben-Sirach who, we know, lived around 180 B.C.E.

In this work Ben-Sirach pays honor to his Jewish ancestors and summarizes their great achievements, listing among them the biblical books in order. Here, not only does he refer to the Torah section but he also mentions the books of the Former and Latter Prophets. This provides us with more proof for the theory that sometime around the year 200 B.C.E., the first two sections of the Hebrew Scriptures must already have been complete.

The Development of the Writings

From the same work of Ben-Sirach we learn that in his day, around 180 B.C.E., the Books of Psalms, Proverbs, Ezra and Nehemiah, and perhaps even Job, were already in circulation. Many scholars believe that by this time, too, the Books of Daniel and I and II Chronicles were also in existence, and that gradually, by about 150 B.C.E., the rest of the books had appeared.

But several centuries elapsed before the entire Writings section was officially completed. We know that even during the lifetime of Flavius Josephus, a Jewish historian who wrote during the latter half of the first century C.E., not all of the books in the Writings had yet been accepted as part of Scripture. In his own words, we find Josephus saying:

> Of these [the books of the Bible], five are those of Moses, which contain the laws and the tradition as to the origin of mankind till his death. . . . The prophets who came after Moses wrote of the things that came to pass in their times. . . . The remaining four books contain hymns to God and precepts [teachings] for the conduct of human life. . . . —*Against Apion,* I: 8

Many interpret this and other evidence to mean that the Writings in the time of Josephus consisted of Psalms, the Song of Songs, Proverbs, and Ecclesiastes. It is also likely, say some, that Josephus included the Books of Ruth and Lamentations in the Prophetic section.

Meanwhile, in addition to the books that now comprise the Writings, many others were in circulation. Some—Ecclesiasticus, Judith, Tobit, and Maccabees, for example—were quite popular with the people. From the Mishnah we know that a number of the early rabbis were very much in favor of including Ben-Sirach's work in the Bible.

But many rabbis objected not only to the inclusion of this book, but even to some that now appear in the Bible. One such book was Esther, which was frowned upon because it did not mention God. The strongest opposition, however, was directed against the Song of Songs and Ecclesiastes. The former was looked upon as mere love poetry; the latter was held to contradict certain teachings of Judaism. However, both were finally included after explanations and additions were made. The Song of Songs was reinterpreted to mean an expression of love between God and His people, Israel.

Some material, especially the conclusion, was added to Ecclesiastes advising the people to keep God's commandments.

How the Bible Was "Closed"

Debates among the rabbis about these and other books continued well on into the second century of the Common Era. Nevertheless, by the end of the previous century, the process of "closing" the Bible—that is, determining which books were to be included in the Writings section—was well on its way.

Apparently two sets of circumstances hastened the decision. One was the unsettled conditions that followed the destruction of Jerusalem by the Romans in 70 C.E. This violent disruption of Jewish life threatened the continued existence of Jewish literature. Evidently, to insure the survival of the most important books, the rabbis were moved to come to a decision about which books should be part of the Bible.

The second circumstance was the rise of Christianity. By the second century C.E., the young Church had not only adopted the "Old Testament" as part of its Scriptures, but had also included within its own version most of the other books about which the Jews still had reservations. As a result, the rabbis were under some pressure to define precisely which books the Jews considered sacred.

By now only a few books among the Writings were still being debated. Popular appeal was given some weight. But for the rabbis, a more important consideration was whether the work had been "properly inspired"—that is, whether it had been written by a prophet or someone else who possessed the prophetic spirit, such as Moses, King David, or King Solomon. And since the rabbis maintained that prophecy had ceased with Ezra, only those books whose authors lived before Ezra could properly receive consideration.

Thus a book like Ecclesiasticus, known to have been written by Ben-Sirach who lived nearly three centuries after Ezra, did not qualify. Nor did the Books of the Maccabees which had to be written sometime after the Maccabean revolt that began in 167 B.C.E. By the time of the rabbinic debates, tradition had already ascribed ancient authorship for books like Esther, Ecclesiastes, and the Song of Songs. King Solomon, tradition said, was supposed to have written Ecclesiastes and the Song of Songs; and Mordecai, the Book of Esther. Hence it was possible for these books to win approval.

Once the rabbis approved inclusion, all the material in the accepted books was regarded as "inspired" by God through the prophetic spirit. All books already included in the Bible were considered sacred. Unquestionably the holiness of the Torah and Prophetic sections had long been accepted. But once the decision was reached about the Writings, its books, too, became sacred. However, of all the sections, the Torah continued to be looked upon as the holiest.

We cannot be sure when the third section was finally closed. The Mishnah tells us the matter was discussed during certain gatherings of rabbis in the years 90 and 118 c.e. By this time, while there appears to have been general agreement about the contents of the Writings section, some authorities still had reservations about certain books.

Eventually, evidently sometime during the second century of the Common Era—perhaps around the year 125—the present thirty-nine books became accepted as the Jewish "canon." This term comes from the Greek word for "rule," and was used by the Christians to refer to the books they considered genuine Holy Scripture.

The Books Outside the Canon

What happened to the books outside the canon—that is, those that were not taken into the Hebrew Bible?

Some disappeared. Many, however, were preserved, and these became part of the Septuagint, the Greek translation of the Bible.

According to a legend, a ruler of Egypt wanted a Greek translation of the Hebrew Bible. Seventy (or seventy-two) Jewish scholars were put into separate rooms, each with instructions to prepare a translation. At the end of seventy days each had completed the task. Miraculously, all seventy versions turned out to be identical! Hence the name given that translation, "Septuagint," from the Latin for "seventy."

The truth is that it was the Jews of Alexandria, Egypt, who undertook to have the Bible translated. Beginning as far back as the Babylonian destruction of Jerusalem in 586 B.C.E., there were settlements of Jews in Egypt. The Book of Jeremiah tells us:

> When Jeremiah finished speaking to all the people [warning them in God's name not to flee from the Babylonians by going to Egypt], Azariah . . . and other insolent men said to Jeremiah, "You are telling a lie. The Lord our God did not send you to say, 'Do not go to Egypt to live there.' But Baruch the son of Neriah [Jeremiah's scribe] has set you against us, to deliver us into the hand of the Chaldeans [Babylonians], that they may kill us or take us into exile in Babylon."

So . . . all the people did not obey the voice of the Lord
[telling them] to remain in the land of Judah. But . . . the
commanders of all the forces took all those who remained
in Judah, . . . including Jeremiah the prophet and Baruch
the son of Neriah. And they came into the land of Egypt,
for they did not obey the voice of the Lord.
    —Jeremiah 43:1–7

In the centuries that followed, more and more Jews went there,
especially after the Greek conquest of the Middle East by Alexander
the Great toward the end of the fourth century B.C.E. Soon most of
the Jews of Egypt spoke only Greek, and they required a Greek
translation of the Hebrew Bible.

Hence, starting with the translation of the Torah section during
the third century B.C.E., the Septuagint slowly came into being.
Gradually over the succeeding centuries, other sections of the
Hebrew Bible were added, until, at its completion, the Septuagint also included fourteen of the books outside the Jewish
canon. Among them were the two Books of Maccabees, Ben-
Sirach's Ecclesiasticus, Tobit, Judith, and the Wisdom of Solomon.

Later, when the Christians accepted the Old Testament as part of
their Bible, they chose, not the Hebrew Scriptures, but the Greek
translation. Hence the Greek name "Esdras" for Ezra in the Catholic
Bible. Furthermore the books outside the Jewish canon were automatically preserved by the Church which looked upon them as also
holy. To this day they are still an official part of the Roman
Catholic Bible.

The fact that the Christians adopted the Greek translation, the
Septuagint, which was arranged differently, likewise explains why
the order of the books in the Catholic and Protestant Old Testaments differs from that in the Hebrew Scriptures.

When Protestantism arose in the sixteenth century its followers
questioned the sacredness of the books outside the Jewish canon.
At first, the Protestants put these "extra" books at the end of their
Bible. Then, about a century and a half ago, they removed them
altogether.

In Judaism, once these books had been excluded from the Bible,
they became known by the Greek word *apocrypha*—works no
longer considered sacred, therefore, "hidden away" or "kept secret."
Yet they have remained one of our most important sources of information about the religious and historical developments that took
place within Judaism during the period between the compilation of
the Writings section and the appearance of the New Testament. In

THE CREATION OF THE BIBLE (*indicates approximate date)

KEY EVENTS	B.C.E.	TORAH	PROPHETS	WRITINGS
Age of the Patriarchs	2000	Beginning of oral traditions		
	1500			
Exodus from Egypt (*1250)		Oldest written material	Oldest material of Former Prophets written	
Start of the Hebrew Kingdom	1000			
Division of the Kingdom (926)				
		Work of J school (to *850)		
Activity of Amos, Hosea, Isaiah, Micah (*750)			Writing of Latter Prophets begun	
		Work of E school (*750-650)		
Fall of Northern Kingdom (721)				
		Book of Deuteronomy found (621)		
Jeremiah's ministry				*Certain psalms, proverbs written
Fall of Southern Kingdom (586)		Work of D school (*621-550)		
Ezekiel and Second Isaiah				
Cyrus permits return of exiles (538)				
	500	Work of P school (*500-400)		
Start of Samaritan conflict (*400)		Torah section completed (*400)		
Conquest of Palestine by Alexander the Great (331)			Prophetic section completed (*200)	Psalms, Proverbs, Ezra, Nehemiah, and other Writings in existence
Septuagint begins				
Ben-Sirach's Ecclesiasticus written (*180)				All books in existence (by *160)
Birth of Jesus (*4)	C.E.			Debate of rabbis about inclusion of various books
Romans destroy Jerusalem (70)				Writings section finally closed (*125)

chapter 4 of I Maccabees, for instance, we learn of the first observance of Chanuko.

Today the fourteen books outside the Jewish canon appear in a
single volume, appropriately named "The Apocrypha."

Only the Half-Way Mark

With the completion of the Torah around 400 B.C.E., of the Prophets
about 200 B.C.E., and of the Writings sometime around 125 C.E.,
the work of creating the Bible came to an end. The experiences of
about two thousand years and the work of innumerable hands had
gone into this task.

Taking all this into account, there is no doubt that the creation of
the Bible is one of the world's most remarkable achievements. For
had the process of collecting, organizing, writing, and editing
ceased at any point, the Bible as we now know it would never
have come into existence.

Still, we have reached only the half-way mark in telling its
history. To have come down to us in the second half of the
twentieth century, the Bible had to survive almost another two
thousand years. That we possess essentially the same Bible as did
our ancestors at the end of the first century C.E. is another extraordinary achievement of history.

For, in the course of the centuries that intervened, thousands of
other important works disappeared. Many of the Greek and Roman
classics written at about the same time our Bible was completed
were totally destroyed in wars, fires, upheavals of empires, and other
disasters that occurred during those long years. Even writings produced much later, like those of Caedmon, an English poet who lived
in the seventh century C.E., have vanished without a trace.

How is it, then, that the Bible has survived?

──────────────── THINGS TO TALK OVER ────────────────

1. Why do the Scriptures appear so much more remarkable from the
standpoint of modern biblical scholarship than from that of tradition?

2. If the decision about which books to include in the biblical canon
were being made today, what would be your position? Why?

3. In what respects do we have a better understanding of the Bible
than people who lived three or four centuries ago?

4. What does the very process by which the Bible came into existence
tell us about the nature of the Jewish religion?

1. In what respects do I and II Chronicles show some of the emphases of the P school? Compare each of the following parallel passages: I Chronicles 15:25–28 and II Samuel 6:12–15; I Chronicles 21:1–30 and II Samuel 24:1–25; II Chronicles 22:10–23:21 and II Kings 11.

2. How do the following passages reveal that the Prophets and Writings sections also underwent rewriting and editing? Compare Joshua 4:8, 4:9, and 4:20; compare Judges 4:4–22 and 5; compare Isaiah 36–39 and II Kings 18:13–20:19; compare Proverbs 10:4 with 10:22.

3. What evidence do we have from the Bible itself that its authors used other sources for some of their information? See Joshua 10:13; II Samuel 1:18; I Kings 11:41; II Kings 1:18; II Kings 15:36.

4. Why would the rabbis have objected to the following in the so-called "disputed" books: Song of Songs 1:2–4; Ecclesiastes 9:2–3? Why would Esther 4:13–14 and Ecclesiastes 5:1–6 have inclined them to view these two books favorably?

——————— FROM THE RABBIS' VIEWPOINT ———————

1. THE PROPHETS SECTION AND ITS AUTHORS: See *Everyman's Talmud*, pp. 130–132, 149–151; and *A Rabbinic Anthology*, p. lxvii, [427–429] pp. 158–159.

2. THE WRITINGS AND THEIR AUTHORS: See *Everyman's Talmud*, pp. 150–153; and *A Rabbinic Anthology*, pp. lxvii–lxviii, [427–429] pp. 158–159, [1060] p. 392 (see footnote).

3. THE "CLOSING" OF SCRIPTURE: See *Everyman's Talmud*, pp. 151–154; and *A Rabbinic Anthology*, [559] p. 206, [1400 and comment] pp. 494–495.

——————— OTHER THINGS TO READ ———————

BROWNE, LEWIS, *The Wisdom of Israel*, Modern Library, Part 2: "Between the Testaments," pp. 87–144.

FREEHOF, SOLOMON B., *Preface to Scripture*, Union of American Hebrew Congregations, Chap. 2: "How the Bible Grew," pp. 13–22.

GOLDMAN, SOLOMON, *The Book of Books—An Introduction*, Harper, Chap. 3: "The Hebrew Canon," pp. 27–38.

MARGOLIS, MAX S., *The Hebrew Scriptures in the Making*, Jewish Publication Society.

ROTH, CECIL, editor, *Standard Jewish Encyclopedia*, Doubleday, "Apocrypha and Pseudepigrapha," pp. 131–133.

Twelve

HOW THE BIBLE CAME TO US

Finding Buried Treasure

IT WAS SOMETIME IN FEBRUARY OR MARCH OF 1947. THE PLACE was the Land of Israel. There, in the foothills overlooking the Dead Sea, a fifteen-year-old Bedouin boy named Mohammad the Wolf was tending a herd of goats. Suddenly he noticed that one goat was missing. Off he went after the stray.

Climbing up the rocky cliff before him, the lad spied the opening to a cave. Thinking perhaps that the goat might have wandered in, Mohammad picked up a stone and threw it inside. There was a loud crash, and he ran away frightened.

A little later he thought about what had happened. His curiosity was aroused; perhaps there was a treasure in the cave. So Mohammad persuaded one of his friends to return with him. Back to the cliff they went. Cautiously they entered the cave. But instead of gold or jewels they found only a few tall clay jars with the fragments of many others scattered about. Standing in some of the broken jars were rolls of old leather wrapped in dirty cloth.

Mohammad and his friend wondered about the unopened jars. The lids were hard to get off because they were so tightly sealed, but they finally managed to open one. Inside was a cylindrical object covered with a black, tar-like substance which they hurriedly removed. Beneath was merely a scroll with faded writing in parallel columns. The other jars contained similar scrolls.

Though Mohammad did not find what he hoped, he did indeed stumble upon buried treasure. For what he discovered, and what others have since found in other caves in the region, were the now-famous "Dead Sea Scrolls," a priceless collection of ancient manuscripts.

Among the most important of these is a scroll of the Book of Isaiah which, according to most scholars, was written during the first or second century before the Common Era.

What the Isaiah Scroll Tells Us

That Isaiah Scroll is the oldest complete manuscript of any book of the Bible we now possess. Its importance lies in the fact that it offers us some very valuable information about how carefully the text of the Bible was transmitted.

We must remember that the material of this Isaiah Scroll is some 2100 years old, which means that it is that much closer to the time the original book was written than our own twentieth century copies of Hebrew Scriptures. But what is the significance of this? Well, we know that up to the time the first complete Hebrew text of the Bible was printed in 1488, every copy of the Bible had to be produced by hand. Therefore, our Hebrew Scriptures today had to undergo about 1600 years more of this handwritten copying than the Dead Sea Scroll; consequently, our Bible today has had far more opportunity to gather errors and changes. For if, in spite of all our modern techniques of typesetting and proofreading, we still come across errors in printed material, we can be sure that in handwritten manuscripts of olden times many more errors were certainly bound to occur.

If you've ever copied a lengthy passage from a book, you know how true this is. Your eye may jump from one word on, say, line five, to the same word say, on line ten, and skip everything in between. Or you might move back to the same word some lines earlier and repeat the very material you have already copied. Sometimes you unconsciously substitute a different word for one in the text, or restate what you are copying in a different way. And of course you may also make errors in spelling, punctuation, and the like.

Ancient copyists did all of this. Our version of Leviticus 20:10 provides a good example. The text there reads:

And the man who commits adultery with another man's
wife, he that commits adultery with the wife of his neighbor, both the adulterer and the adulteress shall surely be
put to death.

Here it is certainly clear that the same phrase, "the man who commits adultery with another man's [neighbor's] wife" has been repeated.

But copyists also made many other kinds of mistakes. Occa-
sionally, when they had difficulty in making out a word, phrase,
or sentence, they would change it or leave it out entirely. We can
see that in the following verse from I Samuel 13:1 several numbers have been omitted:

Saul was ——— years old when he began to reign; and he
reigned ——— and two years over Israel.

Sometimes copyists would incorporate in the text notes that a previous reader had jotted down in the margin, or else add explanations of their own. The statement, "At that time the Canaanites
were in the land," in the following passage from Genesis 12:6 may
well have been such an explanatory note designed to make the
point even clearer to the reader:

Abram passed through the land to the place at Shechem,
to the oak of Moreh. *At that time the Canaanites were
in the land.*

Copyists even edited portions of the manuscript or inserted material they found elsewhere. This undoubtedly happened in connection with Isaiah 2:2–4. There we read the following prophecy:

It shall come to pass in the latter days
That the mountain of the house of the Lord
Shall be established as the highest of the mountains,
And shall be raised above the hills;
And all the nations shall flow unto it,
And many peoples shall come and say:
"Come, let us go up to the mountain of the Lord,
To the house of the God of Jacob;
That He may teach us His ways
And that we may walk in His paths."
For out of Zion shall go forth the law,
And the word of the Lord from Jerusalem.
He shall judge between the nations,
And shall decide for many peoples;
And they shall beat their swords into ploughshares,
And their spears into pruning-hooks;
Nation shall not lift up sword against nation,
Neither shall they learn war anymore.

Now compare this with what appears in Micah 4:1–3. We see that somehow the words of Micah also came to be attributed to Isaiah.

Furthermore we must remember that all errors and changes were automatically perpetuated as each copy in turn served as the model for others. And with every reproduction of the text, still other changes might be introduced.

As a result, over the twenty-one centuries since the Isaiah Scroll was written, we would naturally expect to find a great many differences between it and our own printed Hebrew text.

Strangely, this is not the case. In the main, the texts of both read similarly, and where they differ, our traditional version is far more reliable than that of the Dead Sea Scroll. So much so that recently, when the Protestants were revising the English translation of their Bible, they found only thirteen instances where they preferred the text of the Dead Sea Scroll, and most of the differences were slight indeed. For example, in Isaiah 60:19 the Dead Sea text adds the words "by night" to this passage:

> The sun shall be no more your light by day,
> Nor for brightness shall the moon give light to you [*by night*].

What the Isaiah Scroll tells us, then, is that our traditional Jewish biblical text has remained remarkably faithful to the original over all these centuries. Or, as Millar Burrows, a well-known expert in the field, has put it, "By and large it confirms the antiquity and authenticity of our present Hebrew text."

Yet, this could not possibly be the case unless at a fairly early time certain steps were taken by the Jews to protect the text.

Early Efforts to Protect the Text

The Isaiah Scroll thus confirms what most scholars have long suspected. While specific facts are lacking, they are convinced that in some way the rabbis who lived after the turn of the Common Era succeeded in safeguarding the biblical text.

Some efforts to preserve the text were undoubtedly made even earlier. It is possible, of course, that before the Bible was canonized, people who owned copies of individual books may have felt free to add notes or make other changes in texts that were their personal property. But once the Torah and then the Prophetic sections were definitely completed, people became reluctant to alter "sacred" literature.

Gradually, beginning sometime before the Common Era, it must have become accepted among the Jewish people that the biblical text was not to be changed in any way. Josephus, the Jewish historian of the latter part of the first century c.e, tells us about the Scriptural books of his time:

> . . . No one has been so bold as either to add anything to them, to take anything from them, or to make any change in them. . . . —*Against Apion*, I:8

Undoubtedly the "scribes" who were responsible for copying the biblical books were now carefully trained and instructed in their work. To protect against errors, they were informed of the count of every word in the text, unusual spellings of particular words, and the occurrence of oddities, such as an occasional oversized or undersized letter. Many scholars also believe that the rabbis even prepared a standard Bible text for the scribes' guidance, and statements in the Talmud lead us to believe that this model was deposited in the Temple for safekeeping.

Why was it necessary to take measures to protect the Bible text? There are many reasons. The episode of the Greek Septuagint was a warning and reminder to the rabbis of what might happen if they failed to act. Portions of the Greek translation became corrupted by errors. Moreover, Greek mistranslations of certain Hebrew words were now being used by the Christians to "prove" that the coming of Jesus had been anticipated by Holy Hebrew Scriptures. One extremely important instance shows us how grave a mistranslation could be. The Hebrew text of Isaiah 7:14 uses the word "young woman." The Greek mistranslation stated:

> Therefore the Lord Himself shall give you a sign;
> Behold, a *virgin* shall conceive, and bear a son,
> And his name shall be called Immanuel.

Believing in the "virgin birth" of Jesus, the early Christians proceeded in the Gospel of Matthew [1:23] of the New Testament to cite Isaiah 7:14 as "proof" that the Hebrew prophet had predicted Jesus' coming. Consequently, the rabbis saw that protecting the Hebrew Scriptures against similar tampering was a matter of great urgency.

There was an even more basic reason for safeguarding the text. The people believed in the sacredness of the Bible as the "word of God." Hence, to change the Scriptures by so much as one iota or to permit copyists' errors was to amend God's own statements.

Further, we must realize that all of later Jewish law contained in the Mishnah and G'moro of the Talmud—considered to be the "Oral" word of God, in contrast to the "Written" word of the Bible —was based on interpretations of Scriptural passages. A thoroughly accurate, universally accepted Hebrew text was essential.

An absolutely reliable Hebrew text was especially essential because the rabbis saw their religion as dynamic and believed that opportunity for developing Jewish law had been provided for by God even at the time the Torah was first given. By carefully studying the text of Holy Scriptures, the rabbis felt, they could derive all necessary new legislation. In fact, Rabbi Akiba, who lived during the early portion of the second century c.e., was able to introduce many important new laws by arriving at a different interpretation of just a single Hebrew word!

Hundreds of biblical quotations found in the Talmud follow word for word the same passages in our versions of Scriptures. This leads us to conclude that strict measures must have been introduced early in rabbinic times to standardize the biblical text.

Some Problems with the Text Itself

Despite these efforts to guard the Hebrew Bible text, certain difficulties persisted. Faulty manuscripts remained in circulation and there was always the danger that some copyist would perpetuate their errors. More serious in these times was the fact that the Hebrew Scriptures as yet lacked clear and consistent division between words and sentences; and there existed no standard scheme for pronunciation.

To appreciate some of the problems involved, we must understand that originally the Hebrew Bible text lacked vowels. Hebrew words were made up solely of consonants. So, without vowels, the Hebrew letters KRN could be pronounced either KeReN, "a horn," or KoRaN, "it shone," depending upon the sense of the sentence. (Note that this word is not related to the "Koran," the Moslem Scriptures. The latter is derived from another root meaning "to proclaim.") In some passages a reading of either KeReN or KoRaN might be possible, with each giving a totally different meaning from that which was intended.

Curiously enough, a mistranslation explains a peculiar error in a great work of art, the statue of Moses, by Michelangelo. If you have ever seen a picture or reproduction of this masterpiece you've noticed that Moses has two horns protruding from his head. The great sculptor based his conception upon a mistranslation of Exodus 34:29–30, 35 where the Hebrew word KRN describes Moses' appearance as he came down from Mount Sinai. Although the accurate meaning is that Moses' face *"shone* with beams of light," the Latin translation used by Michelangelo stated that Moses' face "sent out *horns* of light." Hence the magnificent marble statue in Rome today portrays the great lawgiver with horns.

In addition to a lack of vowels, the Hebrew text had no systematic division between words or sentences, and we see how much more difficult it was to be sure of an accurate translation. Here in English is an example of what a Hebrew sentence in the Bible originally looked like:

NDYSHLLLVTHLRDYRGDWTHLLYRHRTWTHLLYRSLN-
DWTHLLYRMGHT

When the proper vowels are added and the letters divided into words, we discover that this is the following well-known passage:

And you shall love the Lord your God with all your heart,
with all your soul, and with all your might.
—Deuteronomy 6:5

However, if we didn't know this particular verse, we might just as easily mistake the first word to mean "no," "in," or "nod." Similarly, although the pronunciation and word-division of most Hebrew biblical passages were quite widely known, nevertheless, there remained a number of passages that were uncertain, obscure, or ambiguous.

Hence, safeguarding the biblical text demanded more than establishing rules for scribes or trying to provide an authorized standard manuscript. Some system of dividing the Hebrew into words and sentences, and of inserting vowels, was also urgently necessary.

The Work of the Masoretes

When scribes began to take on added functions besides that of merely copying the biblical text, they became known as "Masoretes" from the Hebrew word *masorah*. Originally the term meant a "bond" or "fetter," used in the sense here of "binding up" or "holding firm" the text. (See Ezekiel 20:37 where this Hebrew word occurs.) Later *masorah* came to mean "tradition."

The term "Masorete" was evidently applied to certain scribes because they assumed responsibility for determining the biblical text and preserving the traditions about its spelling, wording, pronunciation, and meaning. Although their activity began shortly after the completion of the Bible and continued on as late as the sixteenth century, the bulk of their work was accomplished by the end of the tenth century C.E.

At a very early period, one of the more interesting things the Masoretes did was to introduce into the Bible text substitutes for the names of certain foreign gods. Thus, for instance, they changed the name of Saul's son from Ish-baal, "the man of the god Baal," to Ish-bosheth, "the man of shame." (Compare the name in II Samuel 2:8 with that in I Chronicles 8:33.) They also reworded various expressions, particularly forms of oaths. A good example is seen in Job 2:9 where, reacting to the acute suffering of her husband, Job's wife cries out to him:

> . . . Do you still hold fast to your integrity? *Curse* God
> and die!

Though the meaning is clearly "curse" God, the Hebrew text, thanks to the work of the Masoretes, uses the word "bless."

Their main effort, however, was devoted to the preparation of a standard text of the Bible. In addition to creating special rules for those who copied the Scriptures, the Masoretes undertook to divide the biblical books into words, then verses, and weekly synagogue portions. This task was completed sometime before 500 C.E. Also, to be certain that copyists neither added nor omitted words, the Masoretes took a complete count of all the words of every book of the Bible.

Eventually, with each biblical book, they also marked off the middle words, gave the number of its verses, weekly synagogue portions and sub-sections, and listed all the distinguishing marks of the text. When, at a much later time, chapters were finally introduced, the Masoretes also listed the count of these. All of this information was then put at the end of every book so that on checking back, copyists could be sure they had accurately reproduced the text. As an example of their work, after the close of the Hebrew text of Genesis we find the following Masoretic statement:

> The total number of verses in the Book of Genesis is 1,534.
> And half of them is the verse, "And by the sword you will
> live" [Genesis 27:40]. The weekly synagogue portions are
> twelve in number, the sub-sections are forty-three, the chapters are fifty, the paragraphs whose last lines are open to
> the end of the column are forty-three and those which are
> closed number forty-eight. . . .

The Masoretes were responsible for two additional achievements. One was a system of vowels to insure the correct pronunciation and, therefore, the precise meaning of each Hebrew word. This innovation was introduced sometime during the seventh century c.e., by the Masoretes of Tiberias, in northern Palestine. Their system provided for seven different vowel-sounds corresponding to various symbols placed beneath, above, and alongside the letters. These are the vowels—the dots, lines, and so forth—we find in our present-day Hebrew Bibles and prayer books. Henceforth, no question could exist that the word KRN of Exodus 34:29–30, 35 which prompted Michelangelo to give Moses horns was not pronounced KeReN, "horn," but KoRaN, "shone."

The adoption by all Jews of a single standard text of the Hebrew Bible was the second great achievement of the Masoretes. Even as late as the beginning of the tenth century of the Common Era, different traditions about the biblical text were held by Masoretes of Babylonia and of Palestine. About this time, the two groups produced master texts incorporating their own traditions. Eventually the Palestinian version—the one prepared by Moses ben-Asher of Tiberias—became accepted as *the* standard Hebrew Bible text. This is the one universally used today as our Hebrew Scriptures.

Translations as a Source of Information About the Text

Up to this point we have been dealing only with the transmission of the Hebrew text. Yet in almost every age the Bible has been known to numerous Jews and practically all Christians exclusively through translation. Hence the story of the transmission of the Bible also involves some of the more important translations.

Actually, these Bible translations have been one of our main sources for information about the early Hebrew text. Although we have always had the Hebrew Scriptures themselves, until comparatively recently, when the Isaiah Dead Sea Scroll was discovered, we possessed no ancient Hebrew manuscript of any substantial size older than the tenth century c.e.

For early information about the biblical text, then, scholars have had to depend heavily upon old Septuagint manuscripts. Three of the most important date from the fourth and fifth centuries of the Common Era. Since the oldest complete Hebrew Bible manuscripts come from the tenth century, these Greek Septuagint manuscripts are five or more centuries closer to the original biblical text.

One is named "Vaticanus" because it is housed in the Vatican library in Rome; another is called "Alexandrinus" because scholars believe it was written in Alexandria, Egypt. The third bears the name "Sinaiticus" because it was discovered in an old monastery atop Mount Sinai.

The discovery of this last manuscript is an unusual tale. In the year 1844 a German scholar named Tischendorf made a visit to a Christian monastery located atop Mount Sinai. He noticed during his visit a basket containing some pieces of sheepskin that were about to be burned. On closer inspection, he discovered that they were forty-three pages from a very old manuscript of the Septuagint. A thorough search of the place was immediately undertaken, but not another page of the manuscript could be located.

Then, fifteen years later, Tischendorf again paid a visit to the monastery. Hearing him speak of the Septuagint, a steward disappeared and then returned carrying many more pages of the same Greek manuscript. Today Tischendorf's discovery is housed in the British Museum and its value is listed at over a million dollars.

However, the real value of Sinaiticus and the various other manuscripts of the Septuagint, and other early translations, lies in the information they supply about the original Hebrew text. A careful study of these old manuscripts reveals a great deal about copyists' mistakes, deliberate changes in the text, the meanings of difficult Hebrew words and passages, and the processes of biblical transmission itself.

One error that has come to light by a study of such manuscripts, for instance, is a measurement of the Temple porch constructed by King Solomon. Our Hebrew text of II Chronicles 3:4 reports inaccurately:

> And the length of the porch that was in front [of the Temple] was twenty cubits, equal to its width, and its height was a hundred and twenty cubits. He overlaid it on the inside with pure gold.

The fact is that its height was not the "one hundred and twenty cubits" of the Hebrew version, but rather only "twenty cubits," as the Septuagint records. For, with a cubit measuring approximately a foot and a half, the Hebrew account would have transformed the porch of the Temple into a tower some 180 feet high! Imagine the fantastic cost of overlaying the inside of such a structure with gold!

The Earliest Jewish Translations

Probably the oldest translation of the Bible, or parts of it, was done in Aramaic. This language, similar to Hebrew and using the same characters, was spoken by many people in Palestine, several centuries before the Common Era. Portions of some of the later books of the Hebrew Bible, such as Ezra and Daniel, are written in Aramaic. To this day our prayer book has retained a major prayer, the Kaddish, in that tongue.

Because many Jews of Palestine spoke this language, the early synagogue instituted a practice of repeating the Torah portion in Aramaic translation after it was read in Hebrew. For years this remained only an oral translation. Finally, during the second century c.e., a *targum,* "translation," of the Torah was put into writing. Prepared originally in Palestine, this translation, known as the Targum of Onkelos, was edited in Babylonia and became the official Aramaic version. Later on, several other Aramaic translations were produced.

The first Greek translation of the Bible was, of course, the Septuagint which was undertaken to serve the needs of the Jews of Alexandria, Egypt. However, when the Septuagint was taken over by the early Christians as part of their official Scriptures, Greek-speaking Jews found it necessary to commission a new translation. This was prepared around 130 of the Common Era by a convert to Judaism named Aquila.

In countries north of Palestine, where people spoke a language known as Syriac, the Jews also began to feel the need for a Bible translation. Around 200 of the Common Era the task was begun and it was probably completed within the next century or so. Later on this work was given the name of "Peshitta," meaning "common" or "simple," probably to distinguish it from another, more complicated translation produced by the Christians.

The Aramaic, Greek, and Syriac versions, then, are the oldest of the Jewish translations of the Bible. Apart from the light they shed on the Hebrew text, these versions reveal that the practice of translating the Scriptures was an ancient one among the Jews, beginning even before the Bible itself was completed.

Some Important Christian Translations

Once the Jews established the principle, the Christians began producing translations of their own in Latin, Egyptian, Ethiopic, and other languages. However, we must remember that the original Christian Old Testament was based, not upon the authentic Hebrew text, but on the Greek Septuagint. Therefore, practically all the early Christian translations were based on the Greek.

As we have seen, the text of the Septuagint was not well protected, and many corruptions crept in. A great variety of differently-reading texts were soon in circulation. Therefore, in the beginning of the third century of the Common Era, a Christian scholar named Origen undertook to restore the Septuagint to its original state.

After twenty years of work, which also involved careful study of the Hebrew text, Origen finally produced his great "Hexapla," or "six-column version" of the Bible. It was an enormous manuscript which some think ran to as many as seven thousand pages. Here, in six parallel columns, Origen gave the Hebrew text, its transliteration into Greek letters, the Greek version prepared by the Jew Aquila, a later revision of it, the text of the Septuagint, and its revised version.

The work itself no longer exists; it disappeared from a library in Palestine following the Moslem conquest of the country in 638 c.e. Still, we know of the Hexapla through references to it in a number of old Christian writings and some translations of its version of the Septuagint into other languages.

Apart from the Septuagint, the most influential of all Bible translations among the Christians was that produced in Latin by Jerome, an outstanding Church scholar of the early fifth century. His work is called the "Vulgate," "for the common people," and it was begun at the request of one of the Popes who realized that the existing Latin translation had become hopelessly corrupt. Jerome went to Palestine, learned Hebrew, and was able to read the original Hebrew text, as well as the early rabbinic commentaries. He consulted the Hebrew versions and the Greek Septuagint and prepared a new Latin translation which appeared in 405 c.e.

At first the Vulgate was unacceptable to the Church because it was so different from the existing Latin version. In fact, when it first appeared it even caused riots among the Christians. However, it eventually gained acceptance among Church leaders and over the centuries it has remained the official Latin Bible of Roman Catholicism. Interestingly, the Vulgate was the first Bible to contain our modern chapter divisions, and also the first ever to be printed.

The Earliest English Translations

Of all the translations of the Bible, more have appeared in English than in any other language. The main reason is not too difficult to imagine: English-speaking peoples have been attracted to Protestantism, which places great reliance upon the authority of the Bible. The practice of insisting upon reading Scripture regularly by Protestants has therefore stimulated the production of a great many English translations.

However, even before the rise of Protestantism, certain Englishmen were urging people to read the Bible. But this was impossible for all those who knew no Latin. Roman Catholics—then virtually all the Christians of Western Europe—were permitted to read only the Vulgate, since the Church feared that the use of translations might lead to other interpretations of God's word.

Despite Church opposition, by the year 1384 a brilliant English Christian scholar named John Wycliffe succeeded in translating the Vulgate into English. Though the Church immediately took measures to suppress the Wycliffe translation, it circulated widely among English-speaking masses. Shortly thereafter, in those countries where the Catholic Church did not have as much control, translations in other languages began to appear. By the fifteenth century the Bible had been translated into German, French, Italian, Dutch, Swedish, Russian, and Danish.

The birth of Protestantism in Germany in the early sixteenth century, and its gradual spread among certain groups of Englishmen, created a demand for a new English translation of the Bible. But because of the influence of the Catholic Church, it was not considered safe to attempt to do this in England itself. Therefore, the first printed English Bible was produced on the Continent. This was a translation, never fully completed, prepared by William Tyndale. First he produced the New Testament, and then in 1530 came his version of the Five Books of Moses, translated mainly from the Greek.

The Church attempted to suppress this new translation. Tyndale himself was captured and executed; his body was burned. But by this time King Henry VIII of England broke with the Catholic Church over other issues, and his new Church of England in 1539 issued its own English version known as the "Great Bible." In large part it was made up of Tyndale's translation.

Once the right of translating the Bible into English was firmly established, many different versions appeared. This was due in part to the fact that the various Protestant sects wanted translations of their own. Eventually, the Church of England grew dissatisfied with the "Great Bible," and King James I, a Bible student himself, sponsored a new translation. He appointed a group of more than fifty scholars who labored for about seven years.

The result was the noted King James Version which became the authorized Bible for the Protestant Church. From its publication in 1611, the King James Bible established itself as the most popular of all the English translations, and it exerted a tremendous influence upon the language and culture of all English-speaking peoples.

Why the Necessity for Different Translations?

A great many English translations have been produced since then. In fact, within the past few generations, scarcely a year has gone by without the appearance of another new translation. There are at least three reasons for this:

1. The English language has undergone enormous changes in the last five hundred-odd years. Here, for example, is the first verse of the Twenty-third Psalm as it appeared in the Wycliffe translation of 1384. Below it is the same verse from the latest Revised Standard Version of the Protestant Church:

> 1384: The Lord gouereneth me, and no thing to me shal lacke; in the place of leswe where he me ful sette.
> 1952: The Lord is my shepherd, I shall not want; He makes me lie down in green pastures.

2. There are always new developments in biblical knowledge. Scholars are constantly gaining new understandings about the Bible through the findings of archaeology and the study of ancient languages, texts, and cultures. The discovery of new meanings of Hebrew words, for instance, or additional facts about life in biblical times, is bound to affect existing translations.

Thus, though the Protestants prepared a new American Standard Version in 1901, advances in biblical scholarship, as well as changes in English usage, required still another translation within less than a half-century. Their Bible today is the Revised Standard Version, begun in 1937 and completed in 1952. Among the Protestants of England, work on another new translation was begun in 1948, with the New Testament portion completed in 1961.

3. Each faith must have clear, readable, and up-to-date translations of its own. There are important differences, as we have already seen, between the Jewish Bible and that of the Roman Catholics on the one hand, and the Protestants on the other. In the past, most translations of the Bible have tended to reflect the religious doctrines of the translators. Consequently a version prepared by one religious group would generally not be acceptable to another. For instance, translating the Hebrew word for "young

woman" in Isaiah 7:14 as "virgin," so that it becomes a prediction of Jesus' birth, would certainly be rejected by the Jews.

Thus, it is not at all surprising that Protestants, Catholics, and Jews have each produced English translations of their own. In 1609 the Roman Catholics finally created their own English translation, the Douay Version, named after the city in Belgium where English priests received their training. Within recent years, however, they, too, have felt the need for a better translation, and since 1952 they have been in the process of preparing the new "Confraternity" Bible.

In the United States, the Jews have published two major Bible translations. The first, appearing in 1854, was the work of Isaac Leeser, a well-known rabbi of Philadelphia. The second, produced in 1917, was the work of a group of Jewish scholars under the auspices of the Jewish Publication Society of America. This is the one currently used by American Jewry as a whole. However, since 1955, a group of Jewish scholars under the sponsorship of the Jewish Publication Society has undertaken the task of preparing a new translation.

A Crucial Question About the Bible

This discussion of the latest English translations brings the story of our Bible right up to the present time.

We have now seen how the various books came to be written and how they were compiled into the great collections known as the Torah, the Prophets, and the Writings. We have also noted how the Bible as a whole came to be regarded as sacred literature and how its canon was established. Finally, we have followed the process by which it has been transmitted down to our own time.

More than four thousand years have gone into making and preserving the Bible. While this is impressive, it is even more impressive to consider how the Bible was originally created, how it has survived over these many centuries, and what a powerful influence this ancient work continues to exert today. Almost everything connected with the Bible is quite out of the ordinary!

Yet in modern times we find those who have come to wonder about biblical truth. They may be disturbed over its various contradictions, or they may doubt the accuracy of some of its statements. They are particularly troubled by some of the Bible stories—the account of the creation of the world, for instance, or the tales about Adam and Eve in the Garden of Eden, angels, miracles, and the like.

THE TRANSMISSION OF THE BIBLE (*indicates approximate date)

TRANSLATIONS	HEBREW TEXT
C.E.	C.E.

תנ"ך

TRANSLATIONS

C.E.

1961 New British (Protestant) translation begun

1955 New J.P.S. (Jewish) translation begun

1952 Revised Standard Version (Protestant) issued; Confraternity translation (Catholic) begun

1917 Jewish Publication Society Bible issued

1901 American Standard Version (Protestant) issued

1853 Leeser Bible (Jewish) published

1611 King James Bible (Protestant) issued

1609 Douay Version (Catholic) issued

1539 "Great Bible" issued by Henry VIII

1530 Tyndale's Five Books of Moses published

*1400 Many European translations prepared

1384 Wycliffe's translation (English) completed

*1220 Chapter divisions introduced into Vulgate

405 Jerome's Vulgate (Latin) completed

*400 Sinaiticus, Alexandrinus (Greek) manuscripts; Ethiopic translation begun

*350 Vaticanus (Greek) manuscript; Egyptian translation completed

*250 Origen's Hexapla (Greek and Hebrew)

*200 Peshitta (Syriac) begun; Latin translation completed

*130 Aquila's translation (Greek) prepared

*100 Targum (Aramaic) to Torah produced

B.C.E.

*200 Aramaic oral translation begun

*250 Septuagint (Greek) begun

HEBREW TEXT

C.E.

First complete printing — 1488

Chapter division begun — *1330

Standard Hebrew text of Ben-Asher introduced — *950

Vowel system introduced by Masoretes of Tiberias — *650

Word and sentence division completed by Masoretes — *500

Work of Masoretes begun (to *1500) — *200

Biblical canon fixed — *125

Regulation of scribes begun; Dead Sea Isaiah Scroll produced — *150

Prophetic section completed — *200

Torah section completed — *400

Inevitably then, we are confronted with the very critical question, "Is the Bible true?"

What's the answer? Let us see. . . .

──────────── THINGS TO TALK OVER ────────────

1. What proof have we that the present Hebrew text of the Bible is superior to the Greek text of the Christian Old Testament?

2. In what respects is the transmission of the Bible almost as remarkable as its creation?

3. Do you feel that American Jews need a new translation of the Bible? Why?

4. Why is knowledge of the Bible in Hebrew, rather than through English translation, necessary for a proper understanding of Judaism?

──────── SOME OTHER BIBLE PASSAGES TO CONSIDER ────────

1. What copyists' errors might we find in the following? Compare I Chronicles 9:35–44 with I Chronicles 8:29–38; compare II Samuel 21:18–22 with I Chronicles 20:4–8; compare Jeremiah 27:1 with Jeremiah 27:3; compare Psalm 18 with II Samuel 22.

2. What possible changes did the Masoretes make in the following verses: Exodus 4:18; Judges 18:30; II Samuel 4:4 (compare I Chronicles 8:34); Nehemiah 6:6; II Chronicles 18:14?

3. Using copies of the Jewish Publication Society Bible and the Revised Standard Version of the Old Testament (Vol.1), what do you observe about the differences in the translations of the following: Genesis 4:8; 9:10; Exodus 14:20; I Samuel 18:28?

4. How are the following verses from the Hebrew Scriptures used in the Gospel of Matthew of the New Testament? Compare Micah 5:1 with Matthew 2:3–6; compare Isaiah 42:1–4 with Matthew 12:18–21; compare Psalm 78:1–4 with Matthew 13:34–35; compare Isaiah 29:13–14 with Matthew 15:8–9.

──────── FROM THE RABBIS' VIEWPOINT ────────

1. PRESERVATION OF THE TEXT: See *A Rabbinic Anthology*, pp. lxii–lxvii.

2. TRANSLATION OF SCRIPTURE: See *A Rabbinic Anthology*, [434] pp. 161–162, [1215 and comment] pp. 436–438.

BURROWS, MILLAR, *The Dead Sea Scrolls*, Viking.

FREEHOF, SOLOMON B., *Preface to Scripture*, Union of American Hebrew Congregations, pp. 20–22; Chap. 3: "How the Bible Was Preserved," pp. 23–33.

Holy Scriptures, The, Jewish Publication Society, "Preface," pp. iii–xii.

MARGOLIS, MAX L., *The Story of Bible Translations*, Jewish Publication Society.

Old Testament, The, The Revised Standard Version, Nelson, "Preface," pp. iii–xi.

ROTH, CECIL, ed., *Standard Jewish Encyclopedia*, Doubleday, "Masorah," pp. 1278–1281; "Dead Sea Scrolls," pp. 535–538.

Thirteen

IS THE BIBLE TRUE?

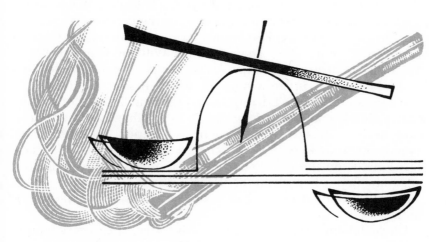

The Bible on Trial!

JULY THAT YEAR WAS ESPECIALLY SULTRY. THE HEAT AND CROWD-ing made the courtroom almost unbearable, but the people who came stayed and listened intently to the proceedings. Outside, hundreds more waited impatiently for some word of what was happening. For this was one of the most celebrated trials in history.

The year was 1925. The place was Dayton, a little country town in the southeastern part of Tennessee. The defendant was John T. Scopes, a science teacher in the local high school. He had been teaching his classes the theory of evolution—that is, that man is descended from the lower animals. But it was then a crime in Tennessee to teach any theory that conflicted with the biblical account of man's creation. So Scopes was arrested and forced to stand trial.

As it turned out, the trial soon involved much more than one man's guilt or innocence. Very quickly it shifted to an investigation of the truth of the Bible itself. Specifically, the issue hung on one question: who was right in explaining the Creation of man? The biblical account in the Book of Genesis, or Charles Darwin and other scientists, who theorized that man evolved over a period of millions of years?

241

This was not the first time the question had been raised. In the late 1800's men like Robert Ingersoll strongly challenged the truth of the Bible. But the Scopes trial dramatized the issue. Here, as many saw it, the Bible itself was being put on trial!

In the courtroom were two of the nation's leading personalities. One was Clarence Darrow, an attorney for the defense. He was unquestionably America's best-known criminal lawyer, a vigorous champion of civil rights. The other was William Jennings Bryan, one of the country's most famous orators and a three-time nominee for the Presidency. Bryan was on the side of the prosecution.

In defending Scopes, Darrow argued that the findings of modern science clearly contradicted the Bible. He produced evidence from many fields to show that the account of Creation in Genesis could not possibly be so. Repeatedly Bryan rose to defend the Bible's teachings. Finally, on the next-to-last day of the trial, Clarence Darrow called Mr. Bryan himself to the witness stand.

Tension mounted in the courtroom as the two men faced one another.

"Do you claim," Darrow asked his adversary, "that everything in the Bible should be literally interpreted?"

"I believe everything in the Bible should be accepted as it is given there . . ." Bryan promptly roared back. Then under extended cross-examination he defended his belief in the biblical stories of the creation of the world [Genesis 1–2:4], Adam and Eve in the Garden of Eden [Genesis 2:8–3:24], Noah and the Flood [Genesis 6–9:17], the sun standing still for Joshua [Joshua 10:1–14], Jonah and the whale [Jonah 2], and others. The most he would concede was that perhaps the biblical "six days of creation" really meant six longer periods of time.

The trial ended the next day. Scopes was found guilty and fined $100, although the verdict was later set aside by a higher court. Gradually the little town of Dayton settled back to normalcy.

But the effects of the Scopes trial were destined to be felt for generations. For many people in the United States and elsewhere, the proceedings had raised serious doubts about the truth of the Bible.

Two Ways of Looking at It

Well, what about it? Is the Bible really true?

This isn't an easy question. The answer depends on what we mean by the word "true." Actually, in speaking about a book like the Bible, there are two possible ways of defining "truth." It can be taken to mean that either:

1. every single fact the Bible presents is completely accurate and reliable;

or

2. although some facts may be erroneous, the underlying teachings in the Bible are nevertheless correct.

Now suppose we apply both definitions to the story of the creation of woman, found in Genesis 2:18–24. The facts given there are that God wished Adam to have a mate. At first He thought He might find one for him among the animals. However, when this proved impossible, Adam was put to sleep and from his rib God fashioned Eve.

According to our first definition, the story would be true only if Eve was actually formed from man's rib. However, the theory of evolution tells us that all human beings, men and women alike, are descended from lower forms of life. Human life as we know it appeared on earth only after an extremely long period of time. Factually, therefore, the biblical account cannot be correct.

But what about the underlying teachings? Isn't it true that man *does* require a mate and that in the process of creation, God *did* produce the male and female of the human species? This is the way God planned it. Sex, marriage, the procreation of children, are all part of human life as He ordered it so that people might fulfil His purposes on earth.

This is the way the religious person finds deeper, underlying truth in the Genesis story while, at the same time, recognizing that the details may not be entirely in line with the latest findings of science. In this respect his position is not so different from that of the scientist. The latter operates in essentially the same way. He knows that today's new discoveries may invalidate yesterday's scientific "facts." Yet he certainly does not abandon the fundamental truths that underlie science itself.

To illustrate, not very long ago the atom was considered the smallest unit of matter. Today we know that the atom is made up of still smaller forms of matter—electrons, protons, neutrons, and a whole host of tiny particles, some of which have not as yet been isolated. Do we then say that science as a whole is not true because in the course of its development it once considered the atom the smallest unit of matter? Hardly! We acknowledge this as an error of fact, but we continue to accept as true the underlying principles of science. One of these principles is that the universe is orderly.

We can look upon the Bible in the same way. Viewing the Genesis account as a story written by people who lived in pre-scientific times, we can agree that the modern theory of evolution forces us to discard the Bible creation story as unfactual. Nevertheless, the underlying belief in an orderly creation by God, according to His plan for man and the universe, remains completely true.

The answer to our question, "Is the Bible really true?" then, depends on what we mean by the "truth" of the Bible.

Fundamentalists Versus Liberals

Here we have the essential difference between the positions of the religious "liberal" and the religious "fundamentalist." To the fundamentalist among both Christians and Jews, every statement of the Bible is completely reliable and accurate, although some leeway in interpretation is possible.

At the Scopes trial, William Jennings Bryan tried to defend the fundamentalist position. Maintaining that the Bible was the actual word of God, he found himself forced to uphold the literal truth of every one of its statements. Although Bryan was prepared to interpret the Bible somewhat, such as his admission about the length of time involved in Creation, he could not permit a single one of its details to be questioned. To him, as to all fundamentalists, the biblical accounts of the creation of the world, the early experiences of man, the activities of angels, miraculous happenings, and the like, were literally so.

The religious liberal rejects this view. He freely admits that the Bible contains legends as well as inaccuracies of fact. Hence he is not compelled to defend the literal accuracy of every single statement in the Bible. It is sufficient for him that the Bible's underlying teachings are true.

Reform Judaism shares the liberal position. Long before the Scopes trial, at the Pittsburgh Conference of 1885, to be exact, Reform's rabbinical leaders had already declared:

> . . . We hold that the modern discoveries of scientific researches in the domains of nature and history are not antagonistic to the doctrines of Judaism, *the Bible reflecting the primitive ideas of its own age and at times clothing its conceptions of divine providence and justice dealing with man in miraculous narratives.*

Consequently, while the Scopes trial dealt a serious blow to the position of the fundamentalist, it in no way affected the Reform Jew's confidence in the underlying truth of the Bible. Thanks to the discoveries of biblical research, he had already come to understand the real nature of Scripture, and this in turn enabled him to answer "yes" to the question, "Is the Bible true?"

The Bible as a Human Document

The Reform Jew was already convinced that the Bible is the work of human beings. To be sure, its writers were gifted individuals and inspired by God Himself. Yet they were human nevertheless, and subject to all the limitations and shortcomings of human beings.

For all their genius, the writers of the Bible were quite limited in their scientific knowledge. By modern standards, they knew pitifully little about history, geography, medicine, and the universe in general. Indeed, none of the ancients possessed the information that we have today. We must remember that it has only been some 450 years since North America was discovered, and just about three centuries since people finally came to accept the theory of Copernicus that the sun, not the earth, is the center of the solar system.

With their limited knowledge, the writers of the Bible could easily believe that woman was originally created from Adam's rib or that man first gained understanding of right and wrong by eating from the "Tree of Knowledge" [Genesis 2:9, 3:1–7]. For want of better information, people who lived as far back as 2,000 B.C.E. simply had to make do with such explanations.

Then, too, the writers of the Bible, just like those who transmitted the text, made mistakes. Sometimes they became confused, or their memories failed, or they made use of questionable traditions. Thus, as we have already seen, they repeated the same incident about both Abraham and Isaac, and they had each refer to his wife as his "sister" to protect her from the same king [Genesis 20:1–18 and 26:1–12]. Sometimes they were also guilty of exaggeration, as when they declared that 600,000 men left Egypt during the Exodus [Exodus 12:37]. Counting all the women and children, this would add up to some two million people! That such a vast multitude could ever have participated in the Exodus, or survived in the desert is hardly conceivable.

Looking upon the Bible as a human document, then, the Reform Jew frankly admits that in certain places its writers give evidence of their human limitations—and, for all we know, their own imaginations! Consequently, not all their statements, even with interpretation, can be accepted as factually correct.

The Bible as a Developing Book

Scientific study has shown that the Bible was produced over a long period of time and therefore it reflects a wide variety of points of view and changing historical circumstances. This in turn accounts for its varying and sometimes even contradictory statements.

As the work of many individuals who lived over the course of some twenty centuries, how natural that the comments of one writer should differ from those of another! For each contributed his own style and insights, the traditions he considered meaningful, and his own personal reaction to the situations of his people and the problems of the day.

The more we look at the Bible, the more clear this becomes. In connection with religious practice, for instance, we find the following statement in Exodus 20:21:

> "An altar of earth you shall make for Me [God] and sacrifice on it your burnt-offerings and your peace-offerings. In every place where I cause My name to be remembered, I will come to you and bless you."

Now compare this with what we find in Deuteronomy 12:5–7:

> . . . You shall seek the place which the Lord your God will choose out of all your tribes to put His name and to make His habitation there. There you shall go and there you shall bring your burnt-offerings and your sacrifices . . . and there you shall eat before the Lord your God. . . .

In the first passage we see that it is quite proper for one to worship at different shrines, but in the second, people must worship only at the Jerusalem Temple.

The reason for this contradiction is not hard to understand. The first statement may have originated with a writer living in the Northern Kingdom of Israel which had no one central sanctuary. The second, however, may have come from the pen of someone from the Southern Kingdom with its one great Temple in Jerusalem.

Similar contradictions in the area of civil and criminal law appear. According to earlier practice, for example, a person who killed another was either to be driven away [Genesis 4:14] or put to death [II Samuel 14:4–7]. However, later law made a distinction between murder and accidental killing. In cases of accidental killing, the individual was now permitted to find safety by fleeing to a designated place of refuge [Deuteronomy 4:41–43].

From time to time, too, different religious customs and beliefs were advocated. On the one hand, Ezra condemns the marriage of Jews to "foreign" women and even compels men to give up their non-Jewish wives [Ezra 9:1–10:17]. On the other hand, Ruth, a Moabite woman, marries Boaz, a Jew, in the Book of Ruth, and the writers of the Bible traced King David's ancestry back to this "mixed" marriage [Ruth 4:17].

Or as we have seen in another connection, an earlier Bible writer states that a person's sins will surely be transmitted to his descendants, even to the generation of his great grandchildren [Exodus 34:6–7]. But later writers deny this and insist that each individual bears responsibility only for his own misdeeds [Deuteronomy 24:16 and Ezekiel 18:19–20].

We are not surprised at this. Recognizing that the Bible was produced by many different people over a long period of time, we know that as life itself changed it was natural for existing laws, beliefs, practices, and thinking to change. The contradictions simply confirm the fact that the Bible is a developing book.

The Bible as a Book of Religious Truth

The findings of biblical research also make it quite clear that Scriptures was never intended to be an encyclopedia of objective fact, scientific or historical. Its authors presented the best information they possessed, but *this was not their main objective!* In fact, in some instances they consciously omitted certain details and referred the reader to other sources that were then in existence, such as The Book of Jashar [Joshua 10:13], The Chronicles of the Kings of Israel [I Kings 14:19], and The Chronicles of the Kings of Judah [II Kings 24:5].

Their primary concern was with religion, and they meant the Bible to be a book of religious truth! In what better way could they present this than through their own knowledge and experience? For to them, as to us, the processes of the universe, nature, history, and human life itself all reveal the workings of God. And by dealing with these, the writers of the Bible were able to discover and pin-point vital, basic religious truths. In this way they were able to inform their people about God and His commandments, the nature of acceptable conduct, and the proper worship of Him.

Historical information, for example, revealed how God's will operated in the affairs of nations. The records of the various kings' reigns reported the moral consequences of their acts. Thus, despite agreement by historians that King Jeroboam of Israel was an exceptionally able ruler, the biblical writers looked more deeply into the moral implications of his conduct. And in this statement they predicted the outcome:

> And . . . Jeroboam did not turn from his evil way, but again appointed priests for the high places [where idolatry was practiced] from among all the people. Any who desired, he consecrated as priests of the high places. And this thing became sin to the house of Jeroboam, so as to cut it off and destroy it from the face of the earth.
> —I Kings 13:33–34

Their judgment proved correct. After his reign, Jeroboam's son was assassinated by conspirators and his whole family was wiped out [see I Kings 15:27–30]. Violation of God's commands, they observed, could lead only to disaster.

Similarly, the descriptions given by the biblical writers of the origins of the universe, the earth, and mankind served to reveal God's role as the Creator and Sustainer of life. Especially is this true in their use of traditions that were current in the ancient Near East.

We can see this from the way they recast one of the Babylonian versions of the Creation story. In its original form, the Babylonian version told of the appearance of many gods who schemed and plotted among themselves. Finally one god, Marduk, emerged supreme and established the world. In the process he also formed man from the blood of the slain rebellious god, Kingu.

To the writers of the early chapters of Genesis, this tale was fundamentally untrue. The fact was that it was the One God alone who planned and created the universe and fashioned man in His own image so that man might carry out His will. The differences in detail were important since they explained basic religious truths.

Another example of how the Bible writers took an ancient legend and gave it a religious emphasis is the story of the great Flood. As presented in a Babylonian tablet dating from the seventh century B.C.E., the Babylonian version related how the gods suddenly decided to overwhelm the earth with a deluge. Because of his rivalry with another deity, however, the god Ea determined to save his favorite, Utnapishtim. He therefore told him of the coming flood and directed him to build an ark.

Note the differences in the Genesis account. Here it is the people's wickedness that prompts God to send the flood, and only because Noah is righteous is he saved [Genesis 6:5–8, 9–14]. As with the Bible's story of Creation, the details here add up to a series of vital religious truths. God is righteous and just, and He demands the same of man. To ignore this is to court catastrophe for the whole human race.

Now we can better understand why the Reform Jew looks upon the Bible not merely as a human and developing document, but also as a book revealing the most profound religious truths known to man.

The Scope of Biblical Religion

Something else that strikes us about the Bible is the great number of subjects it discusses. Biblical material ranges from matters of health—as with the regulations about leprosy [Leviticus 15:1–15] —to explanations of natural phenomena, such as the occurrence of the rainbow [Genesis 9:8–17]. To the writers of the Bible everything in God's universe properly came within their purview since religious truth was intimately concerned with the whole of existence. The rainbow reflected the glory and majesty of its Creator; disease, as a form of evil in the world, was a challenge to man as the guardian of the earth and the partner with God in the continuing work of creation.

However, the biblical authors concentrated upon six main areas that were basic to their religious outlook:

1. The first main area, of course, had to do with God. In nearly every book, His nature, characteristics, demands, and relationships with Israel and mankind are touched upon.

The Book of Amos, as we have seen, portrays God as a just and righteous Lord who expects justice and righteousness from His people [see especially Amos 2:6–7]. If they do evil, God will surely destroy them [Amos 2:4–5, 13–16]. Although Amos and others said repentance was possible, it was Hosea, a prophet who lived at about the same time as Amos, who emphasized that God is merciful and prepared to forgive those who mend their ways [see especially Hosea 14:2–9].

The writers of nearly all the other biblical books approach the subject of God with emphases of their own. The descriptions vary from passage to passage and book to book: He is a mighty Creator in the opening chapters of Genesis; a personal "Shepherd" in Psalm 23; the Sustainer of nature and life in Psalm 104; and the Ruler of history in Psalm 9.

2. Since the writers of the Bible believed that all law originated with God, they presented a wide variety of civil, criminal, and ritual

legislation. The best-known group of these laws is the Ten Commandments [Exodus 20:2–14 and Deuteronomy 5:6–18], but we also find hundreds of others that involve almost every aspect of life.

The Book of Deuteronomy contains many laws dealing with such diverse matters as correct weights and measures [25:13–16], approved court procedures [16:18–20; 19:15–21], humane treatment of the stranger, the orphan, and the widow [24:17–22], and the proper observance of the festivals [16:1–16].

3. The Bible contains a great many rules for worthwhile daily living. Among them are formulas for finding personal happiness, such as avoiding sinners [Psalm 1:1], clinging to God's law [Psalm 1:2], and cherishing wisdom [Proverbs 4:1–13].

The biblical writers set forth numerous prescriptions for wholesome family relationships. Thus, in the story of Joseph and the coat of many colors, we learn the consequences of showing favoritism among one's children. For observe the Bible's keen insight into basic human relations here:

> Now Israel [that is, Jacob] loved Joseph more than any other of his children because he was the son of his old age; and he made him a coat of many colors. But when his brothers saw that their father loved him more than all his brothers, they hated him and could not speak peaceably to him. —Genesis 37:3–4

And in the following passage, note the wise understanding of the Bible about what really is most important to wholesome family living:

> Better is a dry morsel with quiet,
> Than a house full of feasting with strife. —Proverbs 17:1

4. As we have observed, worship was of great interest to the writers of the Bible. Thus they devoted much of the Book of Leviticus to a description of the proper types of sacrifices and burnt-offerings, and several lengthy passages in the Book of Exodus to the nature of the sanctuary [Exodus 25:10–27:21] and the duties of the priesthood [Exodus 28–29].

Naturally the holidays and their observance also received consideration. The Sabbath, we have seen, was described as having been introduced by God Himself following His work of creation [Genesis 2:1–3]. Passover, Shovuos, Sukos, Rosh Ha-shono, and Yom Kippur were dealt with particularly in conjunction with the appropriate Temple offerings [Leviticus 23].

5. The writers of the Bible were very much concerned with re-

ligious ideals. Chief among them were freedom and peace. In connection with the liberation of the Hebrew slaves from Egypt, for example, they glorified liberty as a precious gift from God Himself. For concerning the Exodus, Moses himself said:

> . . . Remember this day on which you came out of Egypt, out of the house of bondage, for by strength of hand *the Lord brought you out from this place.* . . . —Exodus 13:3

And in a prophetic vision of the better world, the writers of the Bible twice repeated the hope that eventually the plough would replace the sword, and wars would be no more [Isaiah 2:4 and Micah 4:3–4].

Among the many other ideals they stressed were fair treatment of one's fellow man [Deuteronomy 24:6–7, 10–15], protection of the rights of the individual even against rulers [I Kings 21:1–26], and concern for the needs of the less fortunate [Deuteronomy 24:17–22]. In fact, they even called for the observance of a Jubilee Year every fifty years when all slaves were to be set free and every man's property was to be returned to him, when indeed:

> . . . You shall proclaim liberty throughout the land to all its inhabitants, . . . when each of you shall return to his property and each of you shall return to his family. —Leviticus 25:10

6. Finally, as we have so clearly seen, the Bible as a book of religious truth was designed to answer certain popular questions about life itself—questions such as the purpose of existence, why there is evil in the world, how one finds happiness, and the like. Whole books, such as Proverbs, Ecclesiastes, and Job, were devoted to such questions.

These, however, were not isolated questions. As we shall see later on, when the questions and the answers are considered together as a whole, they add up to a total view of life with implications of enormous consequences to the individual.

In addition to all six areas we have just examined, the Bible sought to satisfy people's curiosity about a great many other problems and events. To supply the answers and information, the writers of the Bible made extensive use of legends.

About Biblical Legends

It is this legendary material in particular that has prompted most of the doubts about the truth of the Bible. However, now that we understand the nature and development of the Bible, we realize that a book of religious truth in a pre-scientific age had to rely, to a certain extent, on legends. That is the only way the Bible writers could have dealt with certain questions.

Some biblical writers attempted to explain by means of legends how the world and man were created [Genesis 1–2:4], how the animals got their names [Genesis 2:18–20], why people have to work so hard to obtain food [Genesis 2:8–3:19], how murder originated [Genesis 4:1–8], why the snake has no feet [Genesis 3:1–14], and why people speak different languages [Genesis 11:1–9]. Others tried to trace the origin of various place-names, such as Beth-El [Genesis 28:10–19], or personal names, such as that of Isaac, Abraham's son [Genesis 21:1–6].

The early history of the Jewish people was another subject for legend, and because the Bible was a book of religious truth, God's role was central. Legend portrayed Him and His angels as speaking to Abraham [see, for example, Genesis 12:1–3 and 22:11–12]; they even performed marvelous feats for Abraham and his relatives [Genesis 18:16–19:29; 21:1–5]. As the mighty Protector of His people, God demonstrated His power by destroying their enemies. Thus does one of the oldest portions of the Bible, the Song of Moses at the Red Sea, boast of His frightful conquest of the Egyptians:

> Your right hand, O Lord, is glorious in power,
> Your right hand, O Lord, dashes the enemy to pieces.
>   —Exodus 15:6

Naturally, no miracle was impossible for Him. Legend had God devastating Egypt with an assortment of plagues [Exodus 7–12:30], and rescuing the Hebrews from Pharaoh's army by dividing the Red Sea [Exodus 14:21–29]. He granted children to women who were unable to bear them [I Samuel 1:1–20], and even helped Joshua defeat the forces of five kings by making the sun stand still [Joshua 10:12–14].

Some of these legends had their roots in the common traditions of the ancient Middle East. The legends found their way into the Bible after centuries of oral tradition. In many cases the biblical writers developed legends of their own in order to deal with certain puzzling questions. Thus, the Book of Job discusses the problem of evil within the framework of a supposed challenge by Satan [Job 1–2:7]. The story of Jonah and the great fish serves as background for the theme of God's concern for the welfare of all peoples [Jonah 1–2].

Today, of course, we recognize these as legends. Nevertheless, as in the case of other types of biblical material, legends can also contain the most valuable kinds of religious truth. The accounts of miracles testify to the overwhelming power of the Almighty. The legend of Jonah and the great fish affirms the constant watchfulness and universal presence of God, whose will must be done. And the setting for the story of Job merely gives the writer the opportunity to indicate God's capacity to put even the righteous man to the supreme test. Indeed, basic religious truths are often concealed within legend!

The Bible as History

Apart from its paramount concern with religious teachings, the Bible is also invaluable for transmitting two more kinds of truth The first is in the realm of history.

Because its authors drew so heavily upon the events of their own times as background for religious teaching, the Bible offers much reliable information about events that took place in the ancient Near East. In fact, thanks to the expanding research of biblical scholars, experts in ancient languages, historians, and archaeologists, we are coming more and more to recognize how accurate much of the Bible's historical material really is. All this has led the greatest archaeologists of our times to agree that the Bible possesses "an amazing historical memory."

We can be sure that for the most part the biblical reports of political events and military campaigns in the Near East are fact. So, too, are the records of the reigns of the kings of Israel and Judah and the experiences of their peoples.

New evidence is constantly being found to confirm this. For instance, to support the account of the Assyrian siege of Jerusalem reported in II Kings 18:13–17, archaeologists have now discovered a beautifully-preserved Assyrian cylinder which dates to the late eighth century B.C.E. This cylinder relates how the armies of Sennacherib shut up King Hezekiah of Judah "like a caged bird in Jerusalem, his royal city."

Similarly, the reign of King Omri of Israel, in the ninth century B.C.E., described in I Kings 16:23–28, is well attested to by numerous Assyrian inscriptions. The famous Moabite Stone, discovered in 1868, gives us the following statement of Mesha, the king of Moab, himself:

> I am Mesha, son of Chemosh [the god], king of Moab. . . .
> As for Omri, king of Israel, he humbled Moab many years.
> . . . And his son followed him, and he also said, "I will

humble Moab." In my time he spoke this, but I have
triumphed over him and his house. . . .

Note what the Bible has to say about this:

> Now Mesha, the king of Moab, was a sheep-breeder; and he
> had to deliver annually to the king of Israel a hundred
> thousand lambs and the wool of a hundred thousand rams.
> But when Ahab [the king of Israel] died, the king of Moab
> rebelled against the king of Israel. —II Kings 3:4–5

As a result of such discoveries, even some of the material in the
Bible that scholars once regarded as completely legendary has
turned out to have some basis in fact. Here are two examples.

The Bible tells us that after the death of Moses the Hebrew tribes
crossed the Jordan River under the leadership of Joshua. There
they faced their first obstacle to the conquest of Palestine, the
highly fortified city of Jericho. Eventually the order was given for
the people to attack the city with shouting and the blowing of rams'
horns. The Book of Joshua goes on to report:

> . . . And it came to pass, when the people heard the sound
> of the trumpet, that the people shouted loudly, and the wall
> fell down flat. Then the people went up into the city, every
> man directly, and they seized the city. . . . And they
> burnt the city with fire and all that was inside. . . .
> —Joshua 6:20–21, 24

From 1907 to 1909 archaeologists investigated the area described
in the Bible as the site of Jericho. With painstaking and difficult
work, they dug through the layers of soil until, much to their surprise, they uncovered two huge circular walls, one five feet thick,
the other ten feet, made of sun-dried brick. On close examination,
these walls showed traces of a tremendous fire. The ruins of
ancient buildings behind them, too, had been burned. From other
evidence, archaeologists judge that the walls were levelled around
1500 B.C.E., or approximately several hundred years before the
time of Joshua.

Thus, although Joshua himself could not have destroyed Jericho,
evidently the writers of the Book of Joshua recalled the tradition
that the city had once been violently destroyed. This they promptly
ascribed to their great early Hebrew leader. Consequently, although
the details are not as the Bible gives them, the information that
"the city and all that was inside" were "burnt with fire" is historical
fact.

The second case concerns the story of the Flood. In 1929 an

archaeologist named Charles Woolley was excavating the site of the ancient city of Ur, in Mesopotamia, from which Abraham is said to have come [Genesis 11:28, 31]. Digging beneath many layers of soil containing remnants of different settlements, he suddenly came across a large accumulation of what had once been mud, and that could only have been deposited there by water. Continuing to dig, he found that below the "mud" were the remains of the very first settlement on that site. The layer of mud, he concluded, was the result of a severe ancient flood that completely covered the city.

This must have left such a profound impression upon the survivors that their descendants spoke of it from time to time. It became a tradition passed on from generation to generation. It is likely that Abraham and others who came from Ur to settle in and around Palestine brought such memories with them. Flood stories were common in the Middle East, and Abraham's memories made such stories more vivid. The tale ultimately found its way into the Book of Genesis. Thus underlying the legend of the Flood we discover an element of historical truth.

As we observe from these two examples, this does not mean that every bit of historical information in the Bible is fact. We must remember that the writers of the Bible were not historians; nor were they interested in merely presenting history as such. Drawing upon their traditions and experiences, they were chiefly concerned with discovering and revealing religious truth. Sometimes, as in the case of the Book of Esther, they even invented an appropriate historical setting for the story they wished to tell. Nevertheless, we can be absolutely sure that a great many historical statements in the Bible are either completely true or have some basis in fact.

The Bible as a Record of Judaism's Development

The truthfulness of the Bible may be seen in yet another area—the growth of the Jewish religion. Beginning with the time of the Patriarchs, the Bible traces the religious beliefs and practices of successive generations of the Jewish people. This has provided us with an accurate record of Judaism's development.

Here are two illustrations. The first involves the establishment of the priesthood. Originally, as Exodus 20:21 leads us to believe, every person was eligible to offer up his own sacrifices. But by the time of King David, there already appear to be certain individuals who are designated to serve as priests. In fact, two of the king's own sons are specifically mentioned [II Samuel 8:18].

Next, as Deuteronomy 18:1 and 33:8 inform us (the "Thummim" and "Urim" mentioned here were part of the priests' equipment), the priesthood was confined strictly to Levites; that is, members of the tribe of Levi. Finally, only the descendants of Aaron were eligible to be priests [Exodus 29:4–9 and Leviticus 9:1–9]. Thus, from the very pages of the Bible itself we can trace the stages by which the organized priesthood came into existence.

The second example concerns the development of the Festival of Passover. From early statements in the Bible, scholars are sure that Passover must have originated long before the Hebrews ever went to Egypt, perhaps as far back as the time of the Patriarchs. As shepherds, the people each year would celebrate a spring festival on the full moon of the month during which the kids and lambs were born. Then every family would sacrifice one of its sheep or goats and roast it for a special midnight meal. All of this is indicated by the biblical description of the Passover observance in Egypt *before* the Hebrews gained their freedom [Exodus 12:1–11].

Coming into Palestine, the people continued to celebrate their ancient Passover feast. But now, as settled farmers, they were also attracted by a local spring agricultural festival, a barley harvest known as the Festival of Unleavened Bread. Leviticus 23:5–6 and Numbers 28:16–17 make it clear that at one time Passover and the Festival of Unleavened Bread were celebrated on two successive days. Eventually the two were combined into the one great national holiday of Passover, which by then had also come to commemorate the Exodus of the Jews from Egypt [Exodus 12:25–27].

The Bible provides essential information about the development of many other religious beliefs and practices, in addition to the two examples we have just seen. In this respect, then, the Bible serves as a major source of truth about the origin and growth of the Jewish religion.

The Bible and Us

Summing it all up, we have now seen that the Bible is true in a great many ways. Its basic truth may be found in its teachings about God, the universe, man, and life. At the same time, it also contains much that is fact regarding the history of ancient times and the development of the Jewish religion.

We recognize, of course, that as an ancient human document not every single statement in the Bible is fact. Within its pages we do find contradictions, legends, and even outright inaccuracies. This was inevitable, not only because of the limited knowledge of its authors, but also because of the many changes in religious belief and practice that occurred over a period of some two thousand years.

However, once we realize that the Bible is a book of religious truth, not a treatise on history or science, bound to become antiquated with each new discovery, the whole issue appears in a totally different light. For knowing how the Bible came to be and the purpose for which it was written, we can certainly answer the question, "Is the Bible true?" in the affirmative. To us, the real truth of the Bible lies in its religious teachings.

One final question remains. Granted that the Bible is essentially a book of religious truth, how relevant is such a book for people who live in the space age? Or, to put it another way, what can a four thousand year old book mean to us today?

Perhaps this is really the most important question of all. For to the Jew, the Bible cannot be merely an ancient document, treasured like some collection of Dead Sea Scrolls for its historical information about religion and life in the distant past. To be of real value to us, the Bible must be a real and central part of our lives.

Well, then, how is the Bible vital to us today?

THINGS TO TALK OVER

1. How would you answer someone who insisted that various stories in the Bible are not true?

2. How does an understanding of the real nature of the Bible make it all the more remarkable?

3. To what extent does the Bible provide an accurate picture of the history of Judaism and the Jewish people?

4. In the light of modern scientific knowledge, how might we rewrite the Bible's Creation story in line with the underlying truths it contains?

SOME OTHER BIBLE PASSAGES TO CONSIDER

1. From your knowledge of biblical history, how would you explain the differences between the following pairs of passages? I Samuel 9:13–14 and II Chronicles 34:1–3; Leviticus 17:1–9 and Deuteronomy 12:15, 20–22; Leviticus 18:18 and Genesis 29:16–30; Deuteronomy 14:23 and Exodus 20:21.

2. What important underlying truths do the following biblical legends contain? Exodus 7:20; 14:21; 15:22–25; Numbers 20:2–11; I Samuel 7:3–14; II Kings 5:1–19.

3. How do the following passages contribute to our knowledge of the history of Bible times? Genesis 11:28–12:6; Exodus 3:16–17; Judges 1:16–21; I Samuel 13:15–23; II Samuel 5:4–7; I Kings 12:1–17.

4. From what we know about the modern State of Israel, how accurate is the information supplied by the following? Numbers 20:1–5; Deuteronomy 3:16–17; 8:9; I Kings 9:26–28; I Kings 18:20; Psalm 51:20.

———————— FROM THE RABBIS' VIEWPOINT ————————

1. THE BIBLE AS A DEVELOPING BOOK: See *A Rabbinic Anthology*, [347–350] pp. 130–131.

2. BIBLICAL TRUTH: See *Everyman's Talmud*, pp. 132–142; and *A Rabbinic Anthology*, pp. lxi–lxii, lxx–lxxi, [315] pp. 119–120, [322–323] pp. 122–123, [408] p. 150, [422] p. 157.

———————— OTHER THINGS TO READ ————————

ALBRIGHT, WILLIAM F., *The Archaeology of Palestine*, Pelican.

GITTELSOHN, ROLAND B., *Little Lower Than the Angels*, Union of American Hebrew Congregations, Chap. 11: "Religion and Science," pp. 177–195.

GLUECK, NELSON, *Rivers in the Desert*, Farrar, Straus and Cudahy.

KELLER, WERNER, *The Bible as History*, Morrow.

MAZAR, BENJAMIN, ed., *Views of the Biblical World*, International Publishing Co., Jerusalem, Vol. 1: "The Law"; Vol. 2: "Former Prophets"; Vol. 3: "Later Prophets"; Vol. 4: "The Writings."

WRIGHT, G. ERNEST, and FREEDMAN, DAVID N., *The Biblical Archaeologist Reader*, Doubleday, Chap. 3: "Has Archaeology Found Evidence of the Flood?" by John Bright; Chap. 5: "The Manna of Sinai," by F. S. Bodenheimer; Chap. 9: "King Joiachin in Exile," by W. F. Albright; Chap. 20: "New Radiocarbon Method for Dating the Past, etc.," by Donald Collier, Ovid R. Sellers, and G. Ernest Wright.

Fourteen
THE BIBLE AS A LIVING BOOK

The Power of the Bible

AN AMAZING THING ABOUT THE BIBLE IS THE WAY IT CAN AFFECT people's lives.

Here's a striking example. It has to do with the story of the famous "Mutiny on the Bounty," the historical incident that was the foundation of a best-selling novel and a fine movie. Very few, however, know the part the Bible played in the final outcome.

The episode started in 1787 when Captain William Bligh set sail from England on the H.M.S. "Bounty" on a voyage across the Pacific to bring back some breadfruit trees. Bligh was a harsh officer whose strict sense of discipline drove the ship's crew to mutiny on the return trip. Bligh and eighteen others were put off the "Bounty" onto a small, open boat, and set adrift. Only after much hardship did they finally reach the East Indies, some 4,000 miles away.

Meanwhile, the mutineers made for Tahiti where most of them were subsequently captured. A few escaped to lonely Pitcairn Island in the mid-South Pacific. At the beginning, the entire population on Pitcairn consisted of nine white sailors, six natives, ten women, and a girl of fifteen. Soon one of the men discovered a way to distill alcohol, and all fell hopelessly under the influence of drink. Life now degenerated into constant drunkenness and vice.

259

Eventually, only one of the white sailors survived, a man named John Adams. Quite by accident he came across a Bible in a chest taken from the "Bounty." As he read it he fell under its spell. People began to notice that Adams was becoming a different person. When they questioned him he told them something of its teachings. They were impressed and he taught them more of the Bible. Gradually their lives, too, began to change.

Some ten years later, in 1808, the American ship, "Topaz," put in at Pitcairn Island. The American sailors found the settlement vigorous and prosperous. There was no drinking or vice of any kind; the people were honest, hard-working, and conscientious. In fact, the island was a model community.

Such is the power of the Bible!

An Effective Book, Indeed!

We are not surprised. The Bible has always had a great influence upon the lives of people.

We have already seen how it has affected the whole of our Western world and has helped to shape its language, literature, and culture. Our ideals, laws, and institutions, even the democratic way of life itself, derive, to a very great extent, from teachings in the Bible.

Our Bible, to a great degree, has influenced the religious life of Christians everywhere. From the Jewish Scriptures have come their ethical standards, their concept of the good life, many of their most fundamental teachings, as well as some of their actual practices. And the very existence of Protestantism in its various forms can be attributed in part, at least, to the reading of the Bible by its followers and the impact of its teachings upon them.

But the effects of the Bible can be seen in other ways as well, especially in terms of the everyday conduct of people. A number of years ago Edward R. Murrow, the well-known journalist and radio and television personality, began interviewing many of the nation's leading citizens. He asked them what they believed about life and how this in turn had affected them. Their answers have been published in several volumes called *This I Believe,* and it is interesting to see how many have built their whole life upon some particular teaching of the Bible.

The president of one of America's largest corporations declares that a single verse from Ecclesiastes has guided all of his actions. "Cast your bread upon the waters, and you will find it after many days" [Ecclesiastes 11:1], he says, has led him always to do more for others than they can do for him.

A distinguished motion-picture producer always keeps another biblical verse in mind. It is this passage from Micah, "It has been told you, O man, what is good and what the Lord requires of you: Only to do justly, to love mercy, and to walk humbly with your God" [Micah 6:8]. To this producer, Micah's statement is a reminder that only through deeds of justice, mercy, and humility can the individual find genuine achievement and true peace of mind.

The head of a large industrial concern traces his achievements to this biblical verse extolling hard work, "In the sweat of your face shall you eat bread" [Genesis 3:19]. Here, he says, he has found the key to a useful, happy existence.

Belief in God as the Creator has been the dominant force in the life of one of the nation's outstanding physicians. To him the perfection of the human body and the wonders of the universe testify to God's love for mankind. This in turn has impelled him to serve his fellow man with all of his energies.

"You shall love your neighbor as yourself" [Leviticus 19:18], is a source of continuing strength to a distinguished actress. This, she says, is something that has given her courage to face the trials of life and develop a sense of wider purpose for her existence.

What can we learn from these examples? The Bible is a powerful book indeed!

Its Influence Upon Us

But it is upon us as Jews that the Bible has had its greatest influence. For it has shaped our whole way of thinking, our conduct, and our destiny for well over two thousand years.

Perhaps we do not realize to what an extent we are the products of the Bible. We know, of course, that the Bible is the source of most of our religious beliefs and practices. The Bible is the well-spring of our faith in God, and our understanding of His will; it is also the foundation of our Sabbaths and holidays, much of our liturgy, and many of our rituals. From the Bible, too, comes our historic sense of kinship with our people which in our own time has transformed once-desolate Palestine into the flourishing, vibrant, modern State of Israel.

But are we aware of all its other effects upon us? For example, our wholesome attitudes to life, work, marriage, and family living —all are inspired by the Bible. So are our basic standards of ethics and morality, our convictions about justice for all people as the children of God, fairness to minorities, concern for the unfortunate, regard for the rights of the working man, and the like. And long centuries of nurture upon the Bible continue to direct us in the pursuit of world peace, social justice, and the relief of all human suffering.

We are also the beneficiaries of the Bible's high standards and values. Our deep regard for learning and knowledge was inspired directly by the Bible. Down to this very day, when an unusually high percentage of our young people are enrolled in colleges and universities, we Jews have always prized learning. From the Bible, too, we have always been inspired to think for ourselves, and to cherish the freedom to search for truth. These two qualities distinguished the lives of such great men as Brandeis, Einstein, and Freud. These and many other notable Jews throughout history inherited the concepts from generation after generation of Jews who found them in the Bible—in the Book of Proverbs, for example, which emphasizes the pursuit of wisdom; in Ecclesiastes, which shows how Koheleth used his right to think for himself; and in the Book of Job, which recounts the story of a man determined to find an answer to his question, even to the point of challenging God Himself.

The truth is that most of us are what we are and live the way we do because in so many ways we remain very much the "People of the Book."

A Different Age, But. . .

All of this, of course, is part of the answer to our question, "What can the Bible mean to us?" But there is far more to it.

The plain fact is that, as a book of religious truth, the Bible is still indispensable for living today!

Why? Because despite the many technological and scientific advances of our age, we are still human beings. Although outward circumstances have changed, people are not much different today from what they were back in Bible times. We must struggle within ourselves just as hard as they did against virtually all the same evils. As was the case with those who wrote the Bible, temptations also plague us, so do hatred and envy, greed and selfishness, and all the rest.

Moreover, like the biblical authors, we too must face up to all sorts of daily problems. We are constantly confronted by issues such as: Shall we acquiesce to those in authority—parents, teachers, employers, the government—even when we disagree? Shall we go along with the group when we feel it is wrong, or shall we voice our protest to the point of dropping out? Shall we try always to do our very best, or shall we try merely to get by? There are literally scores of such questions that we must answer for ourselves every day of our lives.

Despite human progress, society is a long way from resolving most of its basic problems. As in Bible times, the shadow of war hangs over us and oppression is still prevalent in many parts of the world. Poverty, crime, disease, and human misery abound. Life on all levels is still life.

If anything, our situation is made even more difficult by the advances of our times. The greater abundance of material things simply adds to temptation, widens the gap between classes and between nations, leads to more crime, and invites conquest. The actions of individuals today also carry more serious consequences. A single mistake by the driver of a high-powered car or the pilot of a jet airliner can mean disaster for many. So can a wrong decision by a statesman in this age of missiles, rockets, and multimegaton bombs. And with better means of communication through today's press, radio, and television, any one of our statements or acts may have far-reaching repercussions.

Thus, modern man has even more cause to need guidance and direction. That is why the teachings of the Bible are so vital. For they have grown out of the long experience of people who have had to face the same basic problems and realities of human existence. While they were facing them, they discovered truths for living that have the same validity in our world of today.

Needed: Answers to Man's Deeper Questions

Yet before the writers of the Bible could come to grips with the everyday challenges of life, they first had to answer far deeper questions. For their knowledge of the right course of action could only come from an understanding of the whole nature and purpose of human existence.

In this sense, the writers of the Bible reacted like any of us who plan to take a trip. Before we can decide what route to take, we must know where we are going. Similarly, before the biblical writers could determine the right course for man, they first had to know his ultimate destiny. For without this knowledge, nothing very much matters.

Once they raised this question, however, a great many more arose. What, for instance, is life all about? Is it aimless, or is there some purpose to it? If it has a purpose, what is it? Is life fundamentally good or bad? Why should it often bring us unhappiness and suffering? Why doesn't everything go the way we want it?

The biblical writers asked many, many other questions, among them the following: Have we any real choice over what we do? Are we entirely responsible for what happens to us, or is God responsible, or just chance? What really is right and wrong? Why is the right right and the wrong wrong? Does it make any difference which we do?

They also wondered about God. Does He actually exist, and who is He? What is His nature? What role does He play in our lives? Is He really concerned about us? And, at times, they asked questions about death: Why should people die? Why do we die when we do? Is there any life after death?

The writers of the Bible struggled with these and with other deeper questions of human existence. The answers they found constitute their real achievement. Sometimes, as we have seen, they clothed their answers in legend and allegory; sometimes, in historical incident. More often, however, they spoke their answers simply as prophets, priests, poets, and sages with an urgent message for the people of their time.

Their conclusions, far from being outmoded, represent man's best effort to understand the fundamentals of existence. Indeed, however much humanity has advanced, it has yet to improve upon them. And taken as a whole, they constitute a remarkable philosophy of life. . . .

The Bible—A Religious Philosophy of Life

What do we mean by the term "philosophy of life"? A unified view, a way of looking at the whole of existence—God, the universe, life, man, and everything connected with them. This is what Scriptures presents through its answers to life's deeper questions. And this is what, in the first instance, the Bible has to offer us.

The starting point of this philosophy of life, as we have seen, is God. Indeed, at the very heart of all existence stands the holy, all-righteous, and almighty God. The cosmos, all life, and man himself are of His making; so are the physical laws that regulate the universe and the moral principles that govern society. Everything is in His hands and His will is supreme.

Man has been created in accordance with that will. He has been endowed with freedom to live as he wishes, though he realizes that there are consequences to his acts. Moreover, he has been created for God's purpose, to be the guardian of the earth and to reflect the ways of his Maker. To serve this function, man must engage in work, marriage and family life, study leading to moral improvement, and the promotion of the well-being of all mankind.

Above all, man must worship his Maker with righteousness, for he knows that to do evil is to disobey God. The good, therefore, is obedience to God's commands. And since His moral law always governs the world, wickedness ultimately results in misfortune for both the individual and society; right-doing leads to their well-being. Therefore the true measure of a man's life is not his wealth or social position. The true measure is the degree of a man's holiness—how he worships God through the kind of life he leads. For only in this way can he fulfil God's purposes and help establish His Kingdom on earth.

To this end, life becomes something very precious, the gift of God Himself. Although death is the inevitable consequence of existence as He has created it, it is *life*, not death or life after death, that must be man's chief focus. For it is only in living life to the full that we achieve the purposes for which we were created and find true happiness. And only the living can bring about the establishment of the just, righteous, peaceful society under the fatherhood of God.

Though life is potentially good, we also realize that we must continually struggle against sin, disobedience of God's will. Being human we may, at times, "miss the mark" through sinfulness. Yet, there is always the opportunity for atonement. The way of repentance—being truly sorry for our acts, seeking God's forgiveness, making amends, and resolving to lead holy lives—is always open to us. In the sight of God the penitent can always start life afresh.

Throughout our lives we are sustained by our faith in Him. We know that we can count upon His justice and can turn to Him for love and mercy to help us live in accord with His will. And realizing that we have Him to thank for our existence, for everything we enjoy, and for His ever-present guidance and aid, we remain humbly grateful.

The biblical concept of the Covenant adds special meaning to our lives as Jews. As one of God's chosen people, each of us has a personal mission to perform. We are expected to set an example of righteous living that will hasten the day when, in the words of the *Union Prayerbook:*

. . . All men shall invoke Thy name, when corruption and evil shall give way to purity and goodness, when superstition shall no longer enslave the mind, nor idolatry blind the eye, when all who dwell on earth shall know that to Thee alone every knee must bend and every tongue give homage. —Volume I, p. 151

This, very briefly, is what the Bible has to say. Presented even in abbreviated form, all its teachings give rise to a powerful and positive philosophy of life. Here we have a complete view of existence which gives meaning and purpose to all of life. Now you can understand why one psalmist called the teachings of the Bible "a lamp to his feet and a light to his path" [Psalm 119:105].

The Bible—A Help to Daily Living

Strengthened by this philosophy, the authors of the Bible were able to face life wisely and courageously. We, too, can do the same. For in spite of the fact that we live several thousand years later, we see that we must still wrestle with essentially the same human problems and struggle with the very same basic questions that our ancestors did.

Our forefathers confronted the same problems we confront. From personal experience, Abraham knew the dread of anxiety when he contemplated the sacrifice of his son [Genesis 22:1–19]; and Isaac tasted the bitterness of intrigue within his own family [Genesis 27:1–40]. Jacob knew at first hand the hatred of his twin brother [Genesis 27:41–45], and he suffered the profound remorse of conscience [Genesis 32:4; 33:16]. As a father, Jacob sorrowed over the loss of his favorite son because of the enmity of his own children [Genesis 37:3–36]. A Joseph encountered repeated misfortune [Genesis 37:12–28; 39:5–20]; a Moses had to flee for his life [Exodus 2:11–15]; a Jeremiah felt all too deeply the lash of scorn and hostility [Jeremiah 15:10].

Indeed, all of those who helped write the Bible were personally familiar with the full range of human experience—jealousy, anger, doubt, selfishness, unpopularity, and all the rest. Nor were they spared prejudice, oppression, disgrace, war, and national disaster.

But through their religious philosophy of life they were able to furnish the means by which people of every generation might triumph over such experiences. Here, for example, are some of the teachings they offered for achieving family harmony:

Honor your father and mother. . . . —Exodus 20:12

Behold, how good and how pleasant it is for brethren to dwell together in unity. —Psalm 133:1

. . . Turn the hearts of the fathers to the children, and the hearts of the children to their fathers. . . .
—Malachi 3:24

Better is a dry morsel with quietness, than a house full of feasting with strife. —Proverbs 17:1

And to promote greater harmony between groups and nations in our own world of today, we find no better principles than these:

And God created [every] man in His own image. . . .
—Genesis 1:27

. . . You shall love your neighbor as yourself. . . .
—Leviticus 19:18

Have we not all one father? Has not one God created us all? Why should we deal treacherously, every man against his brother? . . . —Malachi 2:10

. . . Proclaim liberty throughout the land to all the inhabitants thereof. . . . —Leviticus 25:10

. . . Everyone shall sit under his vine and under his fig-tree and none shall make them afraid. . . . —Micah 4:4

Here, then, within the pages of the Bible are those fundamental truths by which we and all other human beings can, in the words of Scriptures itself, "choose life that you may live, you and all your descendants" [Deuteronomy 30:19]. Arising out of a religious philosophy of life, these truths have a timelessness that impels us to return again and again to the Bible for guidance in daily living. And, as so many have found, they can indeed direct one's feet onto paths of blessing.

The Bible—A Guide to Righteous Living

The Bible's outlook on life sheds much light for moderns on the meaning of righteousness. Thus the Bible is a constant, unchanging guide to what is right and wrong in our own age.

This guidance is especially necessary today when so much confusion seems to exist in the minds of people about ethics and morality. Scarcely a day passes that we do not hear of some person in high place—in government, labor unions, business, the entertainment world, or the various professions—who has succumbed to ambition or greed. The recent TV scandals revealed how confused some people are about wrong and right. Many people sympathized with those who were caught, even with those who committed perjury. The general confusion about wrong and right is evident also among young people who all too frequently take the "easy" way out by cheating in examinations or by "cutting corners" to get something they want.

Here the Bible stands as a sentinel, warning us that the principles of honesty, fair dealing, justice, and truth cannot be compromised. For, in unmistakable language it declares:

> You shall not steal, neither shall you deal falsely, nor lie
> to one another. And you shall not swear by My name
> falsely. . . . —Leviticus 19:11–12

The Bible provides us with many examples of how the ancients stood up for the right. Read the stories of Nathan facing King David; of Elijah and King Ahab; and of Amos, Isaiah, Jeremiah, and others who condemned the evil-doers of their times, if you want to see how righteous men confronted men who thought they could "get away with things."

The importance of the Bible's moral standards for the welfare of mankind as a whole can be seen in the recent example of Nazi Germany. There, beginning in 1933 when Adolf Hitler became Chancellor, the definitions of right and wrong were reversed. Murder of innocent people was approved as being in the "best interest of the state." Justice was perverted; truth distorted into lying propaganda. Bearing false witness served as a convenient way of getting rid of the upright. Children were encouraged to betray their parents, and the government openly embarked upon the wholesale slaughter of fellow human beings. Hitler's regime was all too successful in achieving what it called the "New Order."

But there was one set of standards that the Nazis could not alter: the standards defined in the Bible. Because these standards were based on a religious view of life, in which principles of righteousness derive from the very nature of God Himself, right and wrong can never be confused. For mankind there stand these eternal guideposts:

> . . . You shall not bear false witness against your neigh-
> bor. —Exodus 20:13

> ". . . You shall be holy for I the Lord your God am holy."
> —Leviticus 19:2

> ". . . You shall do no unrighteousness in judgment . . .
> but in righteousness you shall judge your neighbor."
> —Leviticus 19:15

Justice, justice shall you pursue that you may live. . . .
—Deuteronomy 16:20

". . . Not by might nor by power but by My spirit," says the Lord of Hosts. —Zechariah 4:6

Thus, because of the Bible, the actions of the Nazis and all those who would turn wrong into right have been immediately recognized for what they are, crimes against God and man.

As a moral guide for ourselves and society, then, the Bible continues to be indispensable.

The Bible—A Source of Comfort and Inspiration

In addition to providing us with a religious philosophy of life, a source of wisdom in daily living, and an unfailing guide to righteousness, the Bible is an ever-present comfort and inspiration in our lives.

Few of us go through life without at one time or another encountering trouble. It may be illness, a serious disappointment, the loss of a job, the death of a loved one, or some other misfortune. At times like these, especially, we can turn to the Bible for comfort, knowing that here we can draw strength from its wonderful outlook upon life.

The Book of Job, for instance, offers us new courage through the example of a man who suffered the loss of everything he possessed, including his children. But he was still able to declare, "The Lord gave, the Lord has taken away; blessed be the name of the Lord" [Job 1:21]. From the tale of King David and the death of his beloved son [II Samuel 12:15–23], we find strength to rise above personal tragedy. And, during times of trial, what greater source of comfort can we find anywhere than this wonderful Psalm:

The Lord is my shepherd, I shall not want.
He makes me lie down in green pastures;
He leads me beside the still waters;
He restores my soul.
He leads me in paths of righteousness for His name's sake.
Even though I walk through the valley of the shadow of death,
I fear no evil;
For You are with me;
Your rod and Your staff, they comfort me.
You prepare a table before me in the presence of my enemies;
You have anointed my head with oil; my cup overflows.

Surely goodness and mercy shall follow me all the days of
my life,
And I shall dwell in the house of the Lord forever.
   —Psalm 23

Even when life moves along smoothly, we still need something to
give us a "lift" above the daily routine, to challenge us to nobler
living. We need the inspiration of great religious poetry and the
example of dedicated people to uplift and stimulate us.

The Bible is a treasure-house of inspiration. A reading of Queen
Esther's courage in going before the king to defend her people
[Esther 4:4–5:8; 7:1–6] renews our own sense of obligation for
heroic living. The firmness of Joseph in rejecting the enticements
of Potiphar's wife [Genesis 39:7–21] encourages us to resist temptation. From the experiences of Jacob we find reassurance that we
can still return to God even though we may have fallen short of the
mark (as, in Jacob's case, the taking of his brother's birthright, in
Genesis 25:24–34, and the stealing of his father's blessing, in
Genesis 27:1–41).

Where indeed can we find greater assurance of God's nearness
than this glorious testimony that He is everywhere:

Whither shall I go from Your spirit?
Or whither shall I flee from Your presence?
If I ascend up into heaven, You are there;
If I make my bed in the netherworld, behold, You are there.
If I take the wings of the morning,
And dwell in the uttermost parts of the sea;
Even there does Your hand lead me,
And Your right hand holds me.
And if I say: "Surely the darkness will cover me,
And the light about me shall be night,"
Even the darkness is not too dark for You,
The night is bright as the day,
The darkness is even as the light.   —Psalm 139:7–12

Or where can we find a higher sense of purpose for Jewish living
than this stirring promise of God to His Servant-people Israel:

"Behold My servant whom I uphold,
My chosen in whom My soul delights;
I have put My spirit upon him,
He will bring forth justice to the nations.
He will not cry or lift up his voice,
Or make an outcry in the street.
A bruised reed, he will not break;
A dimly burning wick, he will not go out;
He will faithfully bring forth justice.

He will not fail or be discouraged
Till he has established justice in the earth,
And all the isles look to his Torah!"

Thus says the Lord God,
Who created the heavens and stretched them out,
Who spread forth the earth and whatever comes from it,
Who gives breath to the people upon it,
And life to those who go upon it:
"I am the Lord, I have called you in righteousness,
I have taken you by the hand and preserved you;
I have given you as a covenant to the people,
For a light to the nations,
To open eyes that are blind,
To bring out the prisoners from the dungeon,
From the prison those who sit in darkness.
I am the Lord, that is My name. . . ." —Isaiah 42:1–8

Reading this, our hearts surge with renewed devotion to our Mission. No ordinary people are we. We are Jews! Our lives are consecrated to the service of the Lord and the blessing of all mankind!

Only the Beginning . . .

What meaning, then, has the Bible for us?

The Bible offers us much that is precious for living in the modern world. It provides us with a religious philosophy of life by means of which we can find meaning and purpose to our existence as both human beings and Jews.

It enables us to answer for ourselves the deeper questions of existence, and to meet the day-to-day problems and challenges of life.

It directs us toward holier living through a clear sense of right and wrong as God—not man—views them.

It affords us the comfort of God's love in our burdens and His inspiration for daily living.

In short, the Bible confers upon us a total way of life that offers blessing for ourselves, and through us, for all God's creation. Taken as a whole, this is what we call "Judaism."

Our religion, as we have seen, did not cease to develop with the completion of the Bible. Many fresh insights and new emphases found their way into Judaism with the work of the rabbis of the Talmud. Inspired men and women of our own generation continue to enrich it.

But the Bible, nevertheless, has always been at the very center of our faith. For this is no ordinary book. The timelessness of its contents makes it a blueprint for life in every age. Indeed, it is a *living* book for *living* people. Anyone who fashions his life according to its teachings, says the Talmud, becomes worthy of many things:

> . . . The whole world is indebted to him. He is called beloved friend, lover of God, lover of mankind. It [the Bible] clothes him with humility and reverence. It fits him to become just, pious, upright, and faithful. It keeps him far from sin, and brings him near to virtue. Through him the world enjoys counsel and sound knowledge, understanding and strength. . . . It gives him sovereignty and dominion and discerning judgment. He becomes like a never-failing spring and like a river that flows on with ever-increasing vigor. He grows modest, long-suffering, and forgiving of insults. It magnifies and exalts him above all things.
> —Mishnah: Ovos 6:1

No wonder, then, that every generation following the Bible's completion has emphasized study of the Bible. Starting with Ben-Sirach's Ecclesiasticus, which calls upon the individual to learn God's Law [Ecclesiasticus 39:1, 8, for instance], we find succeeding generations of rabbis placing increasing stress upon Bible study. Typical of the attitude of the rabbis, for example, are such statements as, "Greater is the study of the Torah than the rebuilding of the Temple" [Talmud: Megillah 16b]; "Be diligent in the study of the Torah" [Mishnah: Ovos 2:14]; and "The study of the Torah takes precedence over all other religious obligations" [Mishnah: Peah 1:1].

And through their own devotion to the Bible, the Sages discovered something even more remarkable! They found that like all living things, the Bible continually grows. Yes, the Bible is like a living plant that has hundreds, thousands of roots. Each time we think we have probed to the very bottom layer, we find we are wrong—there are deeper roots still. Each time we read and reread the Bible, we find deeper and deeper meanings. Therefore, the Bible is not a book that can be read just once. Rather, says one of the rabbis of the Mishnah:

> Turn its pages and turn them again for everything is there. Study it and grow old and grey over it, and never turn away from it, for there is no better rule than this.
> —Ovos 5:25

So while we have learned much about the Bible, we see that we have just begun. For study of THE LIVING BIBLE must always go on . . . and on . . . and on. . . .

1. In what way has your own life been affected by the existence of the Bible?

2. In facing some of the common problems of everyday living, how can the Bible help us?

3. Why is a religious philosophy of life so necessary for us today?

4. In respect to world problems today, what guidance does the Bible offer us?

——————— SOME OTHER BIBLE PASSAGES TO CONSIDER ———————

1. What answers to various family difficulties are suggested by the following? Genesis 33:1–11; 45:1–15; Malachi 2:14–16; Proverbs 1:8–9; 3:1–4; 6:16–19; 10:5.

2. With what deeper questions of life do the following deal? Jeremiah 46:27–28; Zephaniah 3:14–20; Psalm 10; Proverbs 3:11–12; Daniel 12:1–3.

3. How do each of the following reflect the Bible's philosophy of life? Jeremiah 23:23–24; Psalm 32:1–2; Proverbs 2; 5:16–19.

4. In what ways are the following a source of inspiration to us? Exodus 15:1–18; Isaiah 40:1–8; 55:6–11; Psalm 62:6–9; 118.

——————— FROM THE RABBIS' VIEWPOINT ———————

1. THE IMPORTANCE OF SCRIPTURE: See *Everyman's Talmud*, pp. 132–142, 157–167; and *A Rabbinic Anthology*, [306–307] pp. 116–117, [311] p. 118, [314] p. 119, [315]. pp. 119–120, [317] p. 120, [323] pp. 122–123, [327] p. 124, [332–333] pp. 125–126, [342] p. 128.

2. STUDY OF SCRIPTURE: See *Everyman's Talmud*, pp. 142–148; and *A Rabbinic Anthology*, [352–357] pp. 132–133, [368] p. 136, [370] p. 137, [374] p. 138, [394] p. 144, [396] p. 146, [462–475] pp. 175–178.

——————— OTHER THINGS TO READ ———————

BAECK, LEO, *God and Man in Judaism*, Union of American Hebrew Congregations.

FREEHOF, SOLOMON B., *Preface to Scripture*, Union of American Hebrew Congregations, Chap. 4: "The Bible in Worship," pp. 34–41; Chap. 7: "The Bible and the Modern Reader," pp. 65–78.

GOLDMAN, SOLOMON, *The Book of Books—An Introduction,* Harper, Chap. 6: "An Eternally Effective Book," pp. 104–126.

GREENBERG, SIDNEY, *A Modern Treasury of Jewish Thoughts,* Yoseloff, Chap. 7: "Learn and Live," pp. 189–216; Chap. 11: "How Beautiful Is Our Heritage," pp. 265–302; Chap. 12: "Comfort in Sorrow," pp. 303–326.

SILVER, ABBA HILLEL, *Where Judaism Differed,* Macmillan, "Introduction," pp. 1–5; Chap. 1: "One and the Same," pp. 6–10; Chap. 2: "A Pattern in History," pp. 11–21.

STEINBERG, MILTON, *Basic Judaism,* Harcourt, Brace, Chap. 1: "Preliminaries," pp. 3–11; Chap. 2: "Conclusions," pp. 12–17.

Numbers in parentheses indicate the page of this volume

* indicates references mentioned in sections headed "Some Other Bible Passages to Consider"

5: 1–14 (49), 7–9 (34), 15 (25).
6: 20 (152).
7: 4 (152), 5–10 (154), 8–10 (152).
8: 8–9 (213).
9: 21 (4).
10: 1–10* (41), 6–7 (156), 12–13 (35).
11: 21 (113).
12: 1 (108) (113), 13 (114).
13: 23* (15).
15: 5–7 (34), 8–9 (34), 10 (266), 19–20 (100).
16: 6* (182), 6–8* (182), 7 (172).
18: 5–10 (77), 11 (77).
19: 5 (106), 14–20:6 (36).
20: 9 (36), 14 (121), 14–18 (123), 18 (121).
21: 8 (173), 8–10 (72).
22: 13 (139), 15–16 (138).
23: 1–6* (81), 23–24* (15) (273), 23–24 (35) (66), 24 (66).
27: 1* (239), 3* (239), 9 (168).
29: 4–7 (35), 10–14 (90), 12 (92), 14* (61), 19 (73).
31: 31–32 (52), 33–34 (52).
32: 18 (90), 26–30 (70), 33 (154).
33: 20–21 (51).
43: 1–7 (219).
46: 27–28* (273).
50: 4–5 (55), 19 (55), 31 (76).
51: 1–4 (70).

16: 21 (42).
18: 2 (4), 4 (111), 4–9 (74), 7–8 (153), 13 (74), 19–20 (111) (247), 20–23* (81), 23 (73), 29–32* (122), 30–31 (161).
20: 11 (173), 37 (229).
22: 1–16* (122).
24: 17* (182), 17–18 (172).
29: 8–16 (25).
31: 11 (76).
33: 10–12 (170), 11 (174).
34: * (81).
36: 25 (8).
37: 1–10 (178), 12–14 (178).
40: 1 (150).
47: 22–23 (139).

HOSEA

1: 1–3 (32).
2: 4–15 (32), 21–22 (34) (135).
4: 1–2 (49), 1–3* (163), 6 (137) (155), 14 (106), 17–19 (106).
5: 15–6:1 (77).
6: 6 (87) (156).
7: (77).
8: 4 (30).
9: 1–3 (54).
11: 1–4 (32), 8 (32), 9 (32).
14: 2 (32), 2–3 (11), 2–5 (8), 2–9 (249).

EZEKIEL

5: 5–8* (122).
11: 14–21* (62).

JOEL

2: 12–13 (161).
3: 1* (15).

SONG OF SONGS

LAMENTATIONS

RUTH

ECCLESIASTES

GENERAL INDEX *

A

AARON, 25, 111, 129, 145, 172, 185, 186, 198, 256
Ab, the ninth of, 206
ABEL, 66, 85, 87
ABIMELECH, 84, 189
ABRAHAM, 8, 10, 19, 20, 24 f., 45, 54, 59, 66, 84, 85, 93, 107, 111, 133, 149, 156, 185, 187, 188, 196, 207, 245, 252, 255, 266
ABRAM, 225
ABSALOM, 171
ADAM, 22, 66, 67, 71, 107, 130, 132, 172, 185, 188, 207, 237, 242, 243, 245
ADAMS, JOHN, 6
ADAMS, JOHN, 260
Adonoi, 20
Adultery, 47, 48, 133, 225
Afflicted, The, 138
Afterlife, 162, 165 f., 176–181, 265
AHAB, 6, 28, 29, 48, 254, 268
AHRIMAN, 105
AHURA MAZDA, 105
AKHEN-ATON, 193 f.
AKIBA, 79, 228
ALBRIGHT, WILLIAM F., 191
ALEXANDER THE GREAT, 215, 219, 220
ALEXANDRIA, 33, 232, 233
"Alexandrinus," 231 f., 238
ALLAH, 8
Amalekites, 11, 25, 47, 186
Amending one's conduct, 160 f.; *see also* Repentance
AMENOPHIS IV, 193 f.
America, Bible's influence upon, 5–7
America, discovery of, 245
American Jewish Bible translations, 237
American Revolution, 6
American Standard Version, The, 236, 238
AMOS, 25, 30, 31 f., 48 f., 51, 66, 75, 76, 87, 129, 137, 151 f., 153, 204, 220, 249, 268
Book of, 204, 208
Ancestors, deeds of, 90, 91

Angels, 25, 128, 129, 174, 178, 181, 237, 244, 252
Animals, 127 f., 149, 162, 252
Anthropomorphism, 22, 26, 198
Apocrypha, 78, 219, 221
APOLLO, 104
AQUILA, 233, 238
Aramaic, 190, 232 f.
Archaeology, 191 f., 236, 253 ff.
Ark, synagogue, 147
Ark of the Covenant, 187
Assyria and Assyrians, 30, 31, 33, 34, 55, 69, 70, 76, 109 f., 154, 253
Astrology, 168
ASTRUC, JEAN, 189 f.
Atheism, 18, 40, 105
ATHENE, 104
Atom, 243
ATON, 193 f.
Atonement, 91, 159 ff., 161, 265
Day of; *see* Day of Atonement and Yom Kippur
Authorized Version, The, 202
AZARIAH, 218

B

BAAL, 28, 45, 70, 74 f., 106, 230
Babylonia and Babylonians, 9, 11, 28, 33, 34 f., 50, 51, 52–57, 60, 70, 72, 76, 88, 92, 94, 100, 113, 114, 137, 161, 178, 190 f., 192, 193, 206, 213 f., 218, 231, 248
BACON, FRANCIS, 183
Baptism, 8
BARAK, 11
BARUCH, 218 f.
BEL, 28
Beliefs, religious, 13, 85 f., 198, 255 f., 261
BEN-ASHER, MOSES, 231, 238
Benevolence; *see* Charity
BENJAMIN, 176
BEN-SIRACH, 78, 215, 216, 217, 219, 220, 272
Beth-El, 29, 48, 147, 152, 252

* Certain items listed in index denote relative subject matter rather than direct reference.

287

148 ff., 151, 153, 154, 155, 158, 159, 162, 198, 261
Robbery, 153, 160
Roman Catholic Bible, 202 f., 215, 219
Roman Catholicism and Catholics, 166, 219, 234, 235, 236, 237
Roman classics, 221
Romans, 60, 104, 217, 220
Rome, 220, 229, 231
Rosh Ha-shono, 150, 250
Rulers, 251
Russian translation of the Bible, 235
Ruth, Book of, 58, 202, 205, 206, 207, 209, 210, 211, 216, 247

S

Sabbath, 9, 47, 51, 93, 130, 143, 147, 150, 153, 162, 250, 261
SABIN, ALBERT, 121
Sackcloth, wearing of, 89, 98, 171 f.
Sacrifices, 47, 48, 49, 85 f., 87, 88, 93, 147 f., 150, 152 f., 159, 160, 185, 250
SALK, JONAS, 121
Samaria and Samaritans, 29, 69, 214, 220
SAMUEL, 30, 47 f., 84, 85, 86, 92, 132, 167, 204
   Books of, 202, 204, 207, 208 f.
SAMSON, 85, 204
Samson Agonistes, 5
Samson and Delilah, 5
SARAH, 85
SATAN, 116, 206, 252
SAUL, 47, 132, 158, 167 f., 172, 203, 204, 225
Scapegoat, 159
Schools of writers, 195, 210
Science, 241 ff., 244 f.
SCOPES, JOHN T., 241
Scopes Trial, 241 f., 244
Scribes, 227, 229 ff., 232, 238
Scrolls, The Five, 206
Seal of the United States, 6
Security, 59, 138, 139, 267
Seers, 166, 167
SENNACHERIB, 253
Sentence division of the Bible, 228 ff., 238
Septuagint, 218 f., 220, 227, 231 f., 233, 234, 238

Serpent, 107
Servant of the Lord (Israel), 114 f., 135, 141, 270 f.
"Servant Songs, The," 52 ff.
Sex, 169
SHAKESPEARE, WILLIAM, 4, 5, 183
SHAPHAN, 213
Shechem, 225
Shiloh, 84
Sh'ma, 9, 157
Sh'ol, 176 f., 179, 180, 181
Shovuos, 10, 147, 151, 206, 250
Sin and Sinners, 91, 158 f., 250, 265
Sinai, Mt., 11, 12, 17, 23 f., 44, 107, 151, 185, 186, 229, 232
"Sinaiticus," 232, 238
Skin of Our Teeth, The, 5
Slander, 153
Slavery, Egyptian; see Egypt
Slaves, 251
Slums, 139
Snake, 252
Social Action; see Social Justice
Social Justice, 129, 137–140, 262, 265
Sodom, 66, 107, 111, 156
Solar system, 124, 127 f.
Solemn assembly, 153; see also Eighth Day of Solemn Assembly
SOLOMON, 11, 30, 91, 92, 95, 110 f., 147, 148, 159, 172, 173, 184, 187, 203, 205, 207, 209, 217, 232
Song of Solomon, 203
Song of Songs, 132, 184, 203, 205, 206, 207, 209, 210, 216, 217
Sorcery, 168, 193
Sorrow, time of, 269; see also Mourning and Mourners
Soul, 99, 179, 180
Space, outer, 127 f.
Spain, 10
SPINOZA, BARUCH, 188 f.
Spiritualism, 166–169
Stars, 124, 125
Stealing, 267 ff.
STEINBECK, JOHN, 5
"Still small voice, The," 36
Stoics, 105
Strangers, treatment of, 26, 46, 58, 129, 139, 153, 250
Study, 3–14, 136 f., 140, 144, 145, 154 f., 162, 262, 265, 272
Suffering, 108, 109, 115 f., 117, 119 ff., 169, 262
Suicide, 124
Sukos, 9, 151, 206, 214, 250